SMITHSONIAN MISCELLANEOUS C
VOLUME 110, NUMBER 13
(End of Volume)

CONTRIBUTIONS
TO THE ANTHROPOLOGY OF
THE SOVIET UNION

(With Five Plates)

Compiled by
HENRY FIELD

(Publication 3947)

CITY OF WASHINGTON
PUBLISHED BY THE SMITHSONIAN INSTITUTION
DECEMBER 22, 1948

The Lord Baltimore Press
BALTIMORE, MD., U. S. A.

CONTENTS

LIST OF ILLUSTRATIONS

PREFACE

This study, which includes a compilation of anthropological data based on Soviet published and unpublished materials, has been divided into two sections, one dealing with archeology, the other with physical anthropology.

The majority of the archeological publications from which summaries have been translated were given to me while a guest of the Academy of Sciences of the U.S.S.R. during June–July, 1945, in Moscow and Leningrad. The occasion was the Jubilee Session celebrating the 220th anniversary of the founding of the Academy by Peter the Great.

I was the bearer of official greetings from the Smithsonian Institution, the Archaeological Institute of America, the American Anthropological Association, the Library of Congress, the National Archives, and the National Geographic Society. At a full session of the Praesidium of the Academy of Sciences in Moscow I was invited to address the Academy and to present these greetings from the United States, which were officially accepted and warmly reciprocated by President Vladimir Komarov. For an account of this trip the reader is referred to "Anthropology in the Soviet Union, 1945" in the American Anthropologist, vol. 48, No. 3, pp. 375-396, 1946.

Chapter III was translated by Mrs. John F. Normano, the Asia Institute, New York City. Chapters IV and V are based on summaries translated by Eugene V. Prostov prior to 1941. Some sections in chapter IV have been translated from French summaries during 1946 by Mrs. David Huxley, to whom a footnote reference is given. A special introduction to chapter IV, with a list of abbreviations (pp. 114-115), has been included.

While every effort has been made to express clearly and concisely the results obtained by the Soviet archeologists and anthropologists whose work has been translated and summarized, this has proved to be an exceptionally difficult task.

Among other special problems was the fact that work was begun on this publication 10 years ago and during the war years remained untouched. In addition, my collaborator, Eugene V. Prostov, has been on Government service abroad since 1946. However, he has checked the text, particularly the spellings of proper names, but without his customary library and reference works at hand. Hence, some discrepancies and inconsistencies, will appear. Dr. Sergei

Yakobson, Consultant in the Library of Congress, very kindly standardized some of the spellings in order to follow the Library of Congress system of Russian transliteration. Some place names follow
the spelling approved by the Board on Geographical Names. We
noted, but could not correct or change, differences in terminology;
we have kept as close to the original as possible. In some cases we
have made minor additions to elucidate the text either in footnotes
with initials or in brackets.

Since we have often taken considerable editorial license with the
text in the selection and rearrangement of the materials, we decided
to place the name of the author in the first footnote of each article.
On the other hand, there should never be any question as to the
authorship of any statement.

This publication should be considered as complementary to our
previous publications on the U.S.S.R. (see chapter IV, footnotes
1, 2), to my "Contributions to the Anthropology of Iran," and in
particular to my forthcoming "Contributions to the Anthropology of
the Caucasus," wherein will appear my anthropometric data on the
North Osetes and Yezidis as well as Soviet comparative data on
Ciscaucasia and Transcaucasia.

No bibliography has been compiled because, for the sake of convenience, references have been listed in the footnotes.

In the preparation of this material for publication, I have had
some editorial assistance from Miss Morelza Morrow. As already
mentioned, Mrs. John F. Normano and Mrs. David Huxley translated part of the material. The greater part of the text was typed by
Miss Elizabeth Beverly in Thomasville, Ga. Miss Betsy King Ross,
who very kindly assisted in the final stages of preparation, also typed
part of the manuscript. We wish to acknowledge with gratitude all
this assistance. We also wish to thank Dr. T. Dale Stewart, curator
of physical anthropology of the United States National Museum, for
making helpful suggestions regarding certain portions of the manuscript. My wife generously assisted in the compilation of the statistical tables and in proofreading the copy.

We are grateful to Soviet anthropologists, who have contributed so
much to our knowledge of ancient and modern man from the Ukraine
to Siberia and from the Far North to Central Asia.

We received information in 1939 and in 1945 that anthropometric
surveys were in progress in European Russia, in the Caucasus,
Turkestan, Central Asia, and Siberia, and hope that at some not too
distant date we may be able to make the new results available to the

student of Asiatic racial problems, who is either unfamiliar with the
Russian language or does not have access to this important Soviet
literature.

HENRY FIELD

October 28, 1946.
  Cuernavaca, Mexico.

CONTRIBUTIONS TO THE ANTHROPOLOGY OF THE SOVIET UNION

COMPILED BY HENRY FIELD

(WITH FIVE PLATES)

I. ALL-UNION CONFERENCE ON ARCHEOLOGY [1]

This Conference, called by the Academy of Sciences, was held in Moscow during 1945. Represented at the Conference by a total of 156 delegates were the Marr Institute, the Academies of Sciences of the various Union Republics, branches of the U.S.S.R. Academy of Sciences, Peoples Commissariats of Education of the Union and Autonomous Republics, universities, teachers' colleges, central, territorial, regional, and municipal museums, the Commission on the Preservation of Ancient Monuments, and other scientific bodies.

The Conference was opened by V. Volgin, Vice President of the Academy of Sciences and chairman of the committee on organization. In his opening speech Academician Volgin reminded the delegates that the Marr Institute—the leading center of Soviet archeology—had recently celebrated its twentieth anniversary. Founded as the Russian Academy of the History of Material Culture, it succeeded the Committee on Archeology which had been in existence since 1859.

"We no longer support the teachings of former archeologists that the ancient history of our country was represented by separate 'archeological civilizations.' We regard it rather as a harmonious and logically connected chain of consecutive stages in the development of humanity from the Stone Age to the Middle Ages."

The problem of the origin of the Slavs and their relations with neighboring tribes is now presented from a new angle. Archeologists have traced the first stages in the formation of the Slavonic tribes to the beginning of our era. Scientists of today base their conclusions on material found in strata dating back to the Bronze Age and Neolithic civilizations. More and more light is being shed upon the unification of the Slavonic tribes in the first thousand years of our

---

[1] From VOKS Bulletin, 1946. This has been condensed and edited to conform to our style. (H. F.)

era, a factor which exerted a tremendous influence upon the history of Eastern and Central Europe.

Academician B. Grekov delivered a report on the achievements of archeological investigations in the U.S.S.R. He pointed out that interest in ancient cultural remains has long existed in Russia. As early as 1804 a scientific society called the Society of History and Russian Antiquities was founded in Moscow. As stated at the time, this Society was interested, among other things, in collecting antiquities, medals, coins, and other objects shedding light on various events in Russian history.

Pre-Revolutionary archeologists excavated much material connected with the ancient history of the peoples of Russia. The remains of Hellenic civilization in the northern regions of the Black Sea coast, objects excavated from Scythian burial mounds, and other materials cleared up many previously unexplored periods of Russian history. It was mostly due to the efforts of archeologists that a new field of study was opened to historians—the study of the Scythians who inhabited the territory of the present U.S.S.R. before the Slavs. Parallel with these investigations, archeologists unearthed the monuments of ancient Slavs in the Caucasus and Siberia.

In order to clarify previous observations and conclusions, the archeologists established firm ties with paleoanthropology, paleozoology, geology, soil science, philology, and history. At the present time archeology no longer stands apart from the general aims of history, but is itself a historical science solving the same problems and pursuing the same aims in its own specific field.

In recent years the number of sites investigated by archeologists has greatly increased. At the present time there is not a single region or nationality in the U.S.S.R. which has not been the object of study.

Significant achievements have been made in the study of the Stone Age. Hundreds of Paleolithic sites have been discovered and investigated, including those at Kostenki-Borshevo, Gagarino, Timonovka, and Malta and Buret in Siberia. Parallel with these studies, archeologists have charted the various periods in the Russian Paleolithic age, establishing the characteristics of its three main provinces—Asia, Europe Proper, and the regions of the Caspian Sea. These discoveries contributed much that was new to the existing conception of forms of Paleolithic tools and implements and of the art and mode of life of the people of that period.

Thorough investigations of a number of regions (the central part of European Russia, the Karelian-Finnish S.S.R., the Urals, and the Baikal area) made it possible to distinguish between the various

Neolithic civilizations and determine their chronological sequence. The new discoveries made in the course of these investigations, particularly the rock drawings in Karelia, the Gorbunovo turf pit, the Olen-Ostrov burial mound, and others, shed light on the religious conceptions of the Neolithic period, an aspect heretofore little studied.

Extensive investigations of the early Bronze Age have also been made. Excavations along the Dniester and the southern part of the Bug Rivers and at Usatovo near Odessa demonstrated the existence of various stages in the development of Tripolje culture and proved its prevalence in the whole Dnieper and Danube basin during the period from 3000-1000 B.C. Distinctions were established between the Bronze Age cultures in the northern and southern Caucasus, the Shengavit and Angbek cultures attributed to the early Bronze Age, the Kuban burial mounds and Eilar and the excavations at Trialeti,[2] all of which contained remains of highly developed Bronze Age cultures. Excavations at Urartu brought to light considerable material on the history of ancient Armenia. Investigations carried out in the Black Sea regions and in the Ukraine established the chronology of three main cultures—those characterized by pit, catacomb, and hut dwellings. The origin of each of these three types was clearly defined, and investigations were made of settlements of this period for the first time. It was established that the final stage in the development of Bronze Age culture was that of the Cimmerians, who inhabited this region previous to the coming of the Scythians. In the Volga region investigations established the existence of two cultures—that of Poltava (the beginning of the Bronze Age) and of Khvalinsk (the end of the Bronze Age). Investigations in Siberia established three stages of the Bronze Age as represented in the Afanasiev, Andronovo, and Karasuk cultures. A new culture—the Abashev—was discovered in the Chuvash Republic and adjacent regions.

The study of the Scytho-Sarmatian culture is of great significance for a knowledge of the population in the pre-Slavonic era and for determining the ethnogeny of Slavonic tribes. New excavations were carried out on the ancient sites of Kamensk, Sharapovsk, and Nemirov, as well as on the right bank of the Bug River and the western coast of the Black Sea. Excavations were also made of Scytho-Sarmatian burial mounds in the Kuban, the southern regions of the Dnieper, and in other localities.

Soviet archeologists continued the excavations begun in the ancient

---

[2] See Kuftin, B. A., and Field, Henry, Prehistoric culture sequence in Transcaucasia, Southwestern Journ. Anthrop., vol. 2, No. 3, pp. 340-360, 1946, and Microfilm No. 2310, pp. 1-126, in American Documentation Institute.

cities of the Black Sea region—Olbia,[8] Chersonesus, Phanagoria, and Kharabs [Charax?]. Excavations were also begun at other sites.

A more profound comprehension of the Scythian problem, as Academician Grekov pointed out, prepared the ground for a revision of views concerning the origin of the Slavs, particularly of the eastern branch. New investigations have confirmed the ethnogenetic chart outlined by Academician Nikolai Marr confirming the local origin of the eastern Slavs whose roots go back to the tribes of the Tripolje culture, to the Bronze Age civilization in the steppe regions, to the Scythians, and finally to the epoch of field burials. Agricultural tribes of Scythians along the middle course of the Dnieper as well as tribes from the upper reaches of the Dnieper, whose culture has been studied only in the past few years, are now accepted as component factors of the Slavonic ethnogeny.

One of the most important subjects of archeological research has been that of the Antae and their culture. Investigations of this problem can confirm the existence of definite connections between Antean culture and that of the preceding burial-field stage of culture and can also show the more original nature of Antean culture and its higher stage of development. Evidence pointing to this is found in their field agriculture, livestock breeding, skilled arts and crafts, and large settlements of an urban type. Beyond question the center of Antean culture lay in the middle reaches of the Dnieper, in the regions later inhabited by the Polians. Grekov considers it to be an established fact that the culture of Kiev Russ is a successor of Antean culture.

In this connection Academician Grekov dwelt on the researches of Soviet archeologists concerning Russian culture and in particular ancient Russian cities. The first stage in these researches was devoted to revealing the prehistory of these cities, going far back into the prefeudal period. The most important of these ancient cities were those which preceded modern Kiev, the settlements of the eighth and ninth centuries on the ancient site of Riurik near Novgorod, the cultural strata of the fifth and sixth centuries underlying the Pskov Kremlin, and the ancient strata of Staraia Ladoga dating back to the seventh and eighth centuries.

Taken in conjunction with the collections obtained by pre-Revolutionary expeditions, the many handicraft objects found in recent excavations enable archeologists to have a detailed picture of the evolution of urban crafts, their connection with and influence upon rural crafts, the progress and differentiation of technical methods,

[8] See Minns, Ellis H., Thirty years of work at Olbia, Journ. Hellenic Studies, vol. 45, pp. 109-112, 1945.

and the labor skills involved in each particular craft. A study of the cast forms, for example, and of craftsmen's marks, throws light on the social position of the latter, their organizations, and similar matters.

Materials relating to various periods of the Bronze Age have been unearthed at Shengavit settlement, at Shresh-Blur, and in Eilar. Particular interest attaches to the findings made by the expedition of the Georgian Academy of Sciences in the Trialeti burial mounds. Excavations of a tomb near Mtskheta, just north of Tbilisi [formerly Tiflis], furnished valuable material relating to the ancient Georgian kingdom. New finds, which shed light on the later Urartu epoch, have been unearthed on the hill of Kamir-Blur by expeditions of the Armenian Academy of Sciences. Extensive research has been carried on in Azerbaidzhan concerning cyclopean edifices. Investigations of medieval cities in Armenia and Georgia have been launched on a large scale. All these and many other excavations have produced material on the ancient history of the peoples inhabiting the Caucasus and Transcaucasia and their relations with ancient eastern states.

Excavations in Central Asia have unearthed Kelte-Minar and later Tazabagiab cultures which indicate historical connections between the population of ancient Khwarazm (Khoresm) and the north (the Afanasiev and Andronovo cultures), and the east (the Anau culture). Expeditions in Shakhrasiab, Urgench, and Khwarazm, and the excavations of ancient Taraz, all of which unearthed material on a later period in the history of Central Asia, have proved the existence of cultural relations between the ancient population of Central Asia and the Near East.

Prior to 25 years ago only 3 Paleolithic sites were known in Siberia, whereas more than 60 are known today. This has made it possible to establish the various periods in Siberian Paleolithic cultures, and of Neolithic settlements in the lower reaches of the Amur, on the shores of Lake Baikal, on the Angara, the Yenisei, and the Ilim Rivers. A study of the Bronze Age established the first appearance of livestock breeding, agriculture, and the smelting of metal. Three stages of Siberian Bronze Age culture have been established—the Afanasiev, the Andronovo, and the Karasuk. The dissemination of northern Chinese bronze as far west as the present cities of Molotov and Gorki raises the question of the role of cultural relations with the Far East as well as with the Near East, in forming a cultural unity among the peoples inhabiting the territory of the U.S.S.R. in ancient times. Remains corresponding to Scytho-Sarmatian culture in the southern regions of European Russia have been discovered in Siberia.

In archeological research concerning the peoples of the Volga and

Ural regions, particular attention has been paid to the so-called Ananino culture, which is a connecting link between the Bronze Age and the formation of now existing nationalities of these districts. During the Soviet period large-scale investigations have been begun to elucidate the early history of the Udmurts, the Komis, the Bashkirs, and the Mordovian tribes.

Special attention has been given to a study of the Bulgar and Khazar cultures. It is now possible to reconstruct a picture of the life in the Bulgar cities of the Volga region (Bulgari, Suvara, and others) both in ancient times and in the period of the Golden Horde. A systematic study of the material relating to the Khazars has made it possible to elucidate a number of obscure aspects of Russian-Khazar relations in the history of the Slavonic-Russian colonization of the southeast.

Without the efforts of archeologists the early pages of the history of the Bulgars, the Khazars, the eastern Slavs, and the even earlier Scythian and Greek colonies on the north coast of the Black Sea, and of ancient Armenia and Georgia would still remain unknown.

Academician Meshchaninov delivered a report on the planning of archeological expeditions in the U.S.S.R. Many of the archeological investigations, both theoretical and field researches outlined for the 1945-1949 period, are closely linked with key problems concerning the history of Soviet peoples which have been singled out for attention in the last few years. In most cases plans for large-scale excavations provide for the cooperation of several scientific institutes.

The plan also provides for systematic researches covering several years and extensive regions. In liberated cities where reconstruction will be carried out on a large scale, appropriate archeological work is being planned as well as measures for preserving the most important monuments of the past.

One of the tasks confronting Soviet archeologists is that of restoring the collections of many of the museums plundered by the Nazis and the restoration of many treasures of Soviet art and architecture damaged during the German occupation.

Academician Grabar made a report on new legislation concerning the preservation and study of archeological monuments.

II. RECENT WORK IN ANTHROPOLOGY [1]

A. ANCIENT PEOPLES AND THEIR ORIGIN

The discovery of the fossil skeleton of a child in Teshik-Tash cave in the mountains of Central Asia represents one of the most important anthropological finds of recent years.

Southern Bukhara lies in the Hissar Mountains. Teshik-Tash grotto is located in the Zautolos-Sai Canyon of the Beissen-Tad Mountains, belonging to the Hissar Range. This grotto (7 x 20 x 7 m.) stands at an altitude of 1,600 m. above sea level. The central area of the grotto represents a fossil-bearing layer containing animal bones, worked stone, and carbonized materials superimposed on a porous layer of clay. Underneath the clay lies another fossiliferous stratum. Altogether there are five strata with a total thickness of about 1.5 m., of which 40 cm. contain fossils.

In 1938 A. P. Okladnikov discovered the remains of a human skeleton [2] at the base of the first layer at a depth of 25.0 cm. The skull lay in a depression in the non-fossil-bearing layer. The horns of mountain goats arranged in pairs were found in the immediate vicinity. Heaps of charcoal and the remains of fires were found in several places in the fossiliferous stratum. Okladnikov concludes that ritual burials took place here. The alternation of fossiliferous and sterile strata indicates beyond doubt that Teshik-Tash was not permanently inhabited. However, it is evident from the thickness of the non-fossil-bearing strata that the intervals between the use of the grotto were very long.

The geological study of the canyon and grotto yields little for the determination of the epoch to which the fossil-bearing strata of Teshik-Tash belong, but in any case there is nothing to preclude the supposition that they belong to the Pleistocene period.

---

[1] This chapter, by V. V. Bunak, of the Research Institute for Anthropology, University of Moscow, has been edited to conform to our style. Some passages have been condensed; some footnotes have been added. This article appeared in VOKS Bulletin, Moscow, Nos. 9-10, pp. 22-29, 1945. See also Franz Weidenreich, The Paleolithic child from the Teshik-Tash cave in southern Uzbekistan (Central Asia), Amer. Journ. Phys. Anthrop., n.s., vol. 3, No. 2, pp. 151-163, 1945, and Henry Field, Anthropology in the Soviet Union, 1945, Amer. Anthrop., vol. 48, No. 3, pp. 375-396, July–September, 1946.

[2] For illustrations of the Teshik-Tash skulls and reconstructions by M. M. Gerasimov, see Amer. Journ. Phys. Anthrop., n.s., vol. 4, No. 1, pp. 121-123, 1946.

The fossil-bearing strata contain many fragments of bones. According to V. I. Gromov, the following types of mammals are represented: Siberian goat (*Capra sibirica*), horse (*Equus caballus*), wild boar (*Sus scrofa*), leopard (*Felis pardus*), marmot (*Marmotta* sp.). The remains of mountain goats are the most numerous. In general, the composition of the fauna is similar to that of the present day. According to Gromov's supposition, orographic, climatic, and faunal conditions in this part of Central Asia have changed little since the end of the Pleistocene period.

Stone implements were mainly of local siliceous limestone; some were of quartz or quartzite. One implement was made of limestone. The first fossil-bearing stratum contains many so-called "cores," most notable of which are long, massive, oval implements with broad sides and thick round ends fashioned by chipping with a sharp instrument. Flatter scrapers of various forms and sharp-pointed tools of primitive type have also been discovered. Chips and flat pieces of stone for making implements are in abundance. There is a complete absence of objects made of bone and horn. According to Okladnikov Teshik-Tash stone technology corresponds to Mousterian culture in Europe. He also notes the similarity between the typology of Teshik-Tash and the Middle Paleolithic of Palestine and southern Kurdistan in Iraq.

The remains of the human skeleton were brought to the Anthropological Museum of the Moscow State University. Part of the femur, the tibia, the humerus, and both clavicles were in a fair state of preservation. The skull was smashed into more than 150 fragments, but all of them were well preserved and it was possible to restore almost completely the cranium and face. This reconstruction [3] was made by the sculptor and anthropologist, M. M. Gerasimov. Research on the skeleton was conducted by G. F. Debets, M. Gremiatskii (the skull), N. A. Sinelnikov (bones of skeleton), V. V. Bunak (endocranial cast), and others. The results of this work are set forth in a comprehensive monograph now in press.

The preliminary examination revealed that the Teshik-Tash skeleton was that of an 8- or 9-year-old child, probably a boy.

The cranial capacity is large, but the vault of the skull is comparatively low, with an angular occiput, prominent superciliary ridges, and massive bones. The chin is little developed. The teeth are large. The endocranial cast reveals, among others, the following characteristics: a sloping frontal region; a wide fissure between the lobes;

---

[3] I had an opportunity to examine the skull and the reconstruction on June 16, 1945. (H. F.)

impressions of convolutions as far as the frontal protuberances; and a central frontal furrow with a horizontal posterior protuberance.

These characteristics do not identify the skeleton with any variation of modern man even at the lowest stage of his development, but relate the Teshik-Tash skull to the type of fossil man belonging to the end of the Pleistocene period, the Middle Paleolithic, or, broadly, "Neanderthaloid."

This conclusion is beyond doubt, but from the modern point of view it is insufficient. Middle Paleolithic includes many different human types, such as the typical European Neanderthal, fossil remains from Ngandong in Java and from various places in Africa and Palestine. The question arises as to which of these types the Teshik-Tash skeleton most resembles. The extreme youth of the Teshik-Tash cranium renders it difficult to draw a final conclusion, since there is insufficient comparative material for that age. Comparative research in new data, especially the Palestine discoveries, will probably render it possible to clear up this interesting question. Nevertheless, even now the Teshik-Tash discovery is of great interest. First of all, it greatly extends the area in which Middle Paleolithic man existed. All previously found human remains were discovered at comparatively short distances from the sea. The Teshik-Tash skeleton is the first reliable proof of the penetration of Middle Paleolithic man into the interior of the Asiatic continent. Proof that man lived in high mountainous regions is also of great importance. The Teshik-Tash skeleton provides valuable material for the investigation of the variations of the "Neanderthaloid" type and for the study of age peculiarities of ancient man.

A valuable monograph by G. A. Bonch-Osmolovskii entitled "The Hand of Paleolithic Man" was published in 1941 just before World War II. It treats of another most important find of fossil man—the skeleton of a hand found in the Kiik-Koba grotto in the Crimea. Considerable literature has been written about this discovery, but a comparative anthropological study of the skeleton, the skull of which is unfortunately missing, required many years of persevering work. The published monograph treats only of the bones of the hand and is a work of exceptional value as the author is the first to have collected exhaustive material about the structural peculiarities of this important part of the skeleton of modern man, fossil man, and of various groups of *Cercopithecus* monkeys.

As the result of measurements and reconstruction, Bonch-Osmolovskii notes the following peculiarities of the skeleton of the hand of the Kiik-Koba man: relative elongation of the fourth and fifth

2

fingers; very broad carpus, metacarpus, and phalanges, especially the extreme phalanges, which give the hand a peculiar, flattened form; the flatness of certain joints which extend more horizontally giving rise to the conclusion that the Kiik-Koba man was little able to bend his fingers palmward but better able to move them sidewise. The position of the thumb is most peculiar as the joint of the first metacarpal bone is very slightly developed. Bonch-Osmolovskii believes that the ability of this fossil man to move his thumb toward the palm was greatly restricted. The general impression gained is of a wide, flat, pawlike hand. The Kiik-Koba hand is the first to have been studied in such detail and so systematically, but Bonch-Osmolovskii concludes that many of the above-mentioned features are inherent to some degree in skeletons of the European Neanderthal man. At the same time, Bonch-Osmolovskii proves convincingly that the above-described structural type of hand is not similar to that of anthropoid apes but, on the contrary, has developed away from them in the opposite direction.

In general, the Kiik-Koba man had a human hand and could make various stone implements.

Regarding the pawlike hand as the original form in the evolution of man, partially repeated in the individual development of modern man, Bonch-Osmolovskii concludes primitive man's locomotion was not like that of modern anthropoid apes.

The latter are clearly a side branch. The distant ancestors of man were adapted to a different type of locomotion, were less specifically tree forms, and according to the structure of the hand were closer to the modern group of ground monkeys of the Pavian type. This conclusion is supported by interesting facts concerning the type of locomotion of the various Primates, the development of the grasping ability in a child, and other data.

Naturally, Bonch-Osmolovskii's conclusions cannot be regarded as proved beyond doubt, especially those giving general characteristics of the hand of fossil man. The necessary data for this are lacking. The problem of the relation between various forms of Middle Paleolithic man and the modern type remains unsolved. However, Bonch-Osmolovskii's hypothesis that anthropoid apes and their specific type of grasping hand are the result of a new branch developing in a definite direction within the species is shared by many modern authorities. It is quite possible that the hand structure of Miocene Primates (to which both human and anthropoid branches trace their origin) not only lacked the distinctive features of anthropoid apes but was closer to the modern semiground types of Primates. In developing this view, Bonch-Osmolovskii contributed new material of outstanding importance for studying the evolution of man.

The wide dispersal of Neoanthropus at the end of the Pleistocene period and the disappearance of the ancient form (Paleoanthropus) is testified to by many discoveries in various parts of the world. What were the factors which ensured the predominance of Neoanthropus? This problem has been discussed in a number of works, some published and some still in press. The views developed by P. P. Efimenko deserve first mention here. In one of the chapters of his book, "Primitive Society," Efimenko observed during 1938 the significance of strict endogamy (intertribal marriage) which existed in the small hordes of the Mousterian epoch for the fixation of the specific features of the Neanderthal type. The appearance of the new type was conditioned by the formation of broader social groups, the beginnings of the gens organization. This view deserves attention although Efimenko treated the Neanderthal features in a very narrow manner, perceiving in them only signs of degeneration. Actually, it is not degeneration one should perceive but rather specialization.

S. P. Tolstov and A. Boriskovskii stress the great part played in the evolution of man by the development of hunting and technology in the Middle Paleolithic period. Indeed, collective hunting is a most important stimulus to the development of new forms of intercourse among humans, their uniting in large groups, the invention of call signals, the creation of new tools, the acquisition of new materials (horn and bone), and radical alterations in diet.

An interesting view was expressed by G. G. Roginskii, who noted that the small Neanderthal groups themselves presented obstacles to their further development. Unless he was restrained by social motives or self-control, the club-bearing and stone-armed Neanderthal man represented a considerable threat to his fellows in various conflicts for the female and for food.

The development of these two means of restraint are most typical of Neoanthropus. They are closely connected with the development of the brain, especially the frontal region, the formation of which marks the last stage in the physical evolution of man.

A study of the endocranial casts of Neanderthal man stresses the importance of other elements of cranial structure. One of the most striking features of Paleoanthropus is the very slanting frontal region, the high temporal ridge resulting in the feeble development of the lower parietal region (i.e., the region with which conscious speech is connected). Considering that the general brain cavity of Neanderthal man was no smaller than that of modern man, then Bunak's conclusion that a certain reconstruction of the cranium and the development of speech are the most outstanding characteristics of the later stages in the development of man is readily understood. This view is in complete accord with the teaching of Academician Marr on the development of speech and leads one to believe that Neanderthal man possessed only slight powers of speech.

B. MODERN RACES AND THEIR HISTORY

The anthropological study of the numerous nationalities of the Soviet Union provides a key to the solution of many cardinal problems of race formation and race systematization.

In recent years anthropological knowledge of Siberia and the Far East has been increased by extensive research as, for example, the Okhotsk Sea coast by M. G. Levin; the Amur River region by D. A. Zolotarev; among the Nentsi Samoyeds of northwestern Siberia by S. A. Shluger; the Keshms, a small group on the upper banks of the Yenisei River, by G. F. Debets; the Hants and the Mansi or Ostiaks and the Voguls of the lower Ob River by T. A. Trofimova and N. N. Cheboksarov; and the Selkups of the lower Ob by G. F. Debets. The material thus obtained has greatly enriched and rendered more exact existing information about racial types in Asia. It is becoming evident that the most characteristic type for the Asiatic continent, the so-called Mongoloid type, is far from homogeneous. Within this category exist many variations which are either local types or relics of ancient racial formations.

The dolichocephalic or mesocephalic Asiatic anthropological types are widely scattered throughout Siberia and the Far East. Variations are to be found at present among the Trans-Baikal Tungus, in places along the Amur River among the Golds, and on the Okhotsk Sea coast. It is necessary to investigate the relation of this undoubtedly more ancient anthropological type of Central and Eastern Siberia, the so-called Ural type. At present these two variations possess certain features in common, but at the same time there are essential differences in the form of the face and nose, as well as in other respects. The latest research shows that racial characteristics commonly attributed to Asiatic races—coarse hair, heavy upper eyelids with the Mongolian fold, flat faces, and others—do not prevail among the native population of Siberia.

If, in respect to southern Siberians, especially Turki groups, one may assume the blending of European elements in the formation of their type, such an assumption is out of the question regarding the more northern Siberian groups. Among the latter, in some districts there is a definite aquiline nose somewhat resembling that of the North American Indian. Is this type the result of actual genetical relations, however remote? Is this Siberian aquiline nose peculiar to an independent group? Is the aquiline nose merely a secondary trait which arose through the convergent development of separate, isolated groups? These problems may be solved within the next few years.

Much new anthropological information has been obtained about the peoples of Central Asia, especially through the craniological study of medieval and older ethnic groups by V. V. Ginzburg, L. V. Oshanin, and others. More and more facts indicate that the dolichocephalic element of European appearance is widespread in Central Asia and that modern anthropological variations, among which the brachycephalic element is prevalent, are of later formation.

In the Caucasus anthropological research has been conducted for several years, as a result of which a great deal of comparative material [4] has been obtained. Most of this extensive country has been investigated by districts, with the exception of certain regions in Daghestan and in the most mountainous regions of Georgia. The drawing of anthropological maps of the Caucasus is one of the few experiments made in anthropological analysis by districts based upon systematic observations made by groups of research workers. A summary of these data will be published in a special collection about the Caucasus, now being prepared for press by the Institute of Anthropology and Ethnography (IAE) of the Academy of Sciences.

New materials have corrected and complemented former views concerning anthropological types in the Caucasus. The existence of the mesocephalic, long-faced type with a straight nose, dark hair, often with blue or gray eyes, has been established in the northwestern Caucasus. This type is to be found among the Cherkess (Circassian)-Kabardinian peoples in the Kuban region and is clearly a variation of the so-called Pontic race. Morphological and historical data established the unity of the Kuban variation of the Pontic race with lower Danube types in Bulgaria, ancient types in present-day southern Russia, and others. In ancient times the above-described type was very widespread and predominated in what is now western Georgia.

In southeastern Transcaucasia there is another, also mesocephalic type, but it differs from the first in several respects. This type is to be found among Azerbaidzhanis, among a small group called the Tats

---

[4] Cf. my forthcoming Contributions to the Anthropology of the Caucasus. (H. F.)

(remnants of the ancient Iranian inhabitants of this region), the Talyshes, the Kurds, and others. The Transcaucasian mesocephalic type, together with the mesocephalic variation prevalent among the Transcaspian Turkmenians, comprise a special group, the Caspian race, which is also a branch of the great Mediterranean race. Some groups in northern Iran [5] also belong to the Caspian type. A third racial type, Pontozagros or Armenoid, is found in the central Trans-caucasian highlands. This type is composed of several elements, some of more ancient origin than others. The region through which the Pontozagros type is distributed includes districts of southern Daghestan.

The three above-described racial types are also widespread outside the Caucasus. A fourth type, called the Caucasian race proper, is specific for the Caucasus. This type is similar to the Armenoid, but is characterized by a narrower head and a slightly different form of face and nose. This type is found in Georgia and partially in the central Terek region in North Caucasus. The results of the anthropological analysis of the population of the Caucasus fully accord with the latest data of archeology, linguistics, and ethnography, and make it possible to trace the history of modern ethnic types.

In recent years the racial analysis of the population in the European part of the Soviet Union has also advanced considerably.

A series of Neolithic skulls found in the Olonets Lake on Olenii Island and described by E. Zhirov is of great importance in the study of the anthropology of the Far North. This series includes a slightly brachycephalic element which is similar to the Lopar type, but which differs from the latter by virtue of certain Mongoloid features. The great age of this variation in northern Europe is beyond doubt. The connection between this element and the northern forest Neolithic peoples is also evident. The Neolithic brachycephals of the north should occupy a place of their own. There are no data that justify identifying them with the western European Neolithic brachycephalic types of Borreby in Denmark, and Grenelle [6] in France.

A volume of the works of the Institute of Anthropology of the Moscow State University published in 1941 contains a number of essays on the anthropology of various Finnish peoples (articles by G. F. Debets, R. I. Zenkevich, and M. Gremiatskii). As has been observed by previous investigators, anthropologically the Finnish

---

[5] See also Henry Field, Contributions to the anthropology of Iran, Field Museum of Natural History, Chicago, 1939.

[6] This supposedly Neolithic skull, found near Paris in 1870, resembles the Azilian brachycephals of Ofnet in Bavaria. (H. F.)

peoples are not homogeneous. Baltic racial types are clearly distinguished among the Ladoga Finns, for example, among the small groups of Veps, while the Volga Mari (Cheremis) are a variation of the Ural type, and the Udmurts (Votiaks) contain elements close to the Lopar type. In the opinion of the above-mentioned authors it is to be expected that certain Finnish groups contain the neutral proto-Asiatic anthropological element or even more definitely Mongoloid elements. Such an anthropological type is outlined in craniological material belonging to the Iron Age, for example, the skull from Lugov.

In addition to ordinary anthropological investigation, certain other studies of elementary genetic features were conducted among the Finnish tribes—blood groups, reaction in a phenylthio-carbamide solution and especially to color sensitivity. The groups investigated proved very similar in these respects.

Work on the craniology of ancient Slavic tribes is being systematically conducted by T. A. Trofimova, who records differences among the southern Slav group of Severyans and the more northern Krivichi and Vyatichi. The former belong to the dolichocephalic variation, a Pontic form. Trofimova believes that among the latter, together with other elements, there are Asiatic or proto-Asiatic elements.

Several volumes by G. F. Debets treating of the craniology of the population of Russia in the epoch preceding the present one have been prepared for press. Debets has entitled his book "The Paleo-anthropology of the U.S.S.R.," but he includes in it osteological materials belonging not only to the Stone Age or to the prehistoric period in general, but to all later ages up to the seventeenth and eighteenth centuries. Debets has collected a quantity of craniological material preserved in central and local museums, all of which has been carefully checked in respect to dates and classified according to epochs and territories. This comprehensive summary gives a good picture of the craniological types and their alterations beginning with the Neolithic period until modern times through wide sections of Eastern Europe, Siberia, and Central Asia.

These data contain the solution of many anthropological problems in the U.S.S.R. Debets devotes much attention to the local transformation of craniological types, which occurred in many territories, and takes into consideration, at the same time, the change of types which took place as a result of the immigration of separate groups of the ancient population.

In addition to materials about Eastern Europe, the above-mentioned volume of the works of the Institute of Anthropology contains articles by N. N. Cheboksarov on racial types in modern Germany. Based upon the careful study of all the factual material in literature, this work is a most complete and systematic summary greatly superior to anything on this subject heretofore printed. Cheboksarov's work corrects many widespread views concerning the racial composition of the population of Germany. While reaffirming the formerly expressed view concerning the limited distribution of the North European racial type proper and the preponderance of Baltic and Central European types in northern Germany, Debets points out that the Alpine type is also not the main element of which the present population of southern Germany is composed. This type spreads over a very small region. At the same time the existence of a peculiar complex of distinctive features, which Debets classifies with the Atlantic racial form described by Deniker, has been established in the upper Rhine zone.

The great advance in the modern theory of race formation and race analysis as compared with previous views is evident from the above review. The human race is not something unchangeable. In the course of ages the various distinctive features of human groups alter; the size of the population within which marriages among members take place grows or diminishes. As a result, the concentration of various hereditary features varies and under certain conditions changes take place in the average size of the group. At the same time changes in external conditions influence one and the same tendency. The influence of intergroup marriage, as well as group isolation, should be added to these two general factors of racial differentiation.

Considering these facts it would be incorrect to draw a line for racial types based on the absolute existence of one or another trait, or even of several traits. Observing the changes of features within a certain territory one can see that these changes are very gradual; for example, the region with the highest cephalic index is surrounded by a zone where this index is slightly lower, and so forth. The region where a certain feature is most clear is evidently that region where certain hereditary traits are most concentrated, or as it is usually called, the "center of distribution." The entire zone within which the trait alters in one direction (plus or minus) comprises the region of the distribution of one type, despite differences in magnitude. The boundaries of the type are located where the alteration is in the opposite direction, i.e., where, instead of finding a reduction of the average index, it begins to increase.

However, for races the combination of several features in a given territory is always characteristic, as for example, blue eyes, wide heads and tallness. The boundaries of the distribution of the racial type are located where the given combination of features is replaced by another, for example, an increase in height when considered according to territory is accompanied by a darkening of eye color. The race, as a systematic category, is far from being the only taxonomic category. It is necessary to distinguish great races, simple races, subraces, and local races. In such a consecutive subdivision the dynamic essence of the category "race'" is revealed. A most important criterion in determining the race or subrace is the alteration of features according to territory. Those races which by anthropological analysis have been reconstructed in the modern epoch reflect groups that arose in the distant past. Evidently the types of great races arose in the Neolithic period. Outlines of the most primitive forms of some races are found in the Metal Age.

Such are the general views in the study of the race as a historical and dynamic category developed in the above-mentioned works as well as in a number of special investigations (concerning alterations in the length of the body, in the form of the skull, the general conditions of the alteration of the average index in population, the correlation of ethnic and somatic types, etc.).

Among the latest works on general problems in the study of races it is necessary to mention a series of mathematical investigations conducted by M. V. Ignatev, concerning the significance of cross-breeding, isolation, the conditions of the distribution of newly arising traits. G. G. Roginskii investigated the distribution of blood groups from the same viewpoint.

In the study of the geographical distribution of variations of ridge patterns of the fingers, N. V. Volotskoi used the "delta index" which expresses the total number of so-called deltas [triradii] per 10 fingers. Plotting the magnitudes of this index on world geographical maps revealed most important and more or less constant differences in racial groups.

C. VARIATIONS IN THE STRUCTURE OF HUMAN BODIES

The physical types of ancient and modern man is one of the main subjects of study in physical anthropology. However, no less important for this science is wide research in the variation of structure and the laws determining these variations. Only on the basis of a knowledge of ontogenetic alteration, the laws of correspondence and growth of parts of the body, and comparative anatomy can correct racial analyses be made and the earlier stages of the evolution of man be explained.

With the increase in anthropological knowledge, the number of concrete morphological problems grows. Much attention is paid not only to research in the variations of the structure of the skull and individual bones of the skeleton but also to the brain convolutions, the skin and hair, the bones and cartilage, the nose, eyelids, lips, muscles, internal organs, and outer forms of the body, and in the proportion of its parts.

In recent years a number of works in comparative anatomical research, the study of topographical and functional correlations, onto-genetic alterations and the laws of growth have been published.

In the period from birth to approximately 20 years of age, the growth of individual organs and parts of the body differs in respect to speed and length of time. For the organism in general the growth of the total size of the body, its length, weight, and chest measurement, is most characteristic. These measurements determine the size of the body surface and its volume. Available data establish a definite relation between the increase of the total size of the body and its separate parts.

As is known, during the growth period there are 3 to 4 years during which the annual increase in the total size of the body is very great. Some experts regard this so-called puberty phase in boys as extending from the ages of 11 to 15 and others from 12 to 17. An analysis of charts seems to indicate that puberty comes between 13 and 17 years for boys and 13 and 16 for girls. In comparing such widely differing groups in respect to body size as the Japanese and Americans, it is seen that variations in the above-mentioned periods are no more than 4 to 6 months.

At the same time another important circumstance becomes evident: a sharp increase in growth during puberty is characteristic for only one type. If growth is very intensive preceding puberty then the intensity of growth during the period of sexual maturing is hardly noticeable. On this basis it was possible to distinguish several types of growth and to find basic magnitudes according to which it is possible to establish the type of growth of the child in a comparatively short period of observation.

There is little relationship between the type of growth and the final size of the body. Both short and tall persons may grow according to the accelerated as well as the gradual type. At the same time it becomes clear that between the final size and the magnitude of the body at one or another age there is a relation which varies within comparatively narrow limits. In addition to being of great interest for understanding the formative process of an organism, the establishment of these laws is most important for the correct estimation of the physical development of the child by the school doctor. In this respect theoretical anthropological research is closely connected with applied anthropometry.

Research in the physical development of various groups of children is most important and has become the subject of numerous theses written by medical workers. The anthropometric study of the sizes and proportions of bodies was necessary for the standardization of sizes for army clothing. A most important role was played by anthropometric work in controlling methods of physical therapy in treating wounds.

III. PALEOLITHIC SITES [1]

INTRODUCTION [2]

The material [3] based on data available during 1938 has been arranged chronologically from the Clactonian and Primitive Mousterian to the Epipaleolithic, and is divided geographically [4] into the Euro-

---

[1] This excellent study was translated by Mrs. John F. Normano, The Asia Institute, 7 East 70th St., New York City. The text was then edited and condensed. Diacritical marks were omitted. Eugene V. Prostov checked the spellings and made some minor revisions in order to conform to our previously published articles. Under each site the bibliographical references have been omitted because the majority of these Russian publications are not available in United States libraries. However, the entire text in Russian has been placed on Microfilm No. 2414, pp. 1-38, in the American Documentation Institute, 1719 N St., NW., Washington 6, D. C., where a copy may be purchased. Since this list must be considered as separate and usually unrelated items, the names of the excavators have been retained. This volume was given to me by S. P. Tolstov, Director, Ethnological Institute, Academy of Sciences of the U.S.S.R., Moscow, while I was a guest of the Jubilee Sessions of the Academy in Moscow and Leningrad during June–July, 1945. See Anthropology in the Soviet Union, 1945, Amer. Anthrop., vol. 48, No. 3, pp. 375-396, 1946; especially bibliography in footnote 57. There are many references to these Paleolithic sites in our published articles (see p. 66, footnotes 1, 2).

[2] Throughout the text the use of the metric system has been retained and all heights are given as above sea level unless otherwise specified. The abbreviation IAE has been used for the Institute of Anthropology and Ethnography, Academy of Sciences of the U.S.S.R., Leningrad. Some technical descriptions have been included from A. J. H. Goodwin, Method in Prehistory, the South African Archaeological Society Handbook, No. 1, Cape Town, 1945, and from M. C. Burkitt, Prehistory, Cambridge University, 1925. (H. F.)

[3] From P. P. Efimenko and N. A. Beregovaia, Paleolithic Sites in the U.S.S.R., Materialy i Issledovaniia po Arkheologii SSSR, No. 2, pp. 254-290, Moscow and Leningrad, 1941.

[4] According to Prostov, for the convenience of readers having access to other than Soviet maps, the names of various administrative subdivisions of the U S.S.R. have been given in the nonadjectival form of the name of the city after which the subdivision was named. This is followed by the designation in Russian for the type subdivision. This latter, for which there is no exact English equivalent, is given in italics, as follows:

Raion (Aimak in Central Asia and Buriat Mongolia), a rural subdivision corresponding to a United States county.
Okrug, a larger subdivision currently used for several special areas.
Oblast, a major administrative subdivision (province) of a republic.
Krai, a major administrative subdivision in a sparsely populated border area (territory) of the R.S.F.S.R.

20

pean part of the R.S.F.S.R., the Ukraine, Bielorussian S.S.R., the Crimea and Caucasus, and the Asiatic part of the U.S.S.R.

The monuments of the so-called Arctic Paleolithic represent a special group. In view of the numerous Epipaleolithic finds, only the better-known and more thoroughly investigated sites have been included. However, a few well-known sites of doubtful age have not been omitted.

PRIMITIVE MOUSTERIAN AND CLACTONIAN SITES

BLACK SEA LITTORAL: ABKHAZIA [5] AND CRIMEA [6]

1. *Anastasevka.*—Flints of Mousterian type were found on the right bank of Kodor River near this village. A number of flints were collected on exposed areas associated with ferruginous manganese concretions. In addition, on the surface of the fourth terrace occurred older flints of IAshtukh type with a different patina. This material was obtained during 1932 by an IAE [7] expedition.

2. *Apiancha.*—Single flints of IAshtukh type were found on the upper platform of Apiancha Mountain between its two summits at 600 m. above sea level. The flints are distinguished by smooth facets, a deep patina and a brilliant surface. This material was obtained during 1935 by an IAE expedition.

3. *Atap.*—A few characteristic flint implements, including a hand ax, of Acheulian or Primitive Mousterian type were found on the surface of the terrace near this village. On a lower terrace were flints of Upper Paleolithic type. This site was discovered during 1935 on an IAE expedition.

4. *Byrts.*—Single flint flakes of IAshtukh type were collected on the platform of Byrts Mountain near Sukhumi about 450 m. above sea level. The first finds were made during 1934 by L. N. Solovev.

5. *Gali.*—On this site the IAE expedition found an Acheulian hand ax reutilized as a nucleus in Mousterian times.

6. *Gvard.*—Flaked flints, similar to the most ancient group from IAshtukh, were found in a Karstian declivity on the outskirts of the village (450 m.) on the slopes of Gvard Mountain. The first series was obtained during 1934 by L. N. Solovev.

7. *Kolkhida.*—Flints of Clactonian and Primitive Mousterian type were found on the top and on the slopes of the hill, representing

---

[5] Nos 1-14.

[6] No. 15.

[7] Institute of Anthropology and Ethnography, Academy of Sciences of the U.S.S.R., Leningrad.

the 180-m. terrace at this village near Novye Gagry. These surface flints originated in a lower horizon associated with iron manganese concretions. While the material assembled by the IAE expedition during 1935 is not large, its value lies in the uniformity of the series. Some of the flints· bear traces of utilization.

8. *Kiurdere.*—On the surface of an ancient terrace flints of Primitive Mousterian (Acheulian) type were found by S. N. Zamiatnin during 1934 at Kiurdere near Psyrtskhi on the left bank of the Shitskhuara River, near its exit from the gorge. A hand ax and tools made from crude flakes were found not only on the surface of this terrace, but also in the ancient alluvium along the slope of the neighboring limestone ridge.

9. *Okum.*—See No. 48.

10. *Sukhumi.*—Flints of IAshtukh (Primitive Mousterian or Acheulian) type can be found within the city limits, on the banks of the Sukhumka River, which cuts through the fourth terrace at IAshtukh site, as well as in the nearby surrounding area on the top of Cherniavskii Mountain and in the Ostroumov gorge. These discoveries were made during 1935 by an IAE expedition.

11. *Tabachnaia.*—During 1936 on the surface of the 100- to 110-m. terrace at the Zonal Tobacco Experimental Station near Sukhumi, L. N. Solovev found flint flakes of Primitive Mousterian type and a hand ax as well as some flints of Upper Paleolithic appearance.

12. *Tekh.*—In the valley on the road from Tsebelda to Tekh, at 350-400 m. above sea level on the surface of the clayey loam, L. N. Solovev found during 1936 flints of Primitive Mousterian type. Some tools and laminae of Upper Paleolithic appearance were collected.

13. *Chuburiskhindzhi.*—A few crude flakes and implements, including one hand ax, of dark pink and gray Turon flint were collected on the right bank of a stream along the road 12 kilometers southeast of Gali near Satandzhio Mountain. These specimens, contemporaneous with the surviving vestiges of the old fifth terrace, showed signs of utilization and were deeply patined. Ridges between facets were worn smooth. This site was located during 1935 by an IAE expedition.

14. *IAshtukh.*—Flints of Acheulian or Primitive Mousterian type were found on the surface of the fourth terrace (100 m.) near Nizhnii IAshtukh, 3 kilometers north of Sukhumi, in the gorge between Byrts and IAshtukh Mountains. The flints, including discoidal nuclei, massive flakes and implements manufactured from them, as well as hand axes, lay on the large platform, often on the surface, sometimes among pebbles under the diluvial clay. Typologically later flints of

Mousterian and Upper Paleolithic appearance were also found, but are linked stratigraphically with the upper levels of the clayey loam. The first collection was made during 1934 by S. N. Zamiatnin.

15. *Kiik-Koba.*—Remains of Primitive Mousterian type were found in the lower stratum above bedrock in this cave, situated on the right bank of the Zuia River near Kipchak, which lies about 25 kilometers east of Simferopol. Here were excavated by G. A. Bonch-Osmo-lovskii during 1924-1926 numerous flint implements and flakes associated with remains of *Cervus elaphus, Equus, Bos, Saiga, Sus scrofa,* etc.

MOUSTERIAN SITES [8]

16. *Kodak.*—This site, located on the high right bank of the Dnieper 10 kilometers southeast of Dnepropetrovsk, was discovered during 1932 through the accidental finds of several flints associated with Pleistocene fauna. Further investigations were conducted during 1934-1935. These finds lay in the bottom of the deep ravine of Nizhniaia Sazhavka, which cuts the loess bank of the Dnieper, at a distance of 1 kilometer from the river. The stratigraphy consists of 20.0 m. of loess with several horizons of buried topsoil, ancient diluvium from ravines, red-brown clays, variegated clays, and granite bedrock. Nearer to the mouth of the ravine the alluvium of the gulleys is replaced by stratified sands containing fresh-water Mollusca typical of stagnant and slow-flowing waters. Mousterian remains were found in the base of the stratified gray-greenish sands (ravine alluvium) overlain by loess. Below, the sands were mixed with gravel. The cultural stratum was evidently partly washed away. The flints, together with crushed bones, lay in the lower part of the stratum among the pebbles and gravel. Above were also found animal bones. The fauna is represented by *Elephas trogontherii, Rhinoceros tricho-rhinus, Bison priscus, Equus equus, Cervus megaceros, Rangifer tarandus, Felis spelaea, Ursus arctos,* etc.

The several dozen tools were mainly of dark-brown flint, but some were of quartz and compact sandstone. There were: biface points, a discoidal nucleus used as a carinate scraper, scraping tools, broad laminae, etc. Incisions could be seen on the phalanges of the large

---

[8] The geographical distribution of these sites is as follows: The middle course of the Dnieper (No. 16), the basin of the Desna (Nos. 17-18), northern Donets (Nos. 19-21), the Crimea (Nos. 22-28), the coast of the Sea of Azov (No. 29), Kuban (No. 30), Kuma (No. 31), the northern part of the Caucasian coast (Nos. 32-36), Abkhazia (Nos. 37-54), Mingrelia (No. 55), and Uzbekistan (No. 56).

deer; they resembled those found on the "small anvils" of the Mousterian period.[9]

17. *Chulatovo III.*—Rolled flints of Mousterian type were found during 1938 eroded from the bank of the Desna River near Chulatovo near Novgorod-Seversk.

18. *Svetilovichi* (Bielorussia).—Accidental finds on the second terrace above the flood plain of rolled and patined points of Mousterian type were made during 1929 by P. N. Chaikovskii, a teacher who studied the region, on the right bank of the Baseda River in the ravine of Kamennaia Gora near Svetilovichi. These implements were described in 1937 by K. M. Polikarpovich.

19. *Derkul.*—This Mousterian station, largely destroyed by the river, stands near Kolesnikovo farm on the right bank of the Derkul River, a left tributary of the northern Donets River, above its mouth. The Paleolithic remains lie in a stratum of finely rounded flint gravel. This stratum divides two layers of sandy alluvium, of which the lower one, covering the surface of the marl, represents the remnants of the ancient third above the flood-plain terrace of the Derkul River. The only bone found was that of a large mammal. The tools were mainly of quartzite. This site was discovered during 1924 by P. P. Efimenko and studied by him during 1924-1926 and 1930.

20. *Kamenskaia.*—Bones of mammoth and other animals were reported but unconfirmed from the ancient gravel deposits near the Cossack village of Kamenskaia, in the Donets region, near the confluence of the Rychnitsa River with the Northern Donets. The discovery of a discoidal nucleus was reported.

21. *Krasnyi IAr.*—Many large flint flakes and implements of Mousterian type, including points, scrapers, etc., were collected during 1925-1926 by S. A. Loktiushev close to the Northern Donets River, 15 kilometers southeast of Voroshilovgrad [formerly Lugansk]. This station is about 1 kilometer southeast of Krasnyi IAr farm, on the right bank of the river.

22. *Adzhi-Koba.*—This cave of the corridor type, located on the western slope of Korabi-IAila in the mountainous region of the Crimea, was investigated by G. A. Bonch-Osmolovskii during 1932-

---

[9] Cf. at La Quina, Charente district of France, discovered by the late Dr. Henri-Martin and reported from Teshik-Tash near Tashkent. (H. F.) The use of a bone rest or anvil was common in Europe even before the Middle Paleolithic when many large splinters of bone are found to bear indentations and scratches caused by "rest percussion." The bone was used in much the same way that we might use a bench, to steady and support the artifact while fine percussion or pressure was used. (A. J. H. G.)

1933. It contains two horizons: the upper of the Late Paleolithic type of Siuren I with northern deer; and the lower of Mousterian type with saiga antelope, northern deer, rhinoceros, wild donkey, Arctic fox, polecat, etc.

23. *Volchii Grot.*—This Mousterian cave situated on the right bank of the Beshtirek River at Mazanka near Simferopol, was discovered and investigated by Merezhkovskii during 1880. He found, mixed with ashes and charcoal, a Mousterian point, a small hand ax, and remains of mammoth, wild horse, *Bos,* giant deer, and saiga antelope in the yellow Quaternary stratum. During 1938 O. N. Bader discovered here a rich Mousterian deposit.

24. *Kiik-Koba.*[10]—The upper cultural horizon of this cave (see also No. 15) lies in the stratum of yellow clay mixed with crushed rock and is divided from the lower horizon, containing the Lower Mousterian inventory, by a sterile band. The majority of the implements were points (some biface) and scrapers. The fauna included the mammoth, woolly rhinoceros, wild horse, wild donkey, primitive *Bos,* wild boar, cave bear, hyena, fox, rodents, and birds. Some of the bones bore traces of incisions, suggesting use as small anvils [11] or for pressure flaking. This was the site of the destroyed burial containing Neanderthal remains.[12]

25. *Kosh-Koba.*—Traces of an apparently Mousterian cave, 25 kilometers from Simferopol on the right bank of the Zuia River next to Kiik-Koba. During 1923 G. A. Bonch-Osmolovskii found two large hearths, a few flints, and many animal bones, partly split, including mammoth, rhinoceros, cave hyena, giant deer, bison, saiga antelope, horse, wild donkey, fox, marmot, etc.

26. *Chagorak-Koba.*—This Middle Paleolithic cave near Kainaut in the Karasubazar region in the Crimea was discovered by O. N. Bader during 1935 and studied by him during 1936-1937. The fauna, including the woolly rhinoceros, wild horse, saiga, and cave hyena, was found in the Quaternary stratum during 1936. In the following year in the same stratum several flint implements of Mousterian type were unearthed.

27. *Chokurcha.*—An Upper Mousterian cave in the valley of Malyi

---

[10] On July 2, 1945, the Director of the Ethnological Institute of the Academy of Sciences of the U.S.S.R., asked me to transmit to the Chicago Natural History Museum, formerly Field Museum of Natural History, a cast of the Kiik-Koba skeleton. Although since 1942 no longer curator of physical anthropology, I forwarded it to Chicago. (H. F.)

[11] See footnote 9.

[12] One wrist had been found.

Salgir stream near Chokurcha, 2 kilometers northeast of Simferopol, was discovered and investigated by S. I. Zabnin during 1927 and excavated in 1928 and in the following years. The cultural remains of the Quaternary period occur in the yellow clayey loam containing crushed rock, which extends to the rocky bottom of the cave and continues all along the slope where it attains about 4.0 m. in thickness. More than nine thin cultural levels with traces of hearths were recorded in this alluvial deposit. On the slope in front of the cave was found an accumulation of split mammoth bones, associated with a considerable thickness of the cultural stratum. The flint inventory consisted of a large quantity of unifaced and bifaced tools. A few bone awls were found. Included in the fauna were the mammoth, cave hyena, cave bear, rhinoceros, saiga antelope, *Bos, Cervus,* and fox.

28. *Shaitan-Koba.*—A Late Mousterian cave located on the right slope of Bodrak Valley, near a tributary of the Alma River, at Tau-Bodrak near Simferopol. This cave, discovered by S. N. Bibikov during 1928, was investigated by G. A. Bonch-Osmolovskii during 1929-1930. The cultural remains occur in the Quaternary gravels, in the limestone stratum of the rock shelter and also on the scree slopes. Large flint tools of local dark flint were found together with typical Mousterian implements; the inventory included prismatic laminae, scrapers, burins, etc. The fauna included mammoth, cave lion, cave hyena, wild horse, saiga, Arctic fox, rodents, etc.

29. *Bessergenovka.*—During 1933 V. I. Gromov and V. A. Khokhlovkina found Mousterian flakes beneath the Rissian loess near Taganrog on an ancient terrace on the coast of the Sea of Azov.

30. *Ilskaia.*—This Upper Mousterian site lies near the Cossack village of Ilskaia on the left slope going to the valley of the Ilia River. The cultural deposit, 0.5 m. in thickness, extended over a wide area in the upper part of the second terrace, 15.0 m. above the Ilia River. The fauna included a considerable quantity of bones of the primitive *Bos.* The simplest implements were made of bone. Discovered by Baron Joseph de Baye during 1898, investigated by S. N. Zamiatnin in 1925, 1926, and 1928, and by V. A. Gorodtsov in 1936 and 1937.

31. *Podkumskaia.*—A calvarium and other fragmental human bones were found in 1918 at Piatigorsk during sewer construction. These remains were described by M. Gremiatskii. The possibility of assigning these remains to the Mousterian period or to any part of the Paleolithic is now seriously challenged.

32. *Akhshtyr cave.*—Four kilometers from Golitsyno in the Adler *Raion* on the right bank of the Mzymta River, Mousterian flints were

found during 1936 by S. N. Zamiatnin, who continued excavation during the following 2 years. (See pls. 1-4.)

33. *Navalishino cave.*—Located in the Adler *Raion* near Navali-shino, on the Kudepsta River, the lower part of this cave belongs to the Mousterian period. The characteristic flint inventory and numerous cave bear remains were found by S. N. Zamiatnin during 1936.

34. *Khosta* ("The White Rocks").—Mousterian flints were found during 1936 in gullies on the precipitous banks of a ravine about 5 kilometers from Khosta near the paved highway to Vorontsov.

35. *Natsmen.*—Further downstream of the Khosta River than the site of No. 34 and on the opposite bank, on the southern slope of Akhum Mountain in the territory of the Kolkhoz "Natsmen," there was found during 1935 another site with implements and flakes of Mousterian type.

36. *Pauk.*—Crude flints of Mousterian type were found on the plowed surface of the ancient 100-m. terrace in the region of Tuapse, behind Kadoshinskii Cape on the territory of the rest camp near Pauk Mountain.

37. *Anastasevka.*—Here were found Mousterian flints. (See No. 1.)

38. *Akhbiuk.*—Traces of an Upper Mousterian site were identified on the surface of the 80-m. terrace near Akhbiuk Mountain, 6 kilo-meters north of Sukhumi. Discovered by L. N. Solovev during 1935, this open-air station was investigated by an IAE expedition.

39. *Achigvari.*—Typical Mousterian flakes were collected on the surface of the 30-m. terrace.

40. *Bzyb.*—Mousterian flints were found on the right bank of the Bzyb River near Kilometer 16 of the paved highway.

41. *Bogoveshta.*—A few characteristic Mousterian flint implements were collected during 1936 on the surface of the third terrace and along the Pshap River higher on the slope near this village.

42. *Gali.*—Typically Mousterian and Upper Paleolithic flints were found on the surface of the diluvial loam, which covers the ancient 80- to 100-m. terrace. The first discoveries were made by L. N. Solovev during 1935. (See No. 5.)

43. *Ilori.*—Several Mousterian flakes were collected by L. N. Solovev during 1935 in the yellow loam of the 16-m. terrace.

44. *Kelasuri.*—Upper Mousterian implements were found during 1935 by an IAE expedition on the surface of the third terrace and partly also in the slope of the fourth terrace, on the left bank of the Kelasuri River. This site lies on the estate of the All-Union Insti-tute of Sub-Tropical Cultures.

45. *Lemsa.*—On the slopes of the ravine about 300 m. above sea level Mousterian flints were found in a cave and on the edge of the plateau.

46. *Lechkop.*—Mousterian flints were collected on the surface of this terrace near Sukhumi by the IAE expedition during 1935. The same type of implements were also found nearby by L. N. Solovev during 1936 on the 10- to 12-m. terrace.

47. *Mokva.*—Some characteristic Mousterian flints, including discoidal nuclei, were found on the 10- to 12-m. terrace, 2 kilometers from the upper terrace.

48. *Okum.*—A large series of Mousterian flints were found on the tea plantations of the State farm "Chai-Gruzia" near Achigvary on the surface of the 80-m. terrace above the left bank of the Okum River. Among the implements was one finely worked hand ax. The surface of these flint implements bore a characteristic luster and some had traces of iron manganese concretions, which confirms their original location in the ancient horizon. Higher on the same slope typologically older flints were collected. This material was collected by the 1935 IAE expedition.

49. *Ochemchiri.*—Characteristic Upper Mousterian flints were found at the edge of the third (35-m.) terrace, 1 kilometer from Ochemchiri on the paved highway along the Sukhumi River. Lying partly in situ in the loam with iron manganese concretions, the flints appeared dark red with a brilliant, dark-brown patina. The first finds were made by L. N. Solovev. During 1934-1935 this site was explored by an IAE expedition with the participation of two geologists, G. F. Mirchink and V. I. Gromov.

50. *Tabachnaia.*—Mousterian flints were found near here. (See No. 11.)

51. *Tskhiri.*—Some Mousterian flints were found by the 1935 IAE expedition on the surface of the 30-m. terrace.

52. *Esheri.*—A few Mousterian flints were collected on the surface of the eroded 80-m. terrace in a stratum of pebbles near this village by an IAE expedition during 1935.

53. *IAgish.*—A few Mousterian flints were collected by the 1936 expedition from IAE on the elevated plateau 450-500 m. above sea level.

54. *IAshtukh.*—Mousterian flints were found here. (See No. 14.)

55. *Rukhi I.*—On the low ground, which is flooded by the Rukhi River in the spring, about 6 kilometers from Zugdidi, A. N. Kalandadze discovered during 1936 typologically Mousterian flakes.

56. *Teshik-Tash.*—This cave, situated on the northwestern slope

of the Baisun-tau Mountains at 1,500 m., lies 18 kilometers from Baisun in the Turgan-Darya Valley of southern Uzbekistan. Here were discovered five Mousterian strata. The flint inventory consisted of discoidal nuclei, typical triangular flakes, crude chopping tools, scrapers, and small bone anvils.[13] The fauna included *Capra sibirica* and, less often, horse, boar, leopard, marmot, and a rodent (*pishchukha*). The skeleton of a Neanderthaloid child [14] was found here by A. P. Okladnikov during 1938. This represents the first Paleolithic site discovered in Central Asia.

UPPER PALEOLITHIC AND EPIPALEOLITHIC SITES

EUROPEAN PART OF THE R.S.F.S.R.[15]

57. *Anosovka.*—An Upper Paleolithic site was located near Kostenki in the Gremiachenskii *Raion* of the Voronezh *Oblast*. Finds were made by the Kostenkj expedition during 1936. The cultural stratum is stained deeply by red ocher. The animal bones include many fragments of antlers.

58. *Borshevo I* (Kuznetsov Log).—Located on the northern border of this village in the Gremiachenskii *Raion* of the Voronezh *Oblast* on the bank of the Don, the cultural remains and bones of animals, mostly mammoth, lay not very deep in the diluvial deposit along the slope of the gully. The flint inventory is characterized by flint points with lateral flakes removed, which date this site in either the Aurignacian or Solutrean period. Discovered by A. A. Spitsyn during 1905, it was investigated by S. N. Zamiatnin in 1922 and by P. P. Efimenko in 1923 and 1925.

59. *Borshevo II.*—The lower and middle horizons of this site lie on the right bank of the Don near Borshevo, Gremiachenskii *Raion* of the Voronezh *Oblast*. These two horizons, containing mammoth bones (especially numerous in the lower horizon), belong to the

---

[13] See footnote 9.

[14] On June 16, 1945, in the Anthropological Laboratory of the University of Moscow I had the privilege of examining the reconstructed Teshik-Tash skull, which will be published during 1948 by Bunak and Okladnikov. For photographs of this skull and reconstructions by M. M. Gerasimov, see Henry Field, Illustrations of the Teshik-Tash Skull, Amer. Journ. Phys. Anthrop., vol. 4, No. 1, pp. 121-123, 1946.

[15] In the European part of the R.S.F.S.R. will be described the following stations: the Don (Nos. 57-70), the Oka (Nos. 71-79), the basin of the Desna (Nos. 80-85), the Seim (No. 86), the Upper Dnieper (No. 87), the Upper Volga (No. 88), the Middle Volga (Nos. 89-94), the basin of the Kama (No. 95), the southern Urals (Nos. 96-99), and the Sea of Azov coast (No. 100).

Magdalenian period. This site was first located during 1922 by P. A. Nikitin. The excavations were made by P. P. Efimenko in 1923, 1925, and 1929, and by P. I. Boriskovskii in 1906.

60. *Borshevo II.*—The upper horizon corresponding to the stratum of buried soil belongs to the end of the Magdalenian or to the Early Azilian period. No mammoth bones were found. This cultural stratum slopes gradually down to the side of the mouth of the Borshevo gully and finally goes under the level of the Don River. (See No. 59.)

61. *Borshevo III.*—At the mouth of Vishunov ravine, which cuts the high Cretaceous right bank of the Don between Kuznetsov gully and Borshevo ravine, at the time of first excavations made by P. P. Efimenko during 1923, on the terrace of the bank was discovered the accumulation of mammoth bones. Excavation by P. I. Boriskovskii in 1936 also yielded the bones of *Bos* and other animals, and isolated flints.

62. *Gagarino.*—This Aurignacian-Solutrean site, on the left bank of the Don, higher than the mouth of the Sosna River, near Gagarino in the Voronezh *Oblast,* is located on the northern slope of the ravine, which leads to the Don Valley. The cultural remains lie directly under the black earth (*chernozem*) in the upper part of the brown loess. Limestone blocks indicated the walls of the shallow dugouts. Among faunal remains mammoth bones were the most numerous, but there were also represented the woolly rhinoceros, northern deer, bison, Arctic fox, and rodents. The flint inventory is characterized by the presence of points with lateral flakes removed (cf. No. 58). In addition to bone tools, S. N. Zamiatnin found, during 1927 and 1929, female figurines made from the tusk of a mammoth.

63. *Kostenki I.*—This Lower Solutrean site near Kostenki in the Gremiachenskii *Raion* of the Voronezh *Oblast* stands on the right bank of the Don about 30 kilometers south of Voronezh. Here were found the remains of a large encampment, forming an oval plateau covered with traces of habitation, with the line of hearths following its longitudinal axis. This area was occupied by numerous pits used as storerooms. Around this surface construction were found considerably larger pits or storerooms and three dugouts. In addition to a large series of flint implements and animals bones, there were also art objects including 42 female figurines (mainly in fragments), many sculptures of animals, complete figures, heads, etc. Represented in the fauna were a quantity of mammoth bones, as well as the horse, Arctic fox, cave lion, bear, wolf, and hare. Only single finds of musk ox and northern deer came to light. The cultural stratum lies under the fertile black earth (*chernozem*) in the upper part of the diluvial

loess-argillaceous soil. At the base of this clay were discovered, during 1931, traces of an older settlement attributed to the beginning of the Upper Paleolithic. Here were found mammoth, horse, and saiga antelope. The excavations at Kostenki I were made by P. P. Efimenko during 1931-1936. The first account of these Paleolithic dwellings was mentioned by I. S. Poliakov in 1879 and by A. I. Kelsiev in 1881. Some excavations were made by S. A. Krukovskii in 1915, by S. N. Zamiatnin in 1922, and by P. P. Efimenko in 1923. Two nearby sites, similar to the above-described dwellings, were found later by Efimenko.

64. *Kostenki II.*—This Lower Magdalenian site on the right bank of the Don is located at the mouth of Anosov gully, where it merges with the Don Valley. The cultural remains consist of a rich accumulation of mammoth bones with traces of hearths. The fauna also included single examples of the horse, hare, Arctic fox, and bear. The implements, mainly made from flint boulders, consisted for the most part of crude burins. The crudest type of bone tools were also found. This site was discovered and investigated by P. P. Efimenko during 1923 and by S. N. Zamiatnin in 1927.

65. *Kostenki III.*—A Lower Magdalenian station on the bank of the Don near the mouth of Chekalin gully; apparently this location was mentioned by Omelin in 1769. The cultural stratum of yellowish loam, about 2.0 m. deep, lies in a narrow depression in the escarpment. In addition to the mammoth, the fauna is represented by a few bones of the horse, Arctic fox, and hare. The flint tools, of Cretaceous and boulder flint, are small, with primitive chisels prevailing. Rare finds of crude bone implements were made. This site was investigated by P. P. Efimenko during 1925 and by S. N. Zamiatnin during 1927.

66. *Kostenki IV.*—This Lower Magdalenian site stands on the right bank of the Don at the mouth of Aleksandrovskii (Biriuchii) gully. Located at the merging point of the gully and the low terrace, which is partly covered with water in the spring, the cultural stratum lies in the clay at a depth of 1.5 m. In the fauna the mammoth predominated, but there were also represented the horse, hare, and Arctic fox. The flint inventory was more diverse than at Kostenki II and Kostenki III. A few simple bone implements were excavated. Kostenki IV was discovered and investigated by S. N. Zamiatnin in 1927 and by A. N. Rogachev in 1927 and 1928. Rogachev discovered two large, elongated above-ground dwellings. The interior, slightly below the surface of the ground, was filled with refuse. Each building had more than 10 hearths in one line and consisted of four or five round houses 5-7 m. in diameter, closely adjacent and merging

with each other. Part were dugouts with the floor 0.6 m. deep. The general planning of this settlement is slightly similar to that of Kostenki I.

67. *Kostenki V.*—This station lies deeper in Pokrovskii gully than Kostenki I, which faces it on the right side of the gully. In the side fork of the gully (the first from the mouth) are two Upper Paleolithic sites, discovered by Efimenko during 1928. The first, located in the lower part of the side gully near the brook, yielded a great accumulation of mammoth bones and some flint implements. Since the cultural stratum lies beneath the loess and Cretaceous crushed pebbles, this monument should be attributed to the early phase of the Upper Paleolithic. The second Upper Paleolithic site lies higher, on the ascent of the elevation on Mirkina Mountain.

68. *Streletskaia.*—Traces of an Upper Paleolithic site at the mouth of Aleksandrovskii gully near Kostenki in Voronezh *Oblast* were found on the right side of the gully opposite Kostenki IV on the low terrace at the foot of the bank. Zamiatnin discovered here during 1927 typologically Upper Paleolithic flints and bones of mammoth. Excavations made by P. P. Efimenko corroborated the discovery of this site, which was presumably eroded, the result of being only slightly above the waters of the Don.

69. *Telmanskaia Stoianka.*—Situated in the fork of two gullies before they reach the Don Valley, this site is located on Kolkhoz "Telman." Discovered by A. N. Rogachev in 1936 and investigated by S. N. Zamiatnin in 1937, the main excavation revealed a circular dwelling of dugout type with the hearth near its entrance. The flint inventory combines the typical Lower Solutrean implements (laurel-leaf points) and Mousterian forms. In the fauna the mammoth predominated. Many implements were manufactured from bones.

70. *Shubnoe.*—An accumulation of Quaternary animal bones were excavated near this village in Voronezh *Oblast* about 15 kilometers west of Ostrorozhsk. In addition to many bones of the mammoth and horse, there were fewer of *Bos primigenius* and rhinoceros and a few of *Cervus elaphus* and *Cervus megaceros*. At the outlets to the ravine were solitary unretouched flints. This station was discovered by S. N. Zamiatnin in 1925 and investigated by him in 1933.

71. *Gremiachee.*—This Epipaleolithic [16] site stands on the right bank of the Oka River opposite the mouth of its tributary, the Zhizdra. Discovered and investigated by N. I. Bulychev at the end of the 1890's, this station is situated on the sandy hill at the level of the flood plain. The finds lay in the upper stratum of the loamy

---

[16] Attributed to the so-called "Sviderskian Phase" of the Epipaleolithic period.

alluvium. The flint tools were made from knife-shaped laminae. Three arrowheads with handles were found, but no animal bones or bone implements.

72. *Elin Bor.*—This Epipaleolithic [16] site stands on the left bank of the Oka River near Elina, 25 kilometers farther upstream from Murom. Discovered in 1878 by P. P. Kudriavtsev,[17] P. I. Boriskovskii in 1934 investigated the remains of the site on the sandy hill 1 kilometer south of the village. The flint inventory [16] consisted mainly of elongated laminae, nuclei, scrapers, chisels, arrowheads, and many flakes. No bone implement or animal bones were found.

73. *Karacharovo.*—A Lower Magdalenian station on the left bank of the Oka, about 3 kilometers upstream from Murom, was found near this village. Discovered by A. S. Uvarov during 1877, Karacharovo was investigated by him together with I. S. Poliakov and V. B. Antonovich during 1877-1878. Situated on the left slope of the Karacharovo ravine near its mouth, the Paleolithic remains lay in the lower part of the loesslike loam at a depth of 1.0-1.5 m. The cultural stratum, with a disorderly accumulation of animal bones, covers the surface of about 1.5 sq. m. While mammoth remains predominated, bones of *Rhinoceros, Bos,* and *Cervus* were also excavated. The flint implements were made from boulders.

74. *Meltinovo.*—Fragments of bones of fossil animals and some flint flakes were found in the valley of the Dolets, upstream from Belev, along the Oka River, near Meltinovo. The Paleolithic age of the flints has not been determined.

75. *Okskaia.*—K. Lisitsyn described an Upper Paleolithic station in the alluvial deposit of the spring-flooded terrace of the Oka River. The cultural stratum comprises broken and charred bones of *Bos, Sus,* etc., fish vertebrae, and fresh-water Mollusca. It may well be that this site should be attributed to a later era.

76. *Stenino.*—Mammoth bones and flint implements were found in the vicinity of Kozelsk, along Trostianka brook, part of the basin of the Zhizdra River. According to N. I. Krishtafovich the fauna included mammoth, rhinoceros, elk, and deer. The flint and bone tools were not described. The first report was in 1900 from I. Chetyrkin.

77. *Skhodnia.*—Part of a human calvarium was found during 1936 at a depth of 4.0 m. in the valley of the Skhodnia River, a left tributary of the Moskva River, 12 kilometers north of Moscow during the construction of the Volga-Moscow Canal. According to G. F. Mirchink, this find belongs to the end of the Würmian or to the beginning of the following era.

---

[17] He collected surface specimens from local sand dunes during 1878-1894.

78. *IAsakovo.*—A quantity of Quaternary animal bones were found near Troitsa-Pelenitsa on the ancient terrace on the right bank of the Oka River at IAsakovo Station on the Moscow-Kazan Railroad. Discovered by P. P. Efimenko in 1922, this station was investigated in 1934 by P. I. Boriskovskii, who also found here in an untouched stratum several worked flints of Upper Paleolithic type.

79. *IAsnikolskoe.*—Bones of *Cervus megaceros,* horse, and some other animals were found near the efflux of the small riven Aksen, a tributary of the Mostia, on the watershed between the Oka and the Don. The bones were in the alluvial clay beneath a stratum of peat. The so-called flint and bone implements are of doubtful human manufacture.

80. *Timonovka.*—On the right bank of the Desna River near Briansk this Magdalenian site is situated on the side of the ravine which slopes down to the Desna. The finds consist of many flint and bone implements. The fauna is represented by the mammoth, northern deer, Arctic fox, etc. This site was excavated by M. V. Voevodskii in 1926 and by V. A. Gorodtsov from 1928 to 1933. The latter found the remains of houses.

81. *Suponevo.*—This former Magdalenian station stands on the right bank of the Desna, 4 kilometers south of Briansk. Situated on the second terrace above flood plain one can find traces of some kind of constructions and an accumulation of mammoth bones. The fauna included· mammoth, rhinoceros, northern deer, bison, horse, Arctic fox, etc. Suponevo was investigated during 1926-1928 by P. P. Efimenko, B. S. Zhukov, and others.

82. *Eliseevichi.*—On the right bank of the Sudost River, a right tributary of the Desna near this village in the Pochep *Raion,* a Lower Magdalenian station was located. The cultural remains lay in the loess, covering the second terrace of the Sudost River. They consist of dwellings, an accumulation of mammoth skulls and tusks, tablets covered with carvings, and a female figurine of ivory. The fauna consisted almost exclusively of mammoth. The excavations were conducted by K. M. Polikarpovich in 1930, 1935, and 1936.

83. *Kurovo.*—On the right bank of the Sudost River stands this Upper Paleolithic station which was excavated by K. M. Polikarpovich in 1930. The fauna included mammoth, rhinoceros, horse, etc.

84. *Novye Bobovichi.*—In 1927 traces of an Upper Paleolithic station with worked flints and an accumulation of mammoth bones was found on the right bank of the Iput River, left tributary of the Sozh in the vicinity of Novozybkov.

85. *IUdinovo.*—This Upper Paleolithic site stands on the right

bank of the Sudost River, 14 kilometers north of Pogar, on the terrace above the spring floods on Kolkhoz "Pervomaiski." Preliminary excavations were made by K. M. Polikarpovich during 1934. Flint implements and mammoth bones were found in two places 200 m. away from both sides of the ravine.

86. *Suchkino.*—Traces of an Upper Paleolithic station on the left bank of the Seim River near Suchkino, 8 kilometers east of Rylsk, were investigated by S. N. Zamiatnin during 1930. The fauna consisted of mammoth, and the flints were insignificant, mainly flakes.

87. *Gamkovo.*—A large quantity of mammoth bones and rhinoceros were found under the loess in fluvioglacial deposits covering the Riss moraine, 17 kilometers southwest of Smolensk on the watershed of the Ufinia River, the left tributary of the Dnieper. Only one worked flint came to light. This station has been investigated several times since 1910; small excavations were made in 1933 by K. M. Polikarpovich and G. A. Bonch-Osmolovskii.

88. *Skniatino.*—This Upper Paleolithic station is located on the dunes of the left bank of the Nerlia River near its confluence with the Volga. The large flint inventory is Azilian-Tardenoisian (Sviderskian Phase) in character. In 1937 P. N. Tretiakov, basing his study on pollen analysis, found it possible to attribute this site to the boreal phase.

89. *Kuibyshev.*—Mammoth bones were discovered during October 1926, while laying a sewer pipe on the Voznesenskii Spusk on the bank of the Volga. Investigation of this site by M. G. Matkin and A. I. Terenozhkin showed that bones lay at a depth of 3.2 m. under the fertile soil and the reddish-brown clay in a stratum of yellow sand above another arenaceous layer mixed with limestone pebbles. Near the mammoth bones were several small flint flakes.

90. *Mulinov Ostrov.*—Fossil bones were found on this island on the left bank of the Volga opposite the *gorodishche* between Tetiushi and Ulianovsk. Together with the remains of mammoth, Siberian rhinoceros, northern deer, elk, and bison there was found a human mandible. The Paleolithic character of the finds has not been established.

91. *Postnikov Ovrag.*—This Azilian (or even later) station stands at the mouth of the Postnikov ravine, on the northern outskirts of Kuibyshev, near the Postnikov site with the microlithic inventory. P. P. Efimenko and M. G. Matkin discovered on the slope of the bank a cultural stratum comprising microlithic flints and bone implements, including needles, together with faunal remains as yet not investigated.

92. *Undory.*—Fossil bones were found in a sand bar near the right

bank of the Volga on the island near Undory between Tetiushi and Ulianovsk. Together with the bones of mammoth and other animals there were also found two human calvaria, with the dark coloring characteristic of Pleistocene fauna. The age of these finds remains uncertain.

93. *Khriashchevskaia Kosa.*—Fossil bones were found on the left bank of the Volga near Sengilei, farther downstream than this village. Since the end of the 1870's bones of mammoth, Siberian rhinoceros, primitive *Bos,* European bison, northern deer, elk, horse, and camel have been found here. According to P. A. Ososkov this accumulation of bones is the result of human activity since the long bones are often split and bear traces of utilization. In addition, there was found the frontal part of a human skull, which is, however, less deeply colored than the animal bones. The Paleolithic character of the finds remains tentative.

94. *IAblonov Protok.*—Among bones found on the left bank of the Volga on the eroded sandy crest between the IAblonov channel and the Sobachia Prorva channel near Tetiushi were those of mammoth, Siberian rhinoceros, horse, elk, noble deer, bison (*zubr*), and camel. Here also was found a human humerus, covered with the same almost black and brilliant patina as the animal bones. No Paleolithic flints were found.

95. *Ostrov.*—The first find of the Upper Paleolithic period in the Kama basin was made during September 1938 by M. V. Talitskii on the Chusovaia River near Ostrov and Gladenovo. The cultural stratum, 10.0 cm. thick, lies at a depth of 11.0 m. between the deposits covered by spring floods. The fauna included mammoth and northern deer, and apparently also the Siberian rhinoceros. The material consisted of flakes of flint, slate, and rock crystal, as well as knife-shaped laminae and small scrapers. Apparently it is here that occurred the accidental find of a mammoth rib fragment with the engraving in Paleolithic style, which first indicated the existence of this site.

96. *Buranovskaia Peshchera.*—This cave is located 8 kilometers north of Ust-Katav on the bank of the Yuryuzan River in the Cheliabinsk *Oblast.* The cultural stratum, containing the crushed bones of animals, was discovered during 1938 at a depth of 2.0 m. in a yellow clay deposit by S. N. Bibikov. The fauna included *Bos,* horse, northern deer, Arctic fox, wolf, bear, rodents, birds, and fish. A few worked flints were found. This Upper Paleolithic station represents a temporary hunting camp.

97. *Kliuchevaia Peshchera.*—This cave, situated near No. 96, lies farther downstream on the Yuryuzan in the territory of the Bashkir

A.S.S.R. The cultural stratum can be clearly seen. The fauna consisted of Siberian rhinoceros, European bison, northern deer, Arctic fox, and other forms. The few worked flints and flakes were of dark Cretaceous flint unknown in this vicinity and only occurring about 120-150 kilometers distant. This Upper Paleolithic site, a type of hunting camp remote from permanent habitation, was excavated by S. N. Bibikov during 1938.

98. *Ust-Katav.*—During 1937 S. N. Bibikov found a considerable quantity of Pleistocene bones, including mammoth, in this cave near Ust-Katav railroad station in the southern Urals.

99. *Idelbaieva.*—Traces of this Upper Paleolithic site were found on the Guberla River northeast of Orsk in the Orenburg *Oblast*. In addition to flint implements, a large quantity of bones of two species of extinct *Bos,* horse, wolf, elk, northern deer, and dog were found.

100. *Lakedemonovka.*—Upper Paleolithic flints were found by V. A. Khokhlovkina during 1935 in the loess on the northern coast of the Sea of Azov.

UKRAINE [18]

101. *Amvrosievka.*—Of special interest was this Upper Paleolithic site, apparently Magdalenian, near Amvrosievka, Donets region, in the upper part of the Kazennaia ravine, on the right bank of the Krinka River and 2 kilometers distant. Discovered during 1935, this site was investigated in 1936 by the Museum of the Study of the Region in Stalino. Many worked flints were found on the gully slopes over an area of 6 hectares. The finds resemble the flint inventory of Kostenki II and III, Eliseevichi, and the Magdalenian sites along the left bank of the Dniester. The predominant tools were burins. There were also a large quantity of nuclei, indicating that this was an atelier. The finds were not concentrated on some particular level, but could be found from the surface to a depth of 1.25 m. into the loesslike loam. Probably to some later period belong the large campfire and the accumulation of cultural remains, mainly bones of the European bison (*Bison priscus*), no less than 300 animals being scattered over 40 square meters of the excavation. Flint inventories here differ from those mentioned above in the absence of

[18] The following sites have been listed: Donbas (No. 101), northern Donets (Nos. 102-108), the middle Dnieper (Nos. 109-124), the basin of Desna (Nos. 125-138), the basin of Sula (Nos. 139-143), Seim (No. 144), the basin of Pripet (Nos. 145-147), the neighborhood of Odessa (No. 148), southern Bug (No. 149), Dniester (Nos. 150-164), and the neighborhood of Melitopol (No. 165).

burins. Bone points, spindle-shaped, similar to those from Veselogore were also found.

102. *Afrikanova Melnitsa*.—Traces of an apparently Upper Paleolithic site were found near Rogalik-IAkimovskaia at the confluence of the Evsug River and the northern Donets. This site is located on the slope of the high right bank of the Evsug near the mill. The worked flints do not lie deep. According to S. A. Loktiushev, the finds consist of objects similar to those found in Krinichnaia ravine, including burins, scrapers, and knife-shaped laminae.

103. *Beregovaia*.—In the vicinity of Rogalik farm (see No. 106) in the midstream of Evsug River near its confluence with the Donets north of Voroshilovgrad [formerly Lugansk], several flint implements, including two small round scrapers, were found. This station apparently represents the same period [Azilian] as that of Rogalik-IAkimovskaia. (See No. 106.)

104. *Veselogore*.—On a sand bar on the right bank of the Donets, 15 kilometers from Voroshilovgrad, near this village was found accidentally a bone javelin-head of Magdalenian type associated with the bones of mammoth, rhinoceros, *Bos,* horse, etc.

105. *Krinichnaia Balka*.—This Upper Paleolithic station, investigated in 1936, stands on the slope of the high right bank of the river Evsug near its confluence with the northern Donets. At a point 360 m. southwest of the station of Rogalik-IAkimovskaia (No. 106) were found during 1936 burins, scrapers, knife-shaped laminae, nuclei, and other implements of Rogalik type.

106. *Rogalik-IAkimovskaia*.—This typologically Azilian site near Rogalik farm lies on the high right bank of the Evsug River at its confluence with the northern Donets, 35 kilometers northeast of Voroshilovgrad [formerly Lugansk]. This station, discovered in 1926 by S. A. Loktiushev, was investigated in 1927, 1928, 1933, and 1936. The cultural remains, located on the right slope of the IAkimovskaia ravine, lie mainly in sandy loam with a slight admixture of humus, at a depth of 1.86 m. The animal bones were mainly *Equus,* and there were some marine Mollusca. Among the flint tools, which resemble closely those found in the upper horizon of Borshevo II, were such true geometric forms as trapezoids.

107. *Sheishinova Balka*.—During 1936 traces of this Upper Paleolithic site were found at the confluence of the Evsug with the northern Donets in Sheishinova ravine near Rogalik farm. The flint implements, from a depth of 0.25-0.60 m., were similar to those from Rogalik-IAkimovskaia (No. 106).

108. *Shchurovka*.—Mammoth bones and several worked flints,

including angle burins and flakes, were found along the northern Donets near the village of Shchurov Rog, north of Izium. Collected by A. S. Fedorovskii and N. V. Sibilev in 1923, the finds were deposited partly in Kharkov and partly in Izium Museum.

109. *Bairachnaia.*—During 1935 in Bairachnaia ravine near Yamburg, Dnepropetrovsk *Oblast,* there were found typologically Paleolithic flints and an accumulation of Early Quaternary animal bones in a sandy clay deposit of the type of ancient ravine formations.

110. *Burty.*—The remains of an Upper Paleolithic station with flints and bones of fossil animals were found in Burty ravine near Studenitsa in the neighborhood of Kanev, in a stratum of ancient ravine alluvium.

111. *Dubovaia Balka.*—This Upper Paleolithic site, which yielded eight cultural levels, the lower strata of which may be attributed to the Magdalenian period, stands on the left bank of the Dnieper, south of the mouth of the Ploskaia Osokorivka River, opposite Lake Dubovoe in the Dnieper rapids, known as Nenasytets and Volnichskii. Discovered during 1931 by the Dnieprostroi Archeological Expedition and investigated the following years, this station is situated on the left slope of Dubovaia ravine. The cultural remains lay partly in diluvial loesslike clay and partly in the stratified alluvial sands of the second terrace above the flood plain of the Dnieper. Some of the eight cultural levels contained only hearths and animal bones. The fifth stratum was the richest. The bones of *Bos* were in the large majority, although *Equus* and *Lupus* were represented. There were also many bones of *Lepus*. No mammoth bones were found. Among flint implements points predominated. There were also bone tools and shell ornaments.

112. *Kaistrova Balka I.*—This Upper Paleolithic site on the left bank of the Dnieper, south of the mouth of the Ploskaia Osokorivka River, west of Dubovaia Balka (No. 111), in the vicinity of Dnieproges [formerly Dnieprostroi], was discovered and investigated during 1931 by the Dnieprostroi Archeological Expedition. The cultural remains, in the loess of the second terrace above the flood level were partly destroyed by the small gully merging with the ravine. The fauna includes the European bison and horse. The flint inventory is represented mainly by burins and scrapers. The material remains unpublished.

113. *Kaistrova Balka II.*—This is another Upper Paleolithic site in the same vicinity. The cultural remains lie in two adjoining spots in the loess on the right slope of Kaistrova Balka, higher than Kaistrova Balka I at the edge of the gully. The fauna includes the

European bison and horse. The flint inventory is represented mainly by burins and scrapers. Two bones awls were also found. The material has not been published.

114. *Kaistrova Balka III.*—Insignificant traces of a cultural stratum in the loesslike clay occur on the left slope of the Kaistrova Balka, slightly higher than Kaistrova Balka II. Traces of the European bison constituted the only faunal material found.

115. *Kaistrova Balka IV.*—A deposit with an accumulation of flints was found on the left slope of Kaistrova Balka. This stratum was stained red by infiltrations of iron oxides.

116. *Kirillovskaia.*—A Lower Magdalenian site was discovered in 1893 by V. V. Khvoiko on Kirillovskaia Street in Kiev. The lower horizon of several strata yielded an accumulation of large campfires and of bones and tusks of mammoth. This horizon lies on the surface of the clays at the base of the ancient terrace beneath 22.0 m. of postglacial deposits. In addition to mammoth, woolly rhinoceros was occasionally found. Among the few flint implements manufactured from flakes, burins of accidental forms predominated. Khvoiko found in the same horizon the fragment of a mammoth tusk covered with stylized designs. This site was studied from 1893 to 1900.

117. *Kirillovskaia* (upper horizon).—Discovered by V. V. Khvoiko in 1897, this Upper Magdalenian station was investigated by him in 1897 and 1899. The cultural stratum, containing ashes and a few charred animal bones, lay at the base of grayish-green sands, at a depth of 11-16 m. The fauna included lion, wolverine, wolf, and doubtful finds of hyena and mammoth. The flint inventory consisted of many flakes and tools.

118. *Kovalskaia Balka* (Krivoi Rog).—A quantity of flint implements and flakes, as well as mammoth bones, were found about 3 kilometers from Krivoi Rog near the confluence of the Saksagan with the Ingul in Kovalskaia ravine 1.0-1.50 m. into the reddish clay. Discovered by A. N. Pol, this site has not been investigated systematically. The gully is filled with the refuse from the neighboring mine.

119. *Maiorka.*—This Upper Paleolithic (Magdalenian) station stands on the right bank of the Dnieper, farther downstream than Yamburg and Voloskoe, near Maiorka ravine. Found and investigated by I. F. Levitskii during 1932, the cultural remains lay under the thick loess at two points: at the mouth of Maiorka ravine at a depth of 3.6 m.; and higher than its mouth, at a depth of 2.5 m. on the bank of the Dnieper, together with the bones of *Bos*. A few implements were unearthed.

120. *Osokorivka.*—This Upper Paleolithic site on the left bank

of the Dnieper, near the Dnieper Dam, is situated at the mouth of Ploskaia Osokorivka ravine on the second loess terrace. Several cultural horizons were discovered in 1931 and investigated by I. F. Levitskii during 1932. The lower stratum lies at a depth of 5.6 m. at the base of the alluvio-diluvial deposits and apparently belongs to the Magdalenian period. The three upper horizons, at a depth of 3.5 m. in the alluvio-diluvial deposit and 2.0-2.5 m. in the loesslike clay, are probably Azilian. The fauna included bison, horse, mammoth, rhinoceros, beaver, etc. The flint inventory has not been published. Some indications of the dwellings were found.

121. *Protasov IAr.*—Traces of the Upper Paleolithic site were found near the railroad station in Kiev. The finds were made at the beginning of the 1890's during construction work 16.0 m. under the loess. No further studies have been made.

122. *Selishche.*—In 1900 Paleolithic flint implements and associated fauna were discovered by N. I. Krishtafovich near Kanev, on the right bank of the Dnieper. The flints and fauna lay under conditions similar to those at Kirillovskaia (No. 116), where they were found under the thick loess and sand deposits overlying moraine clays.

123. *Skalka.*—In 1922 bones of mammoth and one flint tablet were found near Skalka *gorodishche* in the Kremenchug district.

124. *Yamburg.*—This Upper Paleolithic site stands on the right bank of the Dnieper at the mouth of the Sura River. Discovered and investigated by I. F. Levitskii in 1932, it is situated on the third terrace, common for both the Dnieper and Sura Rivers. The first horizon of the cultural remains lies in the loess clay at a depth of 1.5 m. Levitskii identified nine horizons, which are attributed to the Upper Magdalenian period.

125. *Voronezh.*—This Paleolithic site was found near Glukhov in the Chernigov region. The flints, collected some years ago by Abramov, are deposited in the Hermitage Museum, Leningrad.

126. *Degtiarevo.*—An accumulation of split mammoth bones was discovered in this village in the Novgorod-Seversk district while fencing the church.

127. *Mezin.*—This Paleolithic site, which stands on the right bank of the Desna River downstream from Novgorod-Seversk, belongs presumably to the end of the Solutrean period. It is situated on the left slope of the Mezin ravine not far from its merging with the Desna Valley. In spite of long years of excavation the character of the habitation remains unclear. As a result of excavations during 1909 a dwelling in the form of shallow dugouts may have existed. Flint and bone implements were richly represented. Included in the fauna

were mammoth, rhinoceros, northern deer, horse, Arctic fox, wolverine, and others. Of especial interest were the shells originating near the Black Sea. Mezin was discovered by F. K. Volkov in 1908, investigated by P. P. Efimenko in 1909, by L. E. Chikalenko in 1912-1914, by B. G. Krizhanovskii in 1916, and by M. IA. Rudinskii in 1930.

128. *Novgorod-Seversk.*—This Upper Paleolithic site lies on the bank of the Desna River. The cultural deposits, partly beneath crumbled limestone, were mainly destroyed by quarrying. Many remains of the Pleistocene fauna, including mammoth, northern deer, Arctic fox, and lemming were excavated, associated with flints and worked bones. Among important objects were three gigantoliths, pickax-shaped tools, 0.45 m. long and weighing about 8.0 kilograms, of dark, Cretaceous flint. Found and excavated by I. G. Pidoplichka during April 1936, this site was also investigated in collaboration with M. V. Voevodskii and P. I. Boriskovskii during 1937-1938.

129. *Pushkari I.*—This site, attributed to an early phase of the Upper Paleolithic, stands on the right bank of the Desna River, 20 kilometers north of Novgorod-Seversk. Discovered by P. I. Boriskovskii in 1932, it was partly investigated by him in 1933 and during 1937-1938. The cultural stratum, at a depth of 1.0 m., yielded many flints including points, scrapers, large retouched laminae, and other forms. The faunal remains, including mammoth, Arctic fox, and wolf, were badly preserved.

130-134. *Pushkari II-VI.*—Near this village I. G. Pidoplichka and M. V. Voevodskii discovered several more Upper Paleolithic sites.

135. *Pushkari VII* (Pokrovshchina).—This station, presumably belonging to the end of the Upper Paleolithic, was discovered and investigated during 1938 by M. V. Voevodskii. It is situated near Pushkari, 315 kilometers from the bank of Desna River. The cultural stratum, comprising the accumulation of flints as rounded boulders, flakes, and some finished tools, lay 1.6 m. above the bottom of the gully.

136. *Chulatovo I.*—Discovered and investigated by I. G. Pidoplichka during 1935, this Upper Paleolithic site stands on the right bank of the Desna, 8 kilometers south of Novgorod-Seversk. Quarrying for chalk in the Kreidianyi Maidan destroyed the greater part of the site. The cultural stratum stands 25.0 m. above river level. The fauna was represented by the mammoth, northern deer, horse, Arctic fox, wolverine, and lemming. Part of a human calvarium with traces of sawing [19] were found associated with many flint implements typical

---

[19] Cf. similar marks on Le Placard calvarium. (H. F.)

for the Lower Magdalenian of eastern Europe; these included mainly chisels, some scrapers, and fragments of bone implements.

137. *Chulatovo II* (Rabochii Rog).—This Upper Magdalenian site, 1 kilometer from Chulatovo I, had been partly destroyed by erosion. The cultural stratum was 3.5 m. deep. Some localities showed the manufacturing process of bone tools. The majority of the stone implements were burins, although some nuclei were found. Among the fauna were the mammoth and northern deer. This site, discovered during 1936, was investigated by M. V. Voevodskii in 1937 and 1938.

138. *IUkhnova.*—In the Novgorod-Seversk district near this village were found bones of mammoth and some flint flakes.

139. *Vazovka.*—A chance find of the lower jaw of a mammoth and Paleolithic flint implements, eroded from the ancient clay deposits in the ravine, occurred near this village on the Sula River in the vicinity of Lubny in the Poltava region.

140. *Gai.*—Bones of fossil animals together with crude flint flakes were discovered near Gai farm, Romny district. The finds were deposited in Romny Museum.

141. *Gontsy.*—This Magdalenian site was located on the right bank of the Udai River near this village. Discovered and first excavated by F. I. Kaminskii in 1873, it was investigated by the staff of Poltava Museum during 1914-1915, and by I. F. Levitskii together with A. IA. Briusov and I. G. Pidoplichka in 1935. The Paleolithic remains lay under 3.0-3.5 m. of loess on the edge of the sandy clay alluvium, of which the terrace consists. Mammoth bones were probably associated with the dugouts. In addition, there were also northern deer, hare, etc. The flint implements were small, mainly burins and scrapers. A few bone implements, including a perforated needle, were unearthed.

142. *Zhuravka.*—Standing on the left bank of the Udai River, a right tributary of the Sula, not far from Priluki, was this Azilian station on the alluvio-diluvial deposits of the second loess horizon of the lower terrace. Characteristic were the many bones of rodents (*Marmota bobak* Müll., *Citellus rufescens* K., etc.) and of the flint inventory of Epipaleolithic type. More ancient horizons of the same terrace yielded bones of mammoth. Zhuravka was investigated by an expedition from the Ukrainian Academy of Sciences [A.N.U., later U.A.N.] during 1927-1929.

143. *Sergeevka.*—During 1921 bones of mammoth and a flint lamina were collected in a ravine on the right bank of the Khorol, tributary of the Psel River.

144. *Shapovalovka.*—Bones of mammoth and some small flint laminae were found in the basin of the Seim River by N. D. Zubok-Mokievskii during 1879 on the shore of the lake in a steep escarpment, at the depth of 2.0 m.

145. *Dovginichi.*—In 1929 I. F. Levitskii found traces of this Upper Paleolithic station on the left bank of the Uzh River, a right tributary of the Pripet, near Ovruch.

146. *Iskorost.*—This Upper Paleolithic station stands near the rocky bank of the Uzh River at a depth of 0.5-9.8 m. During the excavations by V. V. Khvoiko in 1911, there were discovered beneath the burial mounds a series of campfires, many worked flints, and a few bones. Khvoiko accumulated here a large number of nuclei and their flakes. This material has not been published.

147. *Kolodeznoe.*—During 1924 I. F. Levitskii reported the accidental finding of bones of horse, mammoth, and other forms in a quarry along the Slucha River at the mouth of its tributary, the Tiukhterevka. The confirmatory excavations by S. Gamchenko in 1926 produced no positive results. The engraved bones published by Levitskii remain of doubtful character.

148. *Nerubaiskoe.*—Quaternary bones, including mammoth, rhinoceros, cave bear, deer, *Bos,* antelope, camel, and horse, were found near Odessa. N. I. Krishtafovich states that during his visit in 1904 he did not discover any worked flints.

149. *Semenki.*—This Upper Paleolithic site stands on the right bank of the southern Bug River near this village in Bratslav district. During 1931 K. M. Polikarpovich found flint implements and animal bones, among them the northern deer and the horse. The fauna has not yet been completely determined.

150. *Bagovitsy.*—An Upper Paleolithic site was located near Kamenets-Podolsk on the bank of the Dniester. The surface finds have not yet been described.

151. *Vrublevtsy.*—This station, situated not far from the Dniester along the Ternovaia River near Kamenets-Podolsk, was first identified in 1881 by V. B. Antonovich. Typologically Lower Magdalenian flints were excavated from the diluvial clay during 1927.

152. *Kalius.*—During 1927 typologically Magdalenian flints were found near this village on the left bank of the Dniester on the plateau near the Kalius River.

153, 154. *Kitai-Gorod I and II.*—Traces of the Upper Paleolithic sites were found on the right bank of the Ternovaia River, a left tributary of the Dniester, near Kamenets-Podolsk. The material has not been fully described.

155, 156. *Kolạchkovtsy I and II.*—Traces of these two Upper Paleolithic sites were found on the right bank of the Studenitsa, a left tributary of the Dniester. The material, which was obtained during 1928, has not been described.

157. *Krivchik.*—A quantity of flint implements were collected at the entrance to the caves situated on the bank of the Dniester near Krivchik at the mouth of the Schusenka River. No further data are available.

158. *Kuzheleva.*—Traces of a site were located on the Ushitsa River, a left tributary of the Dniester near Bolshaia Kuzheleva. No further data are available.

159. *Nagoriany.*—Large stone implements crudely fashioned by percussion flaking were found in this cave situated on the left bank of the Dniester near the Ledava River. The material has not been described.

160. Near the caves situated not far from the Dniester on the left bank of the Smotrich River between Nechin and Zaluch were found stone tools. The material has not been described.

161. *Ozarintsy.*—Several flints and one fragment of mammoth bone with a representation of this animal on it were found during 1912 near this village in the neighborhood of Kamenets-Podolsk in the talweg of the Borshchevetski IAr ravine. The Paleolithic origin of the finds remains doubtful.

162. *Sokol.*—Traces of this Paleolithic site were found on the left bank of the Dniester near this village in the neighborhood of Kamenets-Podolsk. The material has not been described.

163. *Studenitsa.*—This Magdalenian site is situated on the Belaia Gora overlooking the Dniester near the juncture of the Studenitsa River. Paleolithic flints were collected here, on the slopes of this mountain and in its cave, as early as 1883 by V. B. Antonovich. A considerable number of worked flints were found here during 1927.

164. *Ushitsa.*—During 1927 a few typologically Magdalenian flints were found on the surface at this site on the plateau between the Dniester and Ushitsa Rivers.

165. *Kamennyi Kurgan.*—This sandy hill stands on the right bank of the Molochnaia River near Terpene in the Melitopol district, Dnepropetrovsk region. Many engravings were found on the grotto walls formed of sandstone plates. According to O. N. Bader, some of them belong to the Epipaleolithic and even to the Upper Paleolithic periods.

TERRITORY OF THE B.S.S.R.[20]

166. Berdyzh.—This Solutrean site stands in Kolodezhki ravine on the right bank of the Sozh River near this village in the Checherskii district. The cultural remains lie in the sands at a depth of 5.0-6.0 m. The large quantity of mammoth bones were mainly unearthed. In addition, the fauna was represented by the horse, *Bos,* cave bear, Arctic fox, etc. These excavations were conducted during 1926-1929. The site was discovered by K. M. Polikarpovich and investigated by him, by S. N. Zamiatnin, and others. In 1929 there was discovered a pit, 3.0 m. long and 1.5 m. deep, filled with the remains of a dugout. Considerable excavations were made by Polikarpovich during 1938.

167. Kleievichi.—This site stands on the right bank of the Beseda River, a left tributary of the Sozh, near this village in the Kostiukovich district. The finds included a small quantity of mammoth and horse bones together with flints (possibly of natural origin) in the sands of the upper terrace, at about the spring high-level mark. Studies were made here by K. M. Polikarpovich in 1919, 1930, and 1934.

168. IUrovichi.—This Upper Paleolithic site stands on the left bank of the Pripet on the second terrace above the spring high-level mark at the mouth of the ravine near this small town. A few worked flints associated with mammoth and horse bones were found in sands lying about 25.0 m. above the river level.

CRIMEA [21]

169. Adzhi-Koba.—The upper horizon of this cave contained flints of Upper Paleolithic type (see No. 22) similar to those from Siuren I. Above lay a stratum containing implements of microlithic type, excavated by A. S. Moiseev.

170. At-Bash.—This Tardenoisian site lies beneath the rock called At-Bash on the Ai-Petri IAila about 200 m. above sea level on the IAila precipice facing the sea near Siemiz. Investigated during 1927 by B. S. Zhukov and O. N. Bader, the cultural stratum, mostly eroded, lay at a depth of 40-60 cm. below the surface. In the center stood a hearth, surrounded by stone plates 2.5 m. in diameter. The inventory included flints of Tardenoisian type and single bones of deer and boar. The excavators also found fragments of slightly fired pottery, which possibly has no real connection with the Tardenoisian stratum.

---

[20] The following areas have been listed: Sozh Valley (Nos. 166, 167), and Pripet Valley (No. 168).
[21] Nos. 169-188.

171. *Balin-Kosh.*—This Tardenoisian site in located in the Ai-Petri IAila near Bedene-Khyr Mountain and the Balin-Kosh area. Microlithic flint implements were found here by E. I. Visniovskaia and others. T. F. Gelakh found pebbles with an engraved pattern, resembling the painted pebbles (*galets coloriés*) of Mas d'Azil in the Ariège District of France.

172. *Buran-Kaia.*—This cave containing Azilian flints, animal bones, and shells of edible mollusks, stands on the right bank of the Borulcha River near Kainaut, in the Karasubazar *Raion.* Discovered by O. N. Bader in 1935, Buran-Kaia was investigated by him during 1936.

173. *Dzhelau-Bash.*—This open-air Tardenoisian site, in the area known as Dzhelau-Bash or Damchi-Kaia on the Chatyr-Dagh, was discovered and investigated by O. N. Bader in 1930. There were two cultural horizons: in the lower were found geometric microliths; in the upper, microliths with pottery.

174. *Zamil-Koba I.*—This cave, containing Azilian-Tardenoisian remains, was discovered during 1935 near Cherkez-Kermen by D. A. Krainov. The finds were in the lower cultural stratum.

175. *Zamil-Koba II.*—This cave with Tardenoisian remains stands next to Zamil-Koba I. It was discovered and investigated by D. A. Krainov in 1937. The flints were excavated from the lower cultural stratum.

176. *Kachinskii.*—This rock shelter with Upper Paleolithic remains stands above the Kacha River near Pychkhi village close to Bakhchisarai. Discovered by K. S. Merezhkovskii in 1879, it was investigated by him during 1879-1880., He found stone tools and some child's bones. According to G. A. Bonch-Osmolovskii this is a Magdalenian site.

177. *Kizil-Koba.*—This Tardenoisian atelier site stands on the slope of the Dolgorukov IAila near Kizil-Koba village close to Simferopol. During 1879-1880 K. S. Merezhkovskii found a large quantity of flint tools, nuclei, and flakes in the dark brown clay directly beneath the humus, relatively near to the natural location of the flint.

178. *Kukrek.*—This Tardenoisian open-air station stands on the right bank of the Zuia River, 5 kilometers south of Kiik-Koba (see No. 24). Discovered by G. A. Bonch-Osmolovskii in 1926, Kukrek was investigated by him during 1926-1927. The lower stratum of the site, which lay at a depth of 1.5 m. beneath the diluvial strata of clay and gravel, yielded prismatic nuclei, round scrapers, burins, and a quantity of microliths. The upper stratum, at a depth of 0.5 m., was poor in finds but contained typical trapezoids and segments. There

were few remnants of bones and hearths. The fauna included wolf,
wild boar, deer, and hare. The flora of the site was characterized by
the presence of *Quercus*.

179. *Murzak-Koba*.—This Tardenoisian cave, situated on the left
bank of the Chernaia River in Boklu-dere gorge near Balaclava, was
discovered and investigated by S. N. Bibikov and E. V. Zhirov in
1936. The cultural deposits yielded the characteristic flint inventory
and bone tools including awls, a needle, and a double-barbed harpoon.
Among fauna were deer, roe deer, wild boar, bear, fox, domesticated
dog, badger, hare, fish bones, and a large quantity of snails (*Helix
vulgaris*). In addition, here was also found the double burial [22] of the
Tardenoisian period. Excavations by S. N. Bibikov during 1938
revealed Upper Paleolithic strata near bedrock.

180. *Siuren I*.—A rock shelter, possibly Aurignacian, stands on
the right bank of the Belbek River, higher than Biiuk-Siuren, 13
kilometers southwest of Bakhchisarai. Here there were three cultural
horizons with flint implements, similar to those of Aurignacian sites.
In addition, especially in the lower stratum, were found Mousterian
tools including small axes, points, scrapers, and some bone implements. The fauna included the mammoth, cave hyena, northern deer,
Arctic fox, white hare, rodents, northern birds (white grouse), and
remains of fish. A study of the charcoal shows the boreal character
of the vegetation. This site, discovered by K. S. Merezhkovskii in
1879, was investigated by him during 1879-1880, and later by G. A.
Bonch-Osmolovskii in 1926-1929.

181. *Siuren II*.—This Late Azilian (Sviderskian Phase) rock
shelter stands next to Siuren I. Discovered by K. S. Merezhkovskii
in 1879, it was investigated by him during 1879-1880 and later G. A.
Bonch-Osmolovskii in 1924 and 1926. The cultural stratum lies at a
depth of 0.75 m. between limestone fragments. Near the entrance
this stratum becomes about 4.0 m. deeper. The typical flint inventory
includes well-preserved arrowheads of leaf-shaped form. The fauna
has a contemporary character but with some Pleistocene species including cave lion and large deer. Here were also the first finds of
the domesticated dog. A study of the charcoal from the hearth stratum
revealed only aspen.

182. *Fatma-Koba*.—This Azilian-Tardenoisian rock shelter stands
on the right bank of the Kubalar-Su in the Baidar Valley of the
Balaclava district near Urkust. Discovered by S. A. Trusov and

---

[22] A cast of one of the skulls is in the Chicago Natural History Museum.
This was received during 1945 as a gift from IAE, Leningrad, where the original
is on exhibition. See footnote 10. (H. F.)

S. N. Bibikov in 1927, it was investigated by G. A. Bonch-Osmolovskii in 1927. The lower cultural stratum belongs to the Azilian, the upper strata to the Tardenoisian period. In the latter were discovered the burials. The fauna, which was similar in all horizons, included wild boar, deer, wild donkey, horse, saiga, wolf, fox, hare, badger, cave lion, lynx, domesticated dog, and rodents. In the Tardenoisian levels maple and rowanberry were identified.

183. *Chatyr-Dagh.*—Traces of Paleolithic occupation were found in the cave of the Chatyr-Dagh, discovered by K. S. Merezhkovskii in 1879 and investigated by him during 1879-1880. In Bin-bash-Koba cave in the stratum of red clay were found remnants of hearths, bone breccia, and flint and bone implements. In Suuk-Koba cave in the same kind of stratum at a depth of about 1.50 m. were discovered traces of a hearth, crushed bones, and stone tools of Siurenian type. The caves of Chatyr-Dagh were investigated in 1930 by O. N. Bader, who excavated about 3.0 m. of the cultural deposits.

184. *Cherkez-Kermen.*—Two Azilian caves were discovered near this village by K. S. Merezhkovskii in 1880. The finds included stone and bone implements, and the bone of a dolphin. It is probable that these caves are contemporaneous with Zamil-Koba I and II.

185. *Shan-Koba.*—This Azilian-Tardenoisian rock shelter, on the right slope of Kubaral-dere ravine near Urkust in the Baidar Valley, found by S. A. Trusov and S. N. Bibikov in 1927, was investigated by G. A. Bonch-Osmolovskii during 1927-1928 and by Bibikov in 1935-1936. There were found altogether six cultural horizons, five Epipaleolithic with traces of hearths, microlithic flints, bone compressors and needles, borers and points, implements with inserts, and a large quantity of shells of *Helix vulgaris*. The second and third cultural strata belong to the Tardenoisian or Azilian transition period. The fauna included deer, horse, boar, beaver, hare, wolf, fox, lynx, dog, etc. Represented in the flora were birch, mountain-ash, buckthorn, and juniper in the lower strata, and maple and buckthorn in the upper levels.

186. *Shpan-Koba.*—This Tardenoisian rock shelter near Tau-Kipchak was discovered and investigated in 1925 by G. A. Bonch-Osmolovskii and by O. N. Bader a decade later.

187. *IUsuf-Koba I.*—During 1936 E. V. Zhirov discovered a Tardenoisian rock shelter on the eastern slope of Cape Lang near Biiuk-Muskomia in the Balaclava district. The cultural stratum yielded crushed animal bones and an accumulation of the shells of *Helix vulgaris*.

188. *IAila.*—Many Epipaleolithic stations were found on the slopes

of the IAila Plateau, beginning with Chatyr-Dagh and as far as Point Liaspi. One of these sites, Kizil-Koba on the Dolgorukov IAila, was discovered and investigated in 1879 by K. S. Merezhkovskii. In 1913 N. N. Klepnin and N. I. Dubrovskii discovered on the IAila three Tardenoisian sites. Later A. S. Moiseev discovered about 30 more sites. The systematic investigations of the Ai-Petri IAila and Chatyr-Dagh, begun in 1927, were conducted by B. S. Zhukov, O. N. Bader, E. I. Visniovskaia, and others. S. I. Zabnin and Visniovskaia also discovered several sites. In the Feodosia region investigations were conducted by P. P. Zablotskii, N. S. Barsamov, and Bader. Also examined were the sites of Kizil-Koba by Merezhkovskii, At-Bash by Zhukov and Bader, Balin-Kosh by Zhukov, Bader, Gelakh, and others, and the sites of the Chatyr-Dagh, Dzhelau-Bash, Uzun-Koba, Kenavuz-Koba, and others by Bader. Microlithic flint implements were found at all these sites, but other finds, such as a stone lamp and pebbles with incisions, occurred at only a single site.

CAVES IN THE CAUCASUS [23]

189. *Bartashvili Peshchera.*—This Upper Paleolithic cave near Kutaisi, not far from Virchow cave, was discovered and investigated by the expedition led by P. P. Schmidt and L. Kozlovskii in 1914. The results remain unpublished.

190. *Bnele-Klde.*—This Upper Paleolithic cave on the Kvirila River near Chiaturi was discovered by S. A. Krukovskii in 1918 and investigated by S. N. Zamiatnin in 1934.

191. *Virchow Peshchera.*—This Upper Paleolithic cave near Motsameti close to Kutaisi was discovered and investigated by the expedition led by P. P. Schmidt and L. Kozlovskii in 1914 and by G. K. Nioradze in 1936. The flint inventory is characterized by the nuclei-shaped tools and by the large quantity of small laminae with blunt edges, resembling geometric microliths. Represented in the fauna were the strongly mineralized bones of the cave bear.

192. *Gvardzhilas-Klde.*—This Azilian cave, which stands on the left bank of the Kvirila River near Rgani close to Chiaturi, was discovered and investigated by S. A. Krukovskii during 1916-1917. Among the many stone tools were a large quantity of geometric microliths, small crudely fashioned axes, and articles made of bone and horn including a harpoon of Azilian type. In the fauna were *Ursus arctos, Ursus spelaeus, Bison bonasus,* and *Bos taurus.*

193. *Darkveti.*—Traces of an Upper Paleolithic site were found

---

[23] Imeretia (Nos. 189-199), Abkhazia (No. 200), and Adler *Raion* (No. 201).

by S. N. Zamiatnin during 1936 in this cave near Darkveti railroad station on the right bank of the Kvirila River.

194. *Devis-Khvreli.*—This Upper Paleolithic cave, located on the right bank of the Chkherimela River in Khandebi quarry between the Dzeruly railroad station and Kharaguly, was discovered by G. K. Nioradze in 1926 and investigated by him during 1926-1928. Many flint flakes and implements were unearthed. Bone tools, mainly awls and compressors, were present but were not numerous. According to V. I. Gromov and M. V. Pavlova, the fauna consisted of wild boar, wild goat, and bear, all of which were presumably the main objects of the chase. A fragment of a human mandible and two molars were excavated.

195. *Mgvimevi.*—Flint implements and other traces of a cultural stratum of the Upper Paleolithic period were discovered by S. N. Zamiatnin in 1934 near Mgvimevi, 1 kilometer north of Chiaturi on the right bank of the Kvirila River. A row of linear geometric signs was recorded on the surface of the rock along the edge of Rock Shelter No. 5.

196. *Taro-Klde.*—This Aurignacian cave site near Shukrut on the upper course of the Kvirila in the neighborhood of Chiaturi was discovered and investigated by S. A. Krukovskii in 1918. The cultural deposits consist of a flint inventory of Upper Paleolithic type mixed with Mousterian forms and also of a large quantity of bone points.

197. *Uvarova Peshchera.*—This Upper Paleolithic cave, which stands on the left bank of the Krasnaia River (Tskhali-Tsiteli) near Kutaisi and not far from Virchow cave, was investigated in 1914 by an expedition led by P. P. Schmidt and L. Kozlovskii.

198. *Khergulis-Klde.*—This Aurignacian cave is located at Vachevi near Chiaturi on the right bank of the Kvirila. The finds consisted of tools of Upper Paleolithic type and a quantity of surviving Mousterian forms, which, however, were characterized by the perfection of their retouch. The fauna included bear, wild horse, and *Bos.*

199. *Tsirkhvali.*—Traces of an Upper Paleolithic site resembling Gvardzhilas-Klde (No. 192) were found in this cave near Tsirkhvali and the Kvirila River not far from Chiaturi. Tsirkhvali was discovered by S. N. Zamiatnin in 1934.

200. *Planta.*—During 1936 L. N. Solovev found this cave near the confluence of the Amtkel and Kodor Rivers. On the scree slopes and above bedrock were flint implements and flakes of Tardenoisian type, including many geometric forms, associated with animal bones.

201. *Navalishenskaia Peshchera.*—The upper part of this cave in the Adler *Raion* (see No. 33) yielded Upper Paleolithic remains.

OPEN-AIR SITES IN THE CAUCASUS [24]

202. Dafnari.—Several Upper Paleolithic implements were found by A. N. Kalandadze in 1926 on the top of the uplands next to the outlet of the red Turonian flint, near this village 3 kilometers from Lapchkhuti.

203. Liia.—Traces of an Upper Paleolithic site were located during 1936 by A. N. Kalandadze on the ancient terrace of the Ingur River, 1.5 kilometers from the Zugdidi-Dzhvari highway. Near the cemetery, at a depth of 0.8-to1.2 m., were flint nuclei, scrapers, burins, and laminae. The site was destroyed during the construction of this highway.

204. Odishi.—This Upper Paleolithic site, which lies in this village in the Zugdidi *Raion,* was discovered by A. N. Kalandadze during 1936. A large quantity of flint implements including scrapers, burins, nuclei, laminae, and geometric blades were found. In addition, some Neolithic implements such as arrowheads and grinding stones were unearthed in the unplowed part of the small plateau which goes down to the valley of the Dzhumi River. On the Zugdidi-Odishi highway in the vicinity of the Odishi Cooperative were found a few patinated flint tools.

205. Rukhi II.—Traces of an Upper Paleolithic site were discovered by A. N. Kalandadze in 1936 near the school of this village, 6 kilometers from Zugdidi. The nuclear burins, elaborate scrapers, laminae with incisions, knife-shaped tablets, and three points covered with milky patina were accumulated on the surface.

206. Supsa-Shroma.—Traces of this Paleolithic site were discovered by A. N. Kalandadze on the Supsa-Shroma Highway in 1936. Here were found flakes and laminae; in front of the school near Dzharbenadze on the slope near the highway were two scrapers and laminae. At Motsviari on the right bank of the Sefa River flakes were collected.

207. Kheti.—Flint tools were found on the slopes of Urta Mountain by A. N. Kalandadze in 1936. Animal bones, fragments of a human calvarium, and several flint flakes were found on the small elevation. A large, deeply patined flake was collected at the foot of this slope opposite the former Latariia Estate. More to the west, in the escarpment of the brook in situ were two laminae. Traces of the Upper Paleolithic site can also be found on the left bank of the Munchii River, where the slope of Urta Mountain merges with the Kolkhida Valley near the railroad.

---

[24] Mingrelia (Nos. 202-208), Abkhazia (Nos. 209-214), and Sochi *Raion* (Nos. 215-216).

208. *Entseri.*—Traces of this Upper Paleolithic station were discovered by A. N. Kalandadze in 1936 on the left bank of the Ingur River in this village. The inventory included flint laminae, nuclei, scrapers, and multifacetted burins.

209. *Atap.*—Upper Paleolithic flints were collected near this village. (See No. 3.)

210. *Gali.*—Typologically Upper Paleolithic flints were found on the 80-m. terrace. (See No. 5.)

211. *Zakharovka.*—On the elevation over the ravine of the Amtkel River on the surface of the moraine were found Upper Paleolithic flints.

212. *Tabachnaia.*—Flints of Upper Paleolithic type were obtained at the Zonal Tobacco Station on the surface of the 100-m. terrace near Sukhumi. (See No. 11.)

213. *Tsebelda.*—Flints of Upper Paleolithic type were collected on the elevation near Tsebelda. (See No. 12.)

214. *IAshtukh.*—Upper Paleolithic flints were found near Sukhumi. (See No. 14.)

215. *Abazinka.*—Upper Paleolithic flints were collected on the left bank along the Matsesta River, 6 kilometers upstream from Old Matsesta.

216. *Semenovka.*—Upper Paleolithic implements were found on the street and estates of this village which stands beside the Matsesta River.

ASIATIC PART OF THE R.S.F.S.R.[25]

217. *Nizhne-Yeniseiskaia.*—Among the collections made by Sergeev and Markov in 1933 on the right bank of the Biia River, about 12 kilometers from Biisk, were found on the dunes a quartzite *pièce écaillée* and a crude chip of Upper Paleolithic type.

218. *Srostki.*—Traces of this Paleolithic site, as expressed in the finds of crudely fashioned stone tools, mainly quartzite, were discovered in several neighboring locations on the side of the 50-m. terrace on the right bank of the Katun River, 36 kilometers from Biisk. The cultural remains lay at a depth of 1.10 m. in the loesslike sandy loam. The finds consisted of nuclei and tools made of small

---

[25] Western Siberia (Nos. 217-220), the basin of the Upper Yenisei (Nos. 221-255), the basin of the Angara (Nos. 256-277), the basin of the Lena (No. 278), Buriat-Mongolia (Nos. 279-290), Khabarovsk *Krai* (No. 291), and the Primorski [Maritime] *Krai* (No. 292).

See also Henry Field and Eugene Prostov, Results of Soviet Investigations in Siberia, 1940-1941. Amer. Anthrop., vol. 44, No. 3, pp. 388-406, 1942.

flakes resembling those from the Yenisei site (No. 217). The fauna, which was not rich, included horse and possibly deer.

219. *Tomsk.*—A temporary hunting site of the Upper Paleolithic period was discovered and investigated by N. F. Kashchenko in 1896 on the right bank of the Tom River in Tomsk. He found a skeleton of a young mammoth and traces of campfires and flint flakes 3.5 m. deep in the loesslike clay.

220. *Fominskoe.*—Traces of this site were found in 1911 by M. D. Kopytov on the right bank of the Ob River near this village in the vicinity of Biisk. Later finds were deposited in the Biisk Museum. The cultural remains, consisting of rather crudely fashioned points and massive flakes of quartzite similar to those found in Srostki, originated in the lowest terrace only 5.0 m. above river level.

221. *Aieshka.*—Flakes and a scraper of Paleolithic type as well as teeth and fragments of animal bones were found by G. Merhart in 1920 south of this village in the Novoselovo *Raion* on the slope of the first terrace above the Yenisei River.

222. *Anash* (Krasnoiarsk *Krai*).—Several crude stone tools, retouched flakes, and fragmentary bones of mammoth and deer were collected on the surface of the reddish-brown clay in the sandy ravine. These finds were made by G. P. Sosnovskii and M. P. Griaznov in 1923 near this village in the Krasnoiarsk region on the right bank of the Yenisei, 170 kilometers farther downstream than Minusinsk.

223. *Afontova Gora I.*—This Magdalenian site, at the foot of Afontova Mountain on the left bank of the Yenisei near Krasnoiarsk, stands on the slope behind the railroad station. During the preparations for the construction of two brick barns, I. T. Savenkov in 1894 found in the loess clay crushed bones of fossil animals including northern deer, mammoth, *Bos,* horse, and dog, stone and bone tools, and tusks of mammoths.

224. *Afontova II.*—This Paleolithic site near Krasnoiarsk, below the former IUdin Estate, was discovered during 1912. Systematic excavations were conducted by N. K. Auerbakh, V. I. Gromov, and G. P. Sosnovskii during 1923-1925. The cultural strata lay in the deposits of the 15- to 16-m. terrace of the Yenisei. The upper level lay in the sandy loess at a depth of 1.0-3.5 m., the lower stratum in the loessy clay and sandy soil 12.0 m. beneath the surface. Remains of dugouts were found in the lower horizon. The fauna consisted mainly of northern deer, Arctic fox, hare, mammoth, and dog. There were neither mammoth nor Arctic fox remains in the upper level. Together with the numerous stone tools were found bone implements

and also ornaments. In the lower level in trench No. 5 were discovered five human bones.

225. *Afontova III.*—This Paleolithic site, which stands near Krasnoiarsk in the neighborhood of the oil reservoirs, was discovered by I. T. Savenkov in 1914 and investigated by him with the assistance of N. K. Auerbakh in 1925 and 1930. The upper horizon lay at a depth of 0.9-1.5 m. beneath the present surface in the yellow loessy clay soil; the lower horizon, poorer in finds, lay at a depth of 2.0-3.2 m. The fauna of the lower horizon included mammoth, hare, horse, northern deer, and Arctic fox; the upper horizon yielded only the northern deer and *Bos.* Both horizons contained stone and bone implements.

226. *Afontova IV* (Ivanikhin Log).—Near Krasnoiarsk on the upper part of the slope of Afontova Mountain between Afontova II and Afontova III stands this site, discovered by I. T. Savenkov. The strata were similar to the upper horizon of Afontova II. Among fauna were *Bos* and the northern deer.

227. *Achinsk.*—In 1914, during railroad construction, split mammoth bones and charcoal, as well as stone implements, were found in the loessy loam near this town.

228. *Bateni I.*—This Paleolithic site stands on the left bank of the Yenisei River, 150 kilometers downstream from Minusinsk, on the left bank of the Tashtyk River near its mouth. The cultural stratum, discovered in 1925, lay at a depth of 1.0 m. in the loessy loam of the spring-flooded terrace of the Yenisei. Stone and bone implements were found. In the fauna were the northern deer and *Bos primigenius.*

229. *Bateni II.*—The cultural stratum of this Paleolithic site near this village lay in the loessy clay above the spring-flooded terrace of the Yenisei. Stone and bone tools were unearthed. Included in the fauna were *Bos primigenius,* saiga, deer, elk, mammoth, wolf, hare, and *Equus hemionus.*

230. *Bateni III.*—This Paleolithic site, 1.5 kilometers north of this village at IArki, was discovered by I. T. Savenkov during the 1890's. Stone implements were also found here by G. Merhart, G. P. Sosnovskii, and others.

231. *Batoi.*—At this place, 35 kilometers north of Krasnoiarsk, were found the skull of *Cervus elaphus,* bearing traces of human workmanship, and one stone implement.

232. *Biriusa.*—This group of Paleolithic sites on the bank of the Yenisei, at the mouth of the Biriusa River, 50 kilometers upstream from Krasnoiarsk, was discovered by A. P. Elenov in 1890 and was investigated by him in 1891 and by N. K. Auerbakh and V. I. Gromov

in 1926 and 1927. In 1928 these sites were examined by G. F. Mirchink and V. I. Gromov in connection with the study of the terraces of the Yenisei. Biriusa I consisted of three Paleolithic strata lying on the spring-flooded terrace in 2.0 m. of yellow-grayish clay and sand. In the stratum representing the transition from the Paleolithic to the Early Neolithic were found stone implements including nuclei and flakes, and crushed bones of such animals as the large *Bos,* northern deer, horse, noble deer, mountain sheep, wolf, and hare. The upper horizon consisted of an accumulation of large stones and ashes. Here were found stone tools, as well as implements made of bone, such as needles and points. Included in the fauna were the northern deer, *Bos,* hare, mountain sheep, roe deer, and horse.

233. *Bugach.*—This site stands on the left bank of the Kacha River, a left tributary of the Yenisei near its confluence with the Bugach River, 1 kilometer northeast of Krasnoiarsk. Bugach was discovered by G. P. Sosnovskii in 1919 and investigated by him in 1923. The cultural stratum with hearths, flint implements, and flakes was fouund at a depth of 1.0 m. in the loessy clay on the first terrace, which is flooded during the spring high water. The fauna included the Arctic fox, northern deer, hare, and other forms.

234. *Buzunova.*—This group of Paleolithic sites is located on the terrace situated above spring high water on the right bank of the Yenisei, 55 kilometers downstream from Minusinsk. The cultural remains were discovered during 1920 at two points, one above the other below Buzunova. The stone tools and flakes and the fragments of a bone tip were found by G. P. Sosnovskii in 1923 in the hearth level at a depth of 5.5 m. in loessy clay on the right side of the confluence with the river gully. V. I. Gromov and N. K. Auerbakh accumulated new surface material in 1925 from the site above Buzunova.

235. *Voennyi Gorodok.*—This Paleolithic site on the left bank of the Yenisei, 4 kilometers downstream from Krasnoiarsk near the second Korovii Log, was discovered in 1911 by A. IA. Tugarinov and A. P. Ermolaev and investigated by G. P. Sosnovskii in 1919 and 1923 and by V. I. Gromov in 1928. The cultural stratum lies in the loessy clay sand deposits at depths of 2.0 and 4.0-6.0 m. Associated with the stone tools and flakes were implements made of horn and bone. Represented in the fauna were mammoth, northern deer, Arctic fox, wolf, and horse.

236. *Dolgova.*—Stone implements were found in 1885 by I. T. Savenkov at this new settlement near the Chernaia Sopka. Bones of

mammoth, rhinoceros, and other animals were found in the clay near the mill.

237. *Zykovo.*—A fragment of an antler of the northern deer, with incisions, was found by G. P. Sosnovskii in 1925 near Zykovo railroad station. He also found charcoal and animal bones in the loess of the ravine behind Puzyrevo.

238. *Izykh.*—I. T. Savenkov found a Paleolithic scraper on the dunes at the southeastern slope of Izykh Mountain on the right bank of the Abakan River.

239. *Kacha.*—This Paleolithic site, near the factory in the valley of the Kacha River, a right tributary of the Yenisei, was discovered by V. I. Gromov and N. K. Auerbakh in 1928.

240. *Kliuch Gremiachii.*—Traces of this site were located at the efflux of Gremiachii brook on the left bank of the Yenisei, 1.5 kilometers from the railroad bridge over the Yenisei. G. P. Sosnovskii found here in 1919 traces of charcoal, a stone scraper, a fragment of mammoth tusk, and bones of the northern deer and split tubular bones of animals in the loess at a depth of 1.25 m.

241. *Kokorevo I* (Zabochka).—This site on the left bank of the Yenisei stands approximately 500 paces farther upstream than Kokorevo in the northern part of the Minusinsk Valley. Discovered by G. P. Sosnovskii and investigated by him in 1925 and 1928, the cultural stratum lies from 2.6 to 4.15 m. deep in the loesslike sandy loam, which covers the lowest terrace. Here were found four hearths surrounded by stones with the accumulation of cultural remains consisting of stone tools and flakes, a few fragments of bone implements, and crushed bones of such animals as the horse, noble deer, *Bos,* mountain sheep, wolf, and others. The charcoal found in the hearths originated from larch, fir, willow, pine, and birch.

242. *Kokorevo II* (Telezhnyi Log).—This site, located on the left bank of the Yenisei near Kokorevo in the Telezhnyi ravine, was investigated by G. P. Sosnovskii in 1925 and 1928. The cultural stratum was discovered at a depth of 6.2 m. beneath a deposit of buried soil and loessy clay sand covering the lowest terrace. The finds consisted of stone tools, fragments of a few bone implements, charcoal (larch, willow, birch), and of split bones of animals including the mammoth, Arctic fox, northern deer, horse, wolf, hare, and marmot.

243. *Kokorevo III.*—This site, north of Kokorevo in the Kamennyi Log at its merging point with the Telezhnyi Log, was investigated by G. P. Sosnovskii in 1925 and 1928. The cultural stratum lies at a depth of about 1.6 m. in the clay sands of the ancient ravine on the

slope of the 40- to 50-meter terrace. The Paleolithic remains formed small, separate accumulations around the hearth. Among the finds were quartzite tools; crushed bones of northern deer, horse, hare, and wolf; and small pieces of charcoal from larch and fir.

244. *Kokorevo IV.*—This site, situated 2 kilometers farther downstream than Kokorevo in the Kipirnyi Log, was investigated by G. P. Sosnovskii in 1925 and 1928. The Paleolithic remains were in the loesslike sandy loam of the lowest terrace above flood level at a depth of 1.5-2.1 m. In addition to tools there were excavated the bones of animals, including the northern deer, noble deer, bison, and *Equus hemionus*.

245. *Korkino.*—A stone tool and a bone awl were found at the bottom of the ravine, the last one at Korkino on the left bank of the Yenisei River.

246. *Krasnoiarsk.*—During the construction of a brewery, bones of fossil animals with traces of human workmanship and typologically Paleolithic stone tools came to light. Similar discoveries were also made in another part of the city.

247. *Kubekovo.*—Quaternary animals bones, Paleolithic stone tools, and a deer antler with traces of human workmanship were found by N. K. Auerbakh and V. I. Gromov in Lankov Log and in the other ravines near Kubekovo on the left bank of the Yenisei, 23 kilometers upstream from Krasnoiarsk.

248. *Ladeiki.*—Traces of this Upper Paleolithic site were found near this village on the right bank of the Yenisei, 8 kilometers farther downstream from Krasnoiarsk, under the dunes and the pockets of loess among the pebbles. I. T. Savenkov found here in 1883 bones of a large *Bos* and tools of Paleolithic type at the edge of the lowest terrace. The excavations were continued by Baron Joseph de Baye in 1896, by G. Merhart in 1920, and by G. P. Sosnovskii in 1923.

249. *Lepeshkina* (Irdzha).—A group of Upper Paleolithic sites were located on the right bank of the Yenisei near this village, opposite Bateni pier. The first site, which was discovered by G. Merhart in 1920, comprised the material on the slope of Irdzha Mountain, the elevation surrounding the river valley. In 1923 G. P. Sosnovskii discovered in the deposits of eolian sands three hearths surrounded by bones of animals, including bison, stone tools and flakes. The second surface site, yielding stone tools, was found by Sosnovskii in 1923 on the bank of the Yenisei Canal upstream from the village. V. I. Gromov and G. F. Mirchink discovered a thick cultural stratum in 1927 near Lepeshkina.

250. *Pereselencheskii Punkt.*—This Paleolithic site stands on the

right bank of the Yenisei near the canal opposite Krasnoiarsk. The first finds here were made by Baron Joseph de Baye in 1896. The site was investigated by S. M. Sergeev in 1912 and G. P. Sosnovskii in 1923 and 1926. The cultural remains were discovered in the loess of the lowest terrace, where they had the character of patches. It is possible that these are the remains of dugouts. Included in the fauna were northern deer, horse, bison, cave lion, roe deer, rodents, and birds. Together with the stone tools and flakes were found bone tools, fragments of shells, and pieces of coloring matter.

251. *Tes.*—Crude stone implements were found by I. T. Savenkov in 1885 on the dunes near this village on the Tuba River.

252. *Uzunzhul.*—An antler of northern deer with traces of human workmanship, a scraper, and Quaternary animal bones including mammoth and rhinoceros were found in the auriferous gravel of the Uzunzhul River.

253. *Ulazy.*—Traces of this site farther upstream than Ulazy on the right bank of the Yenisei were investigated by G. P. Sosnovskii in 1923 and 1925. On the exposed clay sections he discovered bones of *Bos,* northern deer, and other animals, together with Paleolithic flakes and nuclei.

254. *Chasgol.*—I. T. Savenko found in the auriferous gravel of the Chasgol River at a depth of 4.0 m. a knife-shaped flake of green-stone.

255. *IAnova.*—A typologically Paleolithic stone implement was found by G. P. Sosnovskii in 1925 on the slope of the ravine. This discovery was made at a depth of 1.0 m. in the loess on the left bank of the Yenisei, 1.5 kilometers from this village and 5 kilometers from Novoselovo. In another part of this same ravine were found the jaw of a mammoth and flint flakes.

256. *Badai I.*—The remains of a site of the end of the Upper Paleolithic period were found on the left bank of the Belaia, a tributary of the Angara, near this village on the plowed land along the 40-m. terrace. The site is located in Gluboki ravine near the factory. M. M. Gerasimov accumulated here a large quantity of typical implements, mainly scrapers, small laminae and nuclei.

257. *Badai II.*—This site, which was destroyed by plowing, lay on the right bank of the Belaia River opposite this village.

258. *Buret* (Sukhaia Pad).—This Paleolithic site on the right bank of the Angara near Nizhniaia Buret was discovered by A. P. Okladnikov in 1936. Buret is situated on the slope of the second (15- to 20-m.) terrace above spring high water at the mouth of Sukhaia ravine in the loesslike loam. Among the bones identified were

mammoth, *Equus hemionus,* and northern deer. Together with flint tools were found some sculptures, including the figure of a woman carved from mammoth ivory. This site was excavated by Okladnikov during 1936-1937. The character of finds confirms that the site belongs to the group of more ancient Upper Paleolithic sites of the Angara, i.e., the Malta type.

259. *Verkholenskaia Gora.*—On this mountain near the Angara River and 3 kilometers from Irkutsk were found four Paleolithic stations: Zharnikova Pad, Goriunova Pad, Ubiennykh Pad, and Ushkanka Pad. The first, known under the name of Verkholenskaia Gora, is situated on the southwestern slope of the elevation between the Zharnikova and the Ubiennykh Pad. The cultural stratum was found by M. P. Ovchinnikov as early as 1897. The stone and bone tools and other remains of habitation lay at a depth of 1.5 m. in the loesslike loam. The fauna consisted of northern and noble deer, elk, *Equus hemionus, Bos,* dog, and wolf. The large-horned deer, rhinoceros, and mammoth, found by Ovchinnikov, originated apparently in the lower horizon. This site was investigated at different times from 1919-1928.

260. *Glazkovo.*—In 1897 M. P. Ovchinnikov found stone (flinty schist) tools similar to those from Verkholenskaia Gora, and Quaternary animal bones with traces of human workmanship in the loess on the left bank of the Angara in the suburb of Glazkovo opposite Irkutsk.

261. *Zaitsevo* (Kosoi Vzvoz).—This Upper Paleolithic site, which stands on the left bank of the Angara near Usole at the mouth of the Belaia River, was discovered by A. P. Okladnikov in 1934. The inventory consisted of large scraperlike tools of the same type as those found on Verkholenskaia Gora.

262. *Zvezdochka.*—According to A. P. Okladnikov, remains apparently belonging to the Paleolithic period were discovered on the left bank of the Angara, opposite Irkutsk, on the piece of land called "Zvezdochka" near the ferry.

263. *Irkutsk.*[26]—Paleolithic remains are known from three sites within the city. The first is located on one of the hills along the Ushakovka River. Here in 1871, during construction of the Military Hospital, were found implements made from the tusk of a mammoth (including one with ornamentation), a perforated deer incisor, fragments and points of spherosiderite, and bones of mammoth, rhinoceros, northern deer, horse, *Bos,* and other animals. The second site, located

---

[26] In this area the work of the late B. E. Petri is conspicuously absent. (H. F.)

by M. P. Ovchinnikov, lay not far distant on the bank of the Ushakovka River in the suburb Rabochaia Sloboda. The third, according to A. P. Okladnikov, is in Pshenichnaia ravine.

264. *Kaiskaia Gora.*—M. M. Gerasimov discovered during 1924-1925 Paleolithic traces in the lower part of the loesslike sandy loam on the side of Kaiskaia Mountain at the juncture of the Irkut and Angara Rivers. The finds consisted of roughly fashioned stone tools and flakes, traces of charcoal, and crushed bones of animals, including horse, mammoth, *Bos,* northern deer, elk, rhinoceros, and birds, especially small birds of prey.

265. *Kamenolomnya.*—Here were found traces of an Upper Paleolithic workshop near the old quarry on the right bank of the Belaia opposite Malta.

266. *Kamen.*—Traces of a large Upper Paleolithic site (Badai type) were found on the plowed ground at the edge of the 40-m. terrace on the left bank of the Belaia near Malta. M. M. Gerasimov collected crude nuclei, laminae, and a large quantity of tools, mainly scrapers.

267. *Kova.*—Traces of this Paleolithic station were discovered on the Kova River, a left tributary of the Angara, by this village. The investigation conducted by A. P. Okladnikov in 1937 discovered at a depth of 0.6 m. the remains of campfires and mammoth bones in the loesslike loam.

268. *Malta* (Lower Horizon).—This Paleolithic site stands on the left bank of the Belaia, a left tributary of the Angara, 85 kilometers west of Irkutsk. Led there by local inhabitants, M. M. Gerasimov investigated Malta in 1928 and 1930, 1932, 1934, and 1937. In 1932 S. N. Zamiatnin also worked there, and G. P. Sosnovskii in 1934. The lower horizon, 35.0-75.0 cm. thick, lay in the loesslike sandy loam on the 18-m. terrace. Here were found traces of the surface dwellings and hearths of stone plates. Below the cultural stratum a child's burial was found. Together with numerous stone tools were about 600 bone implements, one-quarter of them ornamented. There were also 20 female figurines made from mammoth tusks, sculptures of birds, etc. The fauna were mainly northern deer; less frequently Arctic fox, rhinoceros, and mammoth; and accidental remains of horse, bison, birds of prey, and other forms. This site belongs to the most ancient monuments of the Upper Paleolithic in eastern Siberia.

269. *Malta* (Upper Horizon).—M. M. Gerasimov discovered this stratum during his excavations in 1932 in the upper part of the loesslike sandy loam 9.45 m. beneath the surface and 0.5 m. above the first cultural horizon (No. 268). Here were found limestone laminae,

fragments of bones of animals, flint flakes, and about 30 large tools of Badai type.

270. *Maltinka.*—Traces of an Upper Paleolithic station were located at the edge of the 40-m. terrace near this village, on the right bank of the Belaia, near the second pond between the Maltinka and Belaia. The finds occurred on a 300-m. stretch of plowed land.

271. *Mondy.*—Typologically Paleolithic stone tools were found by Chastokhin in 1887 on the left bank of the Oka River, a left tributary of the Angara River.

272. *Mozgovaia.*—Traces of this Paleolithic site were found during 1937 by A. P. Okladnikov on the 100-m. terrace on the left bank of the Mozgovaia River, a right tributary of the Angara, along its lower course. This find is of particular significance, because it is the first Paleolithic station reported in this area which lies about 1,800 kilometers from Irkutsk.

273. *Podostrozhnoe.*—This Upper Paleolithic station, discovered by A. P. Okladnikov in 1936, stands on the right bank of Angara on the second terrace above spring flood level. The finds in the loesslike loam consisted of tools made from antlers of the Siberian stag and some stone scrapers.

274. *Ust-Belaia.*—This Paleolithic site lies at the edge of the second terrace at the delta of the Belaia. The cultural deposit lies more than 1.0 m. deep under the Neolithic strata. M. M. Gerasimov in 1936 and 1937 found six large campfires and faunal remains consisting of the deer, elk, beaver, and possibly wolf. The stone inventory is similar to that of Badai (No. 256), mainly large but also some small scrapers, small nuclei and laminae, and two flat bone harpoons.

275. *Ushakovka.*—Stone implements of Paleolithic type were collected by M. P. Ovchinnikov in 1893 on the right bank of the Ushakovka River behind the suburb Rabochaia Sloboda in Irkutsk.

276. *Ushkanka.*—This Paleolithic site on the right bank of the Angara in Ushkanka ravine near Verkholenskaia Gora, was discovered in 1926. The inventory is similar to that found on Verkholenskaia Gora. The fauna included elk and *Bos primigenius.*

277. *Cheremushnik.*—Traces of an extensive Upper Paleolithic site of Badai type (No. 256) were discovered on the plowed land near Badai on the 60-m. terrace on the left bank of the Belaia. This site lies in the Cheremushnik area 2 kilometers downstream from Badai, near the Usolsk Salt Works. M. M. Gerasimov accumulated here a large quantity of flakes and also of finished tools, mainly large scrapers.

278. *Ponomarevo.*—In 1927 A. P. Okladnikov found typologically

Upper Paleolithic implements on the plowed land along the Biriulka River, a right tributary of the Lena, on the edge of the 80-m. terrace near Zalog.

279. *Ara-Tszokui.*—On the right bank of the Selenga, 12 kilometers northwest of Kalinishnaia in the Troitskosavski *Okrug,* in the sands near Nur settlement, the Buriat-Mongolian Archeological Expedition in 1928 found ostrich eggshells and stone tools of Paleolithic type.

280. *Bozoi.*—Traces of this Paleolithic site lay 18 kilometers upstream from Ust-Orda on the right bank of the Kuda River (Ekgirit-Bulagat *Aimak*) on the slope and at the edge of the lowest terrace. Quartzite and flint scrapers and nuclei lay in the black earth (*chernozem*) deposits and in the loesslike sandy loam.

281. *Dureny.*—The material from the sands on the left bank of the Chikoie River, 25 kilometers east of Troitskosavsk, included stone tools, ostrich eggshells, and bones of fossil animals.

282. *Durungui.*—Stone implements of Paleolithic type from the Upper Yenisei and Angara were assembled by S. I. Rudenko in 1923 in the valley of the Onon River at this settlement. Earlier A. K. Kuznetsov also assembled the same kind of tools in the valleys of the rivers Onon and Ingoda.

283. *Zarubino.*—Material from sands in an isolated ravine near this village lying on the left bank of the Selenga downstream from Ust-Kiakhta was obtained by the Buriat-Mongolian Archeological Expedition in 1928 with the participation of G. P. Sosnovskii. They found stone tools, nuclei, flakes, bones of *Equus hemionus,* large deer, mountain sheep, and hare, and ostrich eggshells.

284. *Ivashka.*—Typologically Paleolithic implements were found in Ivashka ravine opposite Ust-Kiakhta.

285. *Mylnikovo.*—Stone implements of Paleolithic type were collected along the Chikoie River near this village.

286. *Nomokhonovo.*—On the right bank of the Selenga, 25 kilometers upstream from Seleginsk in Shirokaia Pad (Mukhor-khundui), which was filled with dune sand, stone implements and flakes, and ostrich eggshells were assembled on the exposed places.

287. *Nialgi.*—Stone implements of Paleolithic type were found in the sand above the mouth of the Dzhida River.

288. *Ust-Kiakhta.*—In exposed sands on the left bank of the Sava River near this village, stone implements, including nuclei and flakes, and ostrich eggshells (one perforated) have been found. The first report was by Mostits in 1894, then by Laptev in 1924, and finally by Debets in 1928.

289. Khara-Busun.—During 1928-1929 stone implements and ostrich eggshells were found on the right bank of the Chikoie River in the sands beside Kudarinskii road about 5 kilometers from Palkanova.

290. Kharankhoi.—This site, discovered in 1927 by the Buriat-Mongolian Expedition in sands on the right bank of the Selenga in Kharankhoi ravine, about 11 kilometers upstream from Ust-Kiakhta. Among objects found were stone tools, ostrich eggshells, and bones of *Rhinoceros, Bos,* and Equidae.

291. Khabarovsk.—M. M. Gerasimov found during 1926-1927 stone implements in the loesslike loam at a depth of 0.75-1.0 m. The period was not determined.

292. Shkotovo.—A Hungarian prisoner-of-war, I. Parkas, discovered a stone tool similar to the Paleolithic implements found in the Ordos.

Arctic Paleolithic [27]

293. Anikieva I.—During 1937 traces of this site were located on the eastern coast of the Rybachii Peninsula, 1 kilometer west of the center of the Tsyp-Navolok settlement at the foot of the southern end of Anikieva Mountain. This site occupied a considerable part of the ancient pebble-covered beach about 37.0 m. above sea level.

294. Anikieva II.—At 31.0 m. above sea level on the western slope of Anikieva Mountain traces of prehistoric occupation were scattered over about 20 square kilometers. The finds were made in 1937.

295. Korabelnaia.—In 1935 B. F. Zemliakov and P. N. Tretiakov discovered traces of this site at 33.0-36.0 m. above sea level on the surface of the bank of the Korabelnyi brook on the western coast of Bolshaia Motka Bay. The material consisted of quartz flakes and crude implements.

296. Log-Navolok.—In 1937 this site was discovered on the northern coast of the Rybachii Peninsula on the crest of the pebbly coastal bank about 20.0 m. above sea level between Cape Log-Navolok and Laush-Guba.

297. Morozova.—B. F. Zemliakov and P. N. Tretiakov in 1935 discovered traces of this site on the eastern coast of the Bolshaia Motka Bay between the valley of the Morozova River and the first brook to the south. A large quantity of quartz flakes and implements were found on the shore of a lake 55.0-60.0 m. above sea level.

298. Ozerko.—In 1935 quartz scrapers and nuclei-shaped burins

---

[27] Northern part of the Kola Peninsula (Nos. 293-304).

were found on the crest of the coastal bank at 42.0 m. above sea level
on the western coast of the Bolshaia Motka Bay at this settlement.

299. *Perevalnaia.*—Traces of this site were found on the eastern
coast of the Rybachii Peninsula, 1 kilometer south of the southern
outskirt of Tsyp-Navolok settlement on the crest of the coastal bank
36.0-37.0 m. above sea level. A quantity of quartz tools and flakes
(also of horn, flint, and quartzite) were assembled in 1937.

300. *Sergeeva.*—Traces of this site were located on the eastern
coast of the Rybachii Peninsula between Cape Sergeeva and Tipunova
River on the pebbly bank 27.0 m. above sea level. Large, crude implements of quartzite and better-finished implements of flint, horn,
and quartz were found.

301. *Tipunova.*—During 1927 large, crude quartzite implements
were found on the eastern coast of the Rybachii Peninsula on the
southern slope of the elevation which divides the valley of the Anikieva
River from the valley of the Tipunova River on the crest of the pebbly
bank 40.0 m. above sea level.

302. *Tsyp-Navolok I.*—Traces of this site were found on the
western coast of Rybachii Peninsula at the southern outskirts of
Tsyp-Navolok settlement on the left bank of the Anikieva River. The
site is situated on the edge of the 25-m. terrace.

303. *Tsyp-Navolok II.*—This site, on the southern outskirts of
Tsyp-Navolok settlement, is situated on the end of the 25-m. terrace,
which surrounds the ancient bay.

304. *Eina-Guba.*—Traces of this site stand on the southern coast
of the Rybachii Peninsula in the vicinity of Eina-Guba settlement on
the crest of the ancient 20-m. terrace.

IV. MISCELLANEA ARCHEOLOGICA

INTRODUCTION

In this chapter some additional archeological data have been assembled from the Ukraine, Crimea, Black Sea coast, North Caucasus, South Caucasus, Armenia, Don region, Urals, Volga region, Central Asia, and Siberia. These miscellaneous notes supplement previously published material [1] on this same subject. In addition, supplementary data have been placed on microfilm.[2]

[1] I am grateful to Soviet anthropologists and archeologists who sent through VOKS from 1934 to 1945 summaries of their results so that these could be made available in English. For convenience there is appended a list of bibliographical references on Soviet archeology. (H. F.)

American Anthropologist, vol. 38, pp. 260-290, 1936; vol. 39, pp. 457-490, 1937; vol. 40, pp. 653-679, 1938; vol. 42, pp. 211-235, 1940; vol. 44, pp. 388-406, 1942; vol. 48, pp. 375-396, 1946. American Journal of Archaeology, vol. 41, pp. 618-620, 1937; vol. 42, pp. 146-147, 295-298, 1938; vol. 43, pp. 331-332, 507, 1939; vol. 44, pp. 138, 535-536, 1940; vol. 45, pp. 113-115, 299-301, 441-444, 626-628, 1941; vol. 46, pp. 144-147, 277-281, 423-427, 568-569, 1942; vol. 47, pp. 355, 486-488, 1943; vol. 48, pp. 201-210, 295, 395, 1944; vol. 49, pp. 102-104, 177-179, 377, 423-427, 1945; vol. 50, pp. 191-192, 307-311, 1946; vol. 51, pp. 201-202, 322-323, 1947. American Journal of Physical Anthropology, vol. 4, No. 4, pp. 501-502, 1946. American Journal of Semitic Languages and Literatures, vol. 52, pp. 138-141, 1936; vol. 53, pp. 123-124, 1937; vol. 55, pp. 109-112, 333-336, 1938; vol. 56, pp. 322-324, 438-440, 1939; vol. 57, pp. 112, 194-196, 327-329, 1940; vol. 58, pp. 109-110, 1941. American Review of the Soviet Union, 1945, pp. 37-39; 1946, pp. 67-75. Antiquity, 1938, pp. 341-345; 1939, pp. 99-101; 1940, pp. 404-426; 1941, pp. 194-196; 1947, pp. 42-45. Ars Islamica, vol. 5, pt. 2, pp. 233-271, 1938; vol. 6, pt. 1, pp. 158-166, 1940; vol. 9, pp. 143-150, 1942; vol. 13, pp. 139-148, 1947. Asia, 1940, pp. 272-277, 327-330; 1941, pp. 243-244, 723-727; 1943, pp. 529-531; 1946, pp. 120-121. Gazette des Beaux-Arts, vol. 23, pp. 129-134, 1943; vol. 29, pp. 65-74, 1946; vol. 31, pp. 123-126, 1947. Southwestern Journal of Anthropology, vol. 2, No. 2, p. 239, No. 3, pp. 340-360, 1946; vol. 3, No. 3, pp. 212-229, 1947.

[2] The following articles have been recorded on Microfilm No. 1605 in the American Documentation Institute, c/o Library, U. S. Department of Agriculture, Washington 25, D. C.: Eneolithic Station at Ochemchiri, Abkhazia, pp. 4-29; Olvia (Olbia) Expedition, pp. 30-42; European Russia: Archaeological Reconstruction in European Russia, pp. 60-66; Archaeological Investigations in the Uzbek S.S.R., by B. Grekov and A. IAkubovskii, pp. 89-93; bibliography, pp. 94-99. There have also been placed on Microfilm No. 2308 Notes on Soviet Museums and Research Institutions, pp. 1-126, and pls. 1-130: Baku, pp. 3-6; Yerevan, pp. 6-7; Tbilisi, pp. 7-8; Ordzhonikidze, pp. 8-9; Moscow, pp. 9-18; Archaeological Reconstruction in European Russia, 1941, pp. 19-25; Excavations

UKRAINE

According to Boriskovskii [3] the earliest site in the Ukraine is the Lower Mousterian station at Kodak, on the right bank of the Dnieper, discovered in 1927 during construction of the dam at Dnepropetrovsk. Flint flakes were found in association with mammoth, Siberian rhinoceros, great-horned deer, reindeer, bison, bear, and lion.

Boriskovskii has given a popular but carefully written presentation,[4] attractively illustrated,[5] of the Paleolithic cultures from the first large-scale excavations by Khvoiko in 1893 to the latest finds up to 1940 at the famous sites of Mezin, Gontsi, and Pushkari.

Boriskovskii concludes with a description of the Neolithic finds at Mariupol, where in 1930 were found 124 burials with rich polished-stone and bone inventories.

CRIMEA

Chersonesus.—Excavations in Chersonesus,[6] begun in 1827 and interrupted in 1914, were renewed in 1926. During this era they were

in Central Asia, pp. 26-35; Soviet Types, pp. 36-39; and List of Scientific Institutions and Branches of the Academy of Sciences of the U.S.S.R., pp. 40-126. The plates include: 1-48, exhibits in IAE; 49-95, Lake Onega rock engravings; 96-101, Minusinsk bronzes; 102-106, gold treasure from Abakan near Minusinsk; 107-111, Central Asia; 112-116, reconstructions by M. Gerasimov; 117-118, leather coat restored in State Historical Museum, Moscow; 119, Zaraut-Sai rock-shelter paintings; 120-130, exhibits in Museum of Oriental Civilizations, Moscow; 131-134, anthropometric form used in Museum of Anthropology and Ethnography; 135, map of Moscow locating museums. Supplementary material has been placed on the following Microfilms in the American Documentation Institute: Nos. 2214, 2307, 2310, 2344, 2414, 2415.

See also Lauriston Ward's Reference List of the Archeology of the Soviet Union, Harvard University, January 1947. (Mimeographed.)

[3] Boriskovskii, P. I., Liudina kamianogo viku na Ukraini [Stone Age man in the Ukraine]. Institute of Archaeology, Academy of Sciences of the Ukrainian S.S.R., p. 128, Kiev, 1940. [In Ukrainian.]

[4] The book is divided into eight chapters: 1, Glacial period; 2, Earliest human traces; 3, Transition to the Upper Paleolithic; 4, Mizin; 5, Lower Paleolithic man near Kiev; 6, Gontsi; 7, End of Lower Paleolithic; 8, Neolithic.

[5] This account has some of the charm of Breasted's "Ancient Times." The interest is particularly enhanced by numerous line drawings, some of them really inspired, of Paleolithic fauna and implements. Illustrations include reconstructions, on the basis of recent finds of such Quaternary fauna as the Siberian rhinoceros, cave bear, and cave lion. Of special interest are the original reconstructions of tools and dwellings. (E. P.)

[6] Translated by Mrs. David Huxley from the French summary in Materialy i Issledovaniia po Arkheologii SSSR, No. 4, pp. 275-278, Moscow and Leningrad, 1941. Minor editorial revisions have been made to conform to our style. (H. F.)

undertaken in a haphazard manner, at several places and without a coordinated plan. During 1931 the question of excavation sites was examined, and it was decided that priority should be given to places which were in the process of destruction from natural causes. It was known that the most threatened area was the northern shore of the Chersonesus, where at the lowest points the archeological stratum was directly encroached upon by the sea. It was here that excavations were started in 1931, with the object of studying the coastal section of the city. An area of approximately 700 square meters was uncovered.

The oldest remains were supporting walls, a pear-shaped cistern, and some wells. In the lowest stratum, close to virgin rock, were found amphora handles, which bore manufacturing marks of Chersonesus, Rhodes, and Cnidus, as well as fragments of black-glazed pottery, both local and imported.

This first period of construction covered from the end of the fourth to the second century B. C.

Dating from the second period were some massive masonry walls and cisterns, paved with bricks (12-20 cm. thick) bound together with cement or simply with mortar. The walls of the cisterns were coated in red parget of the same composition—a mixture of chalk, sand, and finely crushed pottery, which is very durable. Two cisterns are remarkable for their small size; they were placed together and were probably used for the storing of finer grades of fish; the larger tanks were used for salting anchovies (kamsa). The large number of tanks illustrated the extensive development of the fishing industry and the exporting of fish during Roman times.

During the first centuries of our era, one cistern and some of the wells were covered by a layer of earth. In this layer, red-glazed pottery of fine workmanship, dating from the first-second centuries B. C., was found. At other places in this third stratum, silver and bronze coins of the first-fourth centuries A. D. were uncovered, as was a bronze statue of Asclepius, holding in his right hand a rod entwined by a serpent. These cisterns can be ascribed to the first-fourth centuries A. D.

At the base of the second level, well-built walls rested on rock. This layer, filled with refuse, was characterized by a white-glazed clay pottery, decorated with a stamped or painted design, which can be dated from the ninth-tenth centuries; it appears to be of local manufacture. In one section a large quantity of ninth-tenth century coins were found on the ground and also a gold plaque decorated with enamel cloisonné of fine workmanship, showing two peacocks with a vase between them; this plaque was attributed to the ninth-tenth centuries. The constructions of this era disintegrated at the end of the tenth century and were engulfed by a layer of rubble 2 m. deep.

During the following period, a series of buildings were constructed on this foundation, and belonged to several groups of dwelling houses. The walls were poorly built of stones held together with mud; the plan was irregular, the dimensions too small, the furnishings meager, the floors of earth, and the walls unplastered. During this later period (twelfth-fifteenth centuries) this district was rebuilt according to a new plan. Generally, there were inner courtyards; in one courtyard was a well which served four houses. The Roman cisterns, partly covered by the second layer, were then sometimes used as cellars.

Within the houses were unearthed working equipment such as fishing tackle and net weights, boats, dragnets for shell fishing, stone-working and weaving tools, red-glazed pottery decorated with an engraved design, etc. In one well a glazed bowl was found with an interior design showing Theodore Stratilat astride a horse killing a dragon.

The buildings of the late period were destroyed by fire, apparently at the time of the destruction of Chersonesus at the end of the fifteenth century. The floors were covered by thick debris, including fragments of coal, soot, charred wood, and burnt walls and objects.

During 1932 excavations were made to the east of the area explored in 1931; 700 square meters were uncovered.

Architectural remains of the Greek epoch are rare, having been destroyed at the time of the construction of the basilica. In the clay near the rock, amphora handles were found which bore the mark of the Chersonesus astinomes, as were fragments of black-glazed pottery dating from the third-second century B. C.

Near the western street was a large cistern with a flooring of brick and mortar and walls coated in red parget. The bottom of the tank was covered with a layer of salted anchovy, 0.25-1.0 m. thick. The fish formed a compact brown mass. The type of fish was identifiable through the spines. After the cistern was no longer used for salting fish, it had been used as a cesspool. Directly above the fish lay pottery of the later Roman period and coins from the time of Zenon and Justinian the First. During the sixth century, when the basilica was built, it was used as a limekiln; its fourth use was for the storage of provisions; the fifth, during the ninth-tenth centuries, was a final conversion into a cesspool. The finding of this cistern with its fish remains was of great importance, not only for the determination of construction date, but as an indication of the original purpose of the large number of similar tanks found throughout the city. It is certain that they date from the first-fourth centuries. A marble gravestone, with an epitaph in verse, belongs to the third century.

The basilica, found in the eastern part of the district, dates from the sixth century. The dimensions were 26.0 m. long and 16.5 m. wide. It had three naves, with a narthex and pentagonal apse. In the northern colonnade, three marble bases, and next to them a fan-light, are still in place. The marble rood screen in the apse is partially in existence. The side naves had a mosaic floor, whose geometric design was carried out in white, red, yellow, and black in the north nave, and three colors (no black) in the south nave.

Architectural details included marble capitals, fanlights, coignes with carved or polychrome ornamentation. The basilica was destroyed by approximately the end of the tenth century and was subsequently covered by a heavy layer of construction rubble.

Some time later a chapel was built on the ruins of the basilica, the whole being within the apse of the original basilica. Within the chapel, 35 mausoleum tombs were erected, and in the western part, a guard hut with a stove in the eastern corner.

The tombs were in some degree arranged according to a pattern. They contained 10, 15, 25, even 35 and 60 skulls, but very few long bones were found. This shows that when the remains of the dead were transferred from the cemetery to the mausoleum near the temple, it was considered sufficient to take only the skull. In tomb No. 6 the shroud was decorated with bone plates: in the corners are large lamellae with pictures of griffons, a lion, and a hind; lateral bands with circles and squares intersect in the center of the design, also circles made of small squares, lozenges, and triangles, framed with straight and curved lamellae.

Such a design was found for the first time in Chersonesus and constitutes a remarkable example of the local medieval art of bone sculpture. The shroud appears to have belonged to a very wealthy person. Beads were found in tomb No. 20 together with one string of paste beads encrusted with colors and another of lignite and a silver pendant.

Other tombs yielded hollow bronze buttons, decorated bone roundels, and ninth-tenth century coins. The tombs dated from the tenth, eleventh, and later centuries.

In the waterfront section of the district, compounds were uncovered in the first layer which obviously belonged to two houses. Two rooms had been used as food-storage cellars with wooden floors. In one cellar were more than 50 assorted clay vases. Such an abundance of pottery permits the conclusion that at this later date also the art of pottery making in the Chersonesus had reached an extensive degree of development. Tiles with varied brands also confirm this. In the same cellar, two small icons were discovered: one in slate with the image of St. George bearing a lance and shield; the other in bronze with the image of Jesus Christ. Both are covered with gilt, are distinguished by their fine workmanship, and can be ascribed to the ninth-tenth century. Room VII contained wells with a water level of 3.60 m. In other rooms were mills, mortars for crushing grain, fishing tackle, and a quantity of pottery articles. One room had bronze chains with an imperial orb, belonging to an ecclesiastical lamp.

On the floors of rooms of this period, there were also traces of a fire, as in the district excavated in 1931. It is certain that both districts were burned at the same time that the entire city was destroyed by fire at the end of the fifteenth century.

During 1933 excavations were continued along the north shore of the Chersonesus to the east of those undertaken in 1932. Only the top stratum was removed over an area of about 500 square meters; it consisted of an accumulation of debris formed from the destruction of buildings. Their floors were covered with soot, fragments of coal, burnt articles, and pieces of tile.

The walls were of rough stone (*ashlar*) bound together with mud, with wooden beams inserted to connect the walls. The plan of the buildings was usually irregular, the dimensions small, the floors earthen, the walls unplastered or sometimes with a clay coating.

The rooms belonged to two houses. In the first there was an oven, in another two ovens—a small one in the east corner and a large one in the north. These ovens were built of bricks and pieces of tile, bound with clay; they were fitted with an arched "front oven"; the hearth was decorated with squares of baked earth. The roof had an opening for the chimney; tiles pierced with a round orifice and chimney pipes were found. The presence of two ovens in one single room and a third in another room of the same house indicates that this was a large bakery, making bread for sale. This type of stove is rare in houses of the period; normally rooms were heated by simple stone hearths.

The second house was located in the eastern part of the district. In room VIII there was a mortar for grain crushing next to a post with a cavity for a pestle. Similar mortars were found in many rooms of the same period during the 1931-1932 excavations. Room IX was used for food storage: on the floor by the walls were a large number of amphorae containing the remains of fish. Here also were production tools: 2 iron swing-plows, more than 100 bronze fishhooks, 40 net weights, and a quantity of metal articles including padlocks, screw rings, bronze bowls, and others. Room X had a hearth, and on the floor near the west wall were part of a marble column and a cubed stone; this was possibly either a smithy or a workshop. Room XII was a courtyard; in the east corner was the cesspool sump.

The numerous and varied furnishings (work tools and usual articles) allow certain conclusions to be drawn as to the occupations and social organizations of the inhabitants of this dwelling. They engaged in farming, livestock raising, and fishing. Others were artisans such as smiths, locksmiths, builders, and weavers.

It was a regime of small undertakings, sufficient in themselves; trade had evidently ceased at this period since no imported articles were found.

The houses date from the last centuries of the city's existence, or approximately from the fourteenth-fifteenth centuries.

These observations on the latter part of the medieval period, made during 3 years of excavation, can be extended to some degree over the entire city:

1. The economic level of the population during the latter stages of the city's existence was very low.

2. By their occupations and their means of existence, the populations lived mainly in a rural condition through the natural economy of small, independent, and self-sufficient undertakings.

3. In general, the Chersonesus lost its former importance as a large trading center and became a small town with but slender economic connections with its immediate vicinity.

Tiritaka.—Although ancient writers referred to Tiritaka as a city, the excavations by the Bosphorean Expedition of IIMK in collaboration with the Kerch Archeological Museum under the direction of V. F. Gaidukevich [7] disclosed that in general planning and many other essential traits this settlement did not resemble the usual ancient cities.

Tiritaka was a well-developed industrial settlement. An additional group of fish-salting cisterns uncovered during 1939 in the southern part of town evidently belonged to a very extensive establishment. There is no doubt that during the Roman period Tiritaka was one of the most important centers for the export of fish. The 1939 excavations in the western part of the site were a continuation of those of 1938 in the course of which a building of the sixth century B. C.

---

[7] V. F. Gaidukevich, in Kratkie Soobshcheniia, No. 4, pp. 54-58, summarized the 1932-1939 excavations.

containing archaic terra cottas and many other interesting finds had been discovered.

This building was completely excavated, and many service structures surrounding the building were uncovered. These included a barn or storeroom, a paved courtyard, a basement with a flight of steps leading into it, and extensive grain-storage pits lined with stone.

A late Roman dwelling complex discovered in 1939 was buried under a stratum of debris 3.5 m. thick. The walls were preserved to the height of 2.0 m. The main building, paved with stone flags, communicated with a small courtyard also paved with flags. In the floor of the main building opposite the entrance a large sunken pythos with a capacity of several hundred liters was uncovered. This was probably used for grain storage, since many charred grains of wheat were found inside the building close to the pythos, as well as several hand mills. A pit 1.0 m. in diameter and 68 cm. deep filled with ashes, near the pythos, contained a pottery lamp, a bone needle for weaving fish nets, an iron hammer, whetstones, and a gray-ware pitcher of Sarmatian type decorated with a band of intersecting lines formed by polishing.

The finds from the floor of the building included many pieces and fragments of molded pottery, several lamps, a round bronze mirror, clay spindle whorls, fragments of glass vessels, and red lacquer platters of late Roman type, one of which was stamped with the sign of a cross, and several bronze coins. Large pointed amphorae of late Roman type were also unearthed; many had been repaired by means of lead brackets. The building itself had been destroyed by fire; its floor was covered by coal and ashes from the burned wooden parts of the structure. Many of these amphorae had apparently been stored on the second floor of the building but had fallen down in the course of the fire. An outside stone stairway parallel with one of the walls of the building led to the upper story.

The prevalence of burned buildings in Tiritaka, of which several had been previously discovered, suggests that this city was attacked and partially destroyed. The finds from the late Roman building included also the remains of a charred cable, probably a part of some sort of fishing gear, and of two dozen net weights manufactured of stones of varying sizes, each encircled by a shallow notch for attaching to the rope. A small fish-salting cistern, 1.75 x 1.37, and 1.90 m. deep, was found in an adjoining outbuilding.

In the lower part of one of the walls of the main structure was found a clay-covered niche containing the bones of a young pig and a lamb, covered by sea sand containing long scales of *sevriuga*, and sherds of amphorae. The niche also contained a clay lamp. Apparently this niche was connected with some sort of ritual.

A small stone *terapan* (bench for pressing grapes) was found on a dais in the courtyard. Many finds connected with viticulture from 'previous excavations seem to indicate its important role in the economic life of the Bosphorus during the late Hellenistic and Roman periods when the importation of wines from abroad became curtailed. A second large winery of the second century B. C., discovered in 1939, had been partially buried by a railroad embankment. Nonetheless, the large pressing platform was uncovered, together with a gutter leading to a cistern. Both the platform and the cistern were faced with a white cement differing in composition from the Roman cement of that period. On the basis of this and the earlier discoveries, it is now possible to reconstruct the evolution of viticultural technique in Tiritaka from the second century B. C. to the third century A. D.

The 1939 excavations indicated that Tiritaka was sacked during the fourth century A. D. This destruction occurred as a result of one of the mass tribal migrations in the northern Black Sea area, which led to the final dissolution of the Bosphorean State. But Tiritaka did not disappear altogether at that time, as the finds from the excavations include many objects of the Early Medieval period. Thus, in the western part of the site a quantity of pottery of that period had been found, including a pythos stamped with the name of the potter and the incised sign of a cross of the type attributed to the fifth or sixth century A. D. The fisheries continued during this period, although most of the Roman cisterns had become disused. The main occupation of the local population seems to have been agriculture. Tiritaka was abandoned during the seventh or eighth century.

Many sherds of archaic pottery were found, including a fragment of a painted pot. Particularly abundant were the finds from a late Roman house, and also a quantity of objects from the Bosphorean house of the third or fourth century A. D.

A stoppered amphora, attributed to the fourth or fifth century A. D., found near one of the fish-salting complexes, contained nearly 3.5 kilograms of crude oil. The amphora was of the elongated cylindrical type with a conical bottom. The neck had been closed by a bunch of straw which, when permeated with the solidified crude oil, formed a completely hermetical seal. The liquid was analyzed by R. R. IAnovskii of the Leningrad Chemico-Technical Institute. The liquid which was characterized by IAnovskii as "crude oil or a product of crude oil" contained several wisps of straw. According to the classical authors crude oil was used for lighting and also as medicine.

Neapolis.—During the latter part of 1945 an expedition under the leadership of P. Shults was sponsored by the Museum of Fine Arts in Moscow and the Institute for the History of Material Culture (IIMK) of the Academy of Sciences of the U.S.S.R.

Shults began excavations at Neapolis, the Scythian capital, often mentioned by early writers. The numerous finds indicate that Neapolis existed from the fourth century B. C. to the fourth century A. D. This ancient city was encircled by a thick, protective wall of unique masonry. The excavations revealed the first specimen of monumental Scythian architecture consisting of a large house whose basement had been hewn out of rock.

The first Scythian winery to be found contained marble goblets as well as Scythian and Greek pottery of different periods, some of them bearing Greek inscriptions.

The first Scythian mural painting, showing no evidence of Greek influence, came to light. The designs resemble those with which the modern Ukrainians decorate their cottages and household utensils. The clay roof ornaments and animals found during the excavation of another site also resemble Russian roof ornaments and Slavic toys.

Scythian handicrafts, in particular pottery, were as fine as other expressions of art. A complex kiln for pottery making was unearthed.

Archeological surveys were conducted in many parts of the Crimea with a view to establishing the boundaries on this peninsula of the Scythian State, which evidently extended along the Black Sea coast as far as the Danube.

A system of fortifications, consisting of three lines of defense, protected the Scythians from outside enemies:

1. In the north stood the rampart and moat at Perekop.

2. Along the Salgir River.

3. Along the Alma River at the boundary between the foothills and the mountains.

Along these lines stretched a chain of fortress towns. On the western coast there were also Scythian fortifications at intervals of 6 to 8 kilometers. Evidently they protected the Scythians from invasions by sea and at the same time served as ports.[8]

BLACK SEA COAST

Cave excavations.[9]—During 1936-1937 S. N. Zamiatnin excavated two caves in the Sochi and Adler *Raions* of Krasnodar *Krai*. The

---

[8] Quoted from Nina Militsyna in the Moscow News, February 2, 1946.

[9] Translated and summarized from S. N. Zamiatnin, Navalishinskaia i Akhshtyrskaia Peshchery na Chernomorskom Poberezhe Kavkaza, Bulletin de la Commission pour l'Etude du Quaternaire, Nos. 6-7, pp. 100-101, Moscow, 1940. See also Field and Prostov in Amer. Anthrop. vol. 44, No. 2, p. 213, 1942.

work was concentrated in two areas: in the Kudepsta River gorge near Navalishino and in the valley of the Mzymta River and the Akhshtyr Gorge.

Navalishino Cave is situated on the right bank of the Kudepsta River, within 12 kilometers of the seacoast, at a considerable height above the river.

The excavations embraced an area of 22 square meters at the entrance to the cave. In addition, a small excavation was made deep inside the main corridor of the cave.

The upper horizons yielded microlithic implements and the bones of hamster, badger, and *slepysh* [?]. The occasional remains of the cave bear (*Ursus spelaeus*) found here belong to other strata, and are obviously located in a secondary deposit.

Below that lies a stratum containing Upper Paleolithic finds, while the faunal remains are mainly those of cave bear. Here were found also the bones of elk, goat, hamster, fragments of tubular bones of birds, and also shells of *Anodonta* and *Helix*.

The lowest stratum yielded a few typical Mousterian implements. Among the animals represented were cave bear, wolf, and goat.

The character of the finds indicates that Navalishino Cave was not occupied by a permanent settlement, but was rather a seasonal, temporary site.

Akhshtyr Cave (pls. 1-4) is situated on the right bank of the Mzymta River, opposite Akhshtyr, within 15 kilometers of Adler.

The excavators uncovered an area of 60 square meters. The finds from the upper stratum included very late pottery and bones of domestic animals.

Below this were found Upper Neolithic pottery and polished implements. In this stratum also belongs a flexed inhumation of a child. Among faunal remains were wolf, roe, moufflon, and wild pig.

Still lower lies a sterile stratum, below which were found objects of the later stage of the Upper Paleolithic. The fauna included cave bear, fox, wildcat, marten, deer, elk, roe, moufflon, goat, and wild pig.

Beneath the Upper Paleolithic level lay the Upper Mousterian stratum, which yielded a large collection of implements and fauna, the latter, with the exception of the elk, which was absent, being identical with that of the Upper Paleolithic.

The Lower Mousterian was also rich in implements, which permitted comparison with those from Ilskaia, and the finds from the upper horizons of Kiik-Koba in the Crimea.

Since the faunal remains were in a very poor state of preservation, only the following could be identified: large deer [?], cave bear, and wild pig.

The underlying strata are devoid of archeological finds and consist largely of gravel deposited by the floods of the Mzymta River, which since that time has managed to deepen its valley by 120 m., as demonstrated by the marks at the bottom of the cave.

Conference on material culture.—The material culture of the Black Sea coast area in ancient times was the subject of a recent conference [10] in Leningrad attended by specialists from archeology, history, and art research institutes as well as universities in Moscow, Kiev, Odessa, Kharkov, Voronezh, Krasnodar, Saratov, and Leningrad.

The conference heard and discussed more than 30 reports treating various aspects of the life, socio-economic structure, religion, art, and ethnography of the Black Sea coast area at various periods and in many localities. Most of them were summaries of researches by Soviet scientists, in particular field investigations carried out just before the war and during the 1945 season.

Professor Kovalev pointed out that the Black Sea coast area was a flourishing center of culture in antiquity, and exerted its influence on Slavonic tribes.

V. Gaidukevich observed that recent researches have shown that the Greek cities on the Black Sea coast area in ancient times were not isolated seats of culture and that the local population played an active part in building up the ancient culture Soviet archeologists designate as Greco-Scytho-Sarmatian culture. Although the local tribes were subjected to the influence of Greece, in general they retained their own original culture.

This thesis was corroborated by results of numerous excavations reported at the conference, for example, those brought back by the expedition led by P. Shults last summer to the site of the ancient Scythian capital, Neapolis.

A prominent place on the agenda was given to reports on studies of the relations between the local population of the Black Sea coast steppe areas and the Greek colonies. To understand these relations properly it is necessary to know something about the period preceding Greek colonization. This was dealt with in a report by A. Jessen, who mustered facts indicating intensive development of trade and cultural ties as far back as the third millennium B. C. among the tribes living along the Black Sea coast. Archeological data show that articles from the Near East penetrated through the Caucasus into the Kuban

---

[10] Summarized from the Moscow News, June 8, 1946.

area from the western part of Asia Minor, the Aegean basin, and the Balkan Peninsula to the right bank of the Dnieper [present-day Ukraine] as far back as the end of the third and the beginning of the second millennium B. C. Speakers cited many interesting new data on the links between Black Sea coast and Greek cities—Attica, Corinth, and Aeolia—as well as Ionian trade centers.

NORTH CAUCASUS

Adighe A.S.S.R.—A tombstone believed to date back to the first century of our era was recently acquired by the regional museum in Krasnodar. This monument was unearthed in a quarry not far from the place where 2,500 years ago the Greeks founded the town of Sadi (Cepi) which is thought to have been a summer resort for the wealthy slave owners from Phanagoria, the second capital of the Bosphoran Kingdom. It is made of limestone and is in the form of a miniature chapel supported by columns with a niche in which stands a warrior wearing a conical helmet, a short coat, and a sword.

SOUTH CAUCASUS

Kuftin's [11] report is divided into two parts: a description and analysis of the materials excavated near Igdir on the right bank of the Araxes River during 1913 by B. F. Petrov and now in the State Museum of Georgia in Tbilisi [formerly Tiflis]; and the establishment in the South Caucasus during the Eneolithic period of a proper focus of cultural development contemporaneous with the oldest objects found by Petrov.

The upper stratum of the Igdir monument yielded an unusual cemetery columbarium with the ashes of the dead in red polished earthenware pitchers with a round hole pierced in the side. In only one case was there an inhumation. These vessels were placed, together with the personal inventory, in the clefts of a tufa cone. This lava flow covered the ash layers of an ancient settlement, situated to the south of the cemetery beyond the road from Igdir to Markara.

Since evidence of the custom of cremation had not yet been seen in the South Caucasus during the pre-Roman epoch, and because of

---

[11] Kuftin, B. A., Urarsku "Kolumbaru" u podotsvli Ararata i Kuro-Arakssku Eneolit. Acad. Sci. U.S.S.R., Tbilisi, 1943. This study was received from Dr. Kuftin in Leningrad on July 2, 1945, while I was a guest at the Jubilee Sessions in Moscow and Leningrad celebrating the 220th anniversary of the Academy of Sciences of the U.S.S.R. The summary in English has been edited and condensed. See footnote 14. (H. F.)

the presence of the red ware and iron weapons, and, finally, because of the finding in the neighborhood of the cemetery of a silver denarius of Antonius the Pious, the graveyard had been attributed to the Roman epoch.

An analysis of the inventory by Kuftin and his assistants shows the fallibility of thus fixing the date. Fragments of a bronze vessel, found in one of the graves, belonged to the well-known type of bucket from the Colchian-Koban Bronze Age and also found in the Ukraine in pre-Scythian barrows.

Kuftin succeeded in connecting the red polished pottery with a similar type from Toprak-Kala on Lake Van and also from Armavir-Blur,[12] where during 1879 A. S. Uvarov found similar pottery as well as some bichrome ware [13] taken erroneously for late Roman.

Among the beads from the columbarium, which do not reveal any Hellenic or Roman influence, there are three stamp seals with zoomorphic figures: one toggle-shaped bead seal from the grave with the inhumation; and two columnar pendants, in which Kuftin establishes, because of the similarity of the pictures to the earthenware stamps from Toprak-Kala and a series of other correspondences, a type of Urartian seal, little found up to the present, in which is preserved in contrast with the stamp cylinder prevalent in other parts of the Near East, the archaic figure of the stamp seals of Asiatic stock.

Thus, Kuftin came to the conclusion that the cemetery excavated by Petrov does not date from the Roman but from the Van epoch, belonging, as it does, not to the native population, of which the types of tomb and tomb inventory of that time are well known, but evidently to one which had come from Lake Van. Consequently, it must be presumed that there long existed in eastern Anatolia the custom of cremation, a practice not foreign to the early cultures of Mesopotamia and Syria and practiced later in the Kingdom of Mitani and in the burial of the Hittite kings.

The proposed attribution of the columbarium to the Urartians explains the different composition of the necklaces, foreign to the South Caucasus for this date. For example, instead of carnelian, which was the usual material for this period, ribbon agate and colorless glass predominated. In addition, the style of the bronze bracelets with lions' heads was similar to that found at Zakim associated with a bronze belt, the ornamentation of which, in its time, was compared with that of a sword in the Melgunov treasure.

---

[12] This is the town of Argishtichinli of the Urartian inscriptions.

[13] This pottery is probably correlated with the types from Mukhanat-Tepe in Yerevan [formerly Erivan].

By drawing a parallel between this belt and the bronze plate from Shirak in Yerevan Museum and another belt, found in 1905, at Gushi on Lake Urmia [Rezaiyeh] together with the bronze bulls' heads published by F. Sarre and A. U. Pope as Achemenid and Iranian, we try to prove the Urartian origin and age of all these monuments. In this category are also the remarkable bulls' heads, similar to those from Toprak-Kala, on chariot poles in the British Museum, and especially to the Hermitage application to a large bucket or cauldron, found with a handle in the form of a siren of Urartian type.

On the basis of the definite dating which Kuftin obtained for the cemetery with cremation, the previously mentioned discovery in one of the graves of a fragment of a bronze bucket acquires a new significance. This gives a more precise date for the flourishing stage of Koban bronze, which had perhaps been carried back too far, and in which was developed the most skillful molding of bronze weapons (in particular of typical axheads and flat celts with lateral projections), while the territory of Lake Van, poorer in copper ore, had already passed on completely to weapons of iron.

The inventory of the village, which lies beneath the lava flow to the south of the columbarium, is of an entirely different character and is therefore not connected chronologically. The cultural strata consist of huge layers of ashes, used by the peasants for fertilizing the fields, and of large heaps of ruined mud brick. These layers yielded many bones of horned cattle, stone fragments, grain pounders, obsidian flakes, and sherds. There were no traces of metal or of glass, with the exception of a group of beaten-copper ingots perhaps originating here.

The pottery, quite distinct from that of the columbarium, had nothing in common with that from South Caucasian graves of the Bronze Age. It is distinguished by the combination of archaic methods of modeling, without using the potter's wheel, with artistic molding and a fine finish given to the vessels through the use of a slip and elaborate polishing.

The characteristic features include: hemispherical handles, a broad cylindrical neck, a lid, the black shiny outer surface of the sherds with a pink inner surface, and the ornamentation of the neck with a ribbon-like, geometrically cut belt.

Associated with the fragments of a vessel there were pottery fragments, horseshoe-shaped, with a handle behind; these bear some analogy to the "horned altars" from Alishar III and through them with the puzzling Aegean attributes of a goddess on a double ax.

In the absence of any systematic excavation, and because of the haphazard nature of the collected material (in particular the fragment of a bichrome vessel not clearly documented), it is only possible to assign to its approximate chronological place this new type of Igdir ash mound by drawing on a wider range of parallel examples on which more light has been thrown stratigraphically.

The second part of the work, which is devoted to this phase, falls into three parts:

1. The establishing of the presence of parallel monuments among the old collections in the State Museum of Georgia.

2. A survey of corresponding materials obtained from Kuftin's excavations.

3. An attempt to establish the existence, prior to the third millennium B. C., of a singular, highly developed Eneolithic phase in the central part of the Kura-Araxes basin, as a local basis for the development of the flourishing cultural focus of the Bronze Age, revealed by the excavations in Trialeti.[14]

The accurately documented excavation of an ash grave carried out by E. G. Pchelina during 1923 in Kiketi near Tbilisi, assigned by Kuftin to this level, together with the pottery from the Igdir ash mound, proved to be a key to the understanding of the Eneolithic objects in the old collections in the Georgian State Museum. This ash grave, with a burnt earthenware coating, yielded several groups of earthenware vessels which now appear as one contemporaneous culture complex. The following vessels were unearthed: (a) a large, finely polished black vessel with a pink inner surface, ornamented with large double spiral figures (like eyeglasses) in relief; (b) and (c) pinkish-brown urns with a slip and miniature handles at the base of the neck, one with single birdlike (ostrich ?) figures in flat relief on the neck, the other with a cut angular design on the shoulders; (d) a tureen, thick-walled, roughly modeled with layers of carbon in the clay but a glossy-black surface; and (e) a gray vessel painted red.

Thus, by a comparative analysis of the pottery Kuftin succeeded in establishing that in the Armavir mound A. S. Uvarov touched not only the Urartian stratum, unnoticed by him, but also the most ancient Eneolithic level, both in the settlements and in the graves, also not understood by him. In addition to the characteristic vessels, the finding of fragments of a horseshoe-shaped stand of the above-mentioned Igdir type is significant. This seems to be a leading type for the

---

[14] Kuftin, B. A. Prehistoric culture sequence in Transcaucasia, Southwestern Journ. Anthrop., vol. 2, No. 3, pp. 340-360, 1946, and pp. 1-26 on Microfilm No. 2310 in American Documentation Institute. The summary in English has been edited and condensed by Henry Field.

stratum in the South Caucasus with which we are concerned and has been found near Karakurt in Kars Province of Nakhichevan and in Shengavit near Yerevan.

In making a stratigraphic study of the horizon with which we are concerned, some help is afforded by the short account by E. Lalaian of the excavations during 1904 in Nakhichevan, of the ash mound of Kul-Tepe with cultural level many meters in depth in which strata containing painted pottery overlie a deposit with black ware.

To this latter, supposedly, must be assigned three remarkable vessels polished black, with hemispherical handles, narrow concave bases and specific ornamentation, bearing witness to the absolutely original artistic style inherent in this culture. A main characteristic is the dynamism of the linear movement inside the externally balanced, closed, curvilinear figures, executed concavely and convexly, and with spiral tailpieces, adorning only the front of the body of the vessel, while around the neck runs a cut-out belt of rhythmically recurring rectilinear geometric elements.

Lalaian did not pay due attention to these vessels nor did he distinguish a grave with a finely molded scoop and a goblet, of the shape in question, from the usual Late Bronze and Early Iron Age tombs discovered by him during 1905-1906 on the west bank of Lake Sevan.

The first substantial material for judging the cultural layer characterized by this ceramic complex is given by Lalaian's excavations during 1927 on Eilar mound, where he found a cyclopean fortress with an inscription of Argishti concerning the conquest of Darani. In addition, Lalaian excavated during 1913 Shresh-Blur tumulus at Echmiadzin.

Lalaian assigned the lower cultural strata of these two mounds to the Neolithic period on the basis of a mistaken interpretation of the stone querns, flaked pebbles, flint and obsidian flakes, and bone bodkins. This was in direct contrast to the rooted prejudice of reckoning cultural life in the South Caucasus as beginning only from the Late Bronze Age, immediately before the Urartian expansion.

The pottery from the lower stratum of Eilar is relatively poorly decorated, i.e., with bosses and hollows forming a kind of facial pattern on one side of the body of the vessel, like that on the pitcher found during 1869 in Zaglik. The molding and the shape of the vessels are especially similar to the Igdir pottery, while at Shresh-Blur and Kul-Tepe the designs are distinguished by one-sided but complicated geometric compositions, symmetrically balanced, with the spiral tailpieces replaced by isolated concentric circles. This is particularly clear when comparing them with the ornamentation, carried out in relief, of the black polished urn, also Eneolithic, from Frangnots near Echmiadzin.

The presence in this stratum with similar pottery of "round dwellings with one entrance" of the "tholos" type discovered by Lalaian at Eilar was confirmed later by excavations at Shengavit, where, because of the construction of the walls from river boulders and mud brick, these dwellings come particularly close to the circular buildings revealed recently in the lower levels at Tell Halaf and at Al Ubaid, as well as the settlements of Arpachiyah, Kidish Saghir, and Tepe-Gawra in Upper Mesopotamia.

Lalaian also discovered at Eilar, at the centers of double concentric rings of stones, numerous holes faced with stone and filled with layers of ash containing the remains of human bones, and also a singular hollowed-out stone sarcophagus attributed by him to this same level.

Special significance in establishing the Eneolithic phase in the South Caucasus belongs to the excavations of the Georgian Department for the Preservation of Monuments of Culture, and of the Georgian Academy of Sciences during 1936-1940 at Trialeti, and of the Armenian Department for the Preservation of Monuments of Culture, and of the Armenian Branch of the Academy of Sciences during 1936-1938 at Shengavit.

The first gave stratigraphic material, already partly published;[15] and established a series of ceramic modifications of the Eneolithic layer on the site of the cyclopean town of Akhillar near Beshtashen. This determined the relation of this layer and the usual South Caucasian cemeteries with the blackish-gray ware to the flourishing Trialetian Bronze Age barrow culture with painted pottery and to the preceding culture of the oldest Trialetian barrows. The second excavations made it possible to determine that this settlement belonged to one homogeneous Eneolithic stratum.

The unusual combination in one complex of many types of pottery occurs in the Kiketi tomb and at Trialeti. Here were found heaps of potter's slag and a developed culture emphasized by the skill of the firing. Portable ceramic hearths of a special form, found in Shengavit in an unbroken state in the center of circular buildings, are characteristic of this deposit.

The polished black ware from Shengavit is distinguished by inherent details, strictly peculiar to it, both of shape (the barrel-shaped body and sharply conical narrow lower part of the vessel) and of

---

[15] Kuftin, B. A., Archaeological excavations in Trialeti, vol. 1, pp. 106, 118, and 168, and About the question of the early stages of bronze culture in the Territory of Georgia, pp. 13-14, 20-24.

ornamentation (the characteristic development of the drawing in the upper rectilinear geometric frieze and the decorative fretting of the clear-cut outlines of the closed design in relief on the body), so that it may be connected with the comparatively late stage of the Shengavit Eneolithic.

In any event in this connection the finding in Shengavit of a fragment of an oval cup with two bends is significant, being a type well known from the Kizilvank complex with painted pottery, but with the black polishing of the outer surface inherent in the Shengavit types. A cup of this light ware, recalling by its shape a section of a human skull,[16] also came from the excavations by Lalaian on the west bank of Lake Sevan and was erroneously imputed to a Late Bronze Age tomb. There was also a fragment of a similar cup in the upper level of the Eneolithic stratum at Akhillar.

The horseshoe-shaped stands from Shengavit have a special form with a female anthropomorphic figure in the center, in relation to which the bends of the horseshoe play the part of embracing arms. This confirms the connection between these stands and the cult of a female goddess (in the present case, of the hearth) and at the same time may be used as an argument for the hypothesis concerning the origin of the form of the Aegean "horned altars" through the symbolic simplification of the idol of the goddess with the hands held up in prayer. Of other figurative motifs in sculpture the attention is arrested by the sheeplike tailpieces on another kind of horseshoe-shaped stand from Shengavit, by the massive figure of a bull from Shresh-Blur, and also by a kind of hearth stand and separate rude sculptures of animals and man.

The flint inventory from Akhillar and Shengavit included arrows, knives, sickle-teeth, and especially perforated stone implements. In addition, a fragment of a wedge-shaped ax and a marble cask-shaped hammer have particular significance in dating this level. Metal was very rare and consisted of small fragments of pins and of a copper awl, rhombic in outline, characteristic of the early stages of copper production.

The survey of these data, unusual for the South Caucasus, makes it possible to establish the existence, at the dawn of the knowledge of metal or at least prior to the third millennium B. C., in the central part of the Kura-Araxes basin of a cultural layer absolutely homogeneous from Karakurt to Nakhichevan and from Tbilisi to Ararat. This level is characterized by a ceramic production, finely developed

---

[16] Cf. Human calvaria from Paleolithic deposits at Le Placard, France. It is suggested that these were used as ceremonial drinking vessels. (H. F.)

artistically and yet archaic, with cattle-raising, agricultural settlements with protective cyclopean walls, circular houses, built with mud bricks, with high flues raised above the hearths, and traces of the cult of the domestic fire and of a female goddess.

The development of artistic pottery took place locally, not in the direction of the application of colored painting (Tell Halaf, Samarra, Al Ubaid, Elam styles), but along the lines of the refined use of the still earlier traditions of black polishing and of a gutterlike design of the pottery. This had a pink inner surface of the type from Sakchegozy and proto-Hittite Akhlatlibel near Ankara, with its suspected western connections on which depend the peculiarities of the South Caucasian Chalcolithic stage. For example, here developed the spiral motif, foreign to Mesopotamia; the unusual restriction of the design to only one side, the front of the vessels, springing perhaps from the facial urn of western Asia Minor; the presence of earthenware hearth stands of the Alishar and Aegean "horned altar" type; and finally, partly the construction of "tholoi," which are completely absent, for example, in the corresponding lower layer of Persepolis.

All this taken together changes radically the customary historical perspective and opens up new possibilities for the understanding of the early processes of the cultural and ethnic formation of the South Caucasus. This throws light on the conditions causing the appearance of the brilliant cultural rise in the Middle Bronze Age, revealed in Trialeti, and on the proposition made by Kuftin concerning the aboriginality of Georgian culture in the Caucasus.

ARMENIA

Georg Goyan reports [17] from Yerevan that his recent researches on the history of ancient Armenian drama reveal that in 58 B. C. the theater was on a high professional level, performing in both Greek and Armenian, the latter being the official language during the reign of Tigranes. Plutarch, for example, recorded that Euripides' "Bacchante" was presented in Artashat in 58 B. C. in honor of the victory of the Armenians and Parthians over the Roman legions of Marcus Crassus. Excavations are now in progress.

DON REGION

Tsymliansk gorodishche.—The Sarkel expedition of IIMK, under the leadership of Liapushkin,[18] resumed work in 1939 after a 3-year

---

[17] From the Moscow News, February 9, 1946.
[18] Liapushkin, I. I., in Kratkie Soobshcheniia, No. 4, pp. 58-62.

interruption on the right bank of the Don River, 8 kilometers below Tsymlianskaia Cossack settlement. This *gorodishche* was located on a platform, 70.0 m. above the river level, formed by the delta of two ravines. This highly fortified *gorodishche,* commanding the important waterway connecting the steppes with the cities beside the Sea of Azov and the Black Sea and with the Caspian by way of the Volga, existed from the eighth-tenth centuries.

Three cultural levels were uncovered. The lowest stratum was well preserved because of a sterile layer (clay floor of a building); the few finds included iron slag, bones of animals, and some hand-made pottery. Of particular interest were the remains of a dwelling of the semidugout type, probably a conical structure of yurt type. The lower part consisted of an oval pit (2.5 x 1.8 m.), plastered with clay on the walls and the floor, and with a round hearth pit at the north wall. Hand-made pottery, largely flat-based pots with slightly convex walls and sharply flaring lips decorated with notches of the type known from Maiatskaia settlement, was found both inside and outside the dwelling.

The second period is represented by ruins of brick and mortar buildings, very similar to those of the left-bank site where stands the Sarkel *gorodishche.*

To this period also belong the remains of strong fortress walls, 4.5 m. thick with round towers, built of dressed white limestone.

The finds of the three upper levels are very closely related. The pottery, almost entirely wheel-made, was represented by the following types: (a) pots with incised linear and wavy ornament; (b) various shapes of polished ware of Saltovo type; (c) egg-shaped amphorae; and (d) unornamented well-made pots of hard gray clay.

This second period was also characterized by a profusion of iron objects including arrowheads and spearpoints, bits and stirrups, and various implements such as knives, fragments of buckets, sickles, axes, fishhooks, and others. Among personal ornaments were beads, fragments of metallic mirrors, an earring, and several belt buckles. All pottery and objects from this period have analogies in the finds from the Saltovo and Maiatskaia sites and burials. The existence of the second period was terminated by the destruction of the fortifications. In the third period the building materials from these fortifications were widely utilized in construction. This destruction could have occurred during the capture of the Khazar city of Belaia Vezha by Sviatoslav Igorevich, Prince of Kiev, in the year 965, as recorded in one of the old Russian chronicles. This identification of the right-bank site with the Belaia Vezha city had been anticipated by M. I. Artamanov.

The third period is characterized by yurtlike semidugout dwellings closely related to those of the first period. Their remains consist of clay-paved circular or oval shallow pits, occasionally double, 2.5-3.0 m. in diameter, with a hearth in the middle. Many of the dwellings contained human skeletons in various positions, showing no signs of orientation or proper grave inventories. On the other hand, the finds from many of the dwellings were numerous and variegated. Iron was widely represented by such objects as fishhooks, chisels, scythes, plowshares, spades, sickles, and others. Most of these were found in the dwelling pits which had been filled by bricks, fragments of mortar, stone, mineral, and fishbones, and potsherds.

The abrupt cessation of the third period probably occurred during one of the invasions of the steppe tribes at the end of the tenth or at the beginning of the eleventh century, at which time, after the downfall of the Khazar Kaganate, these nomads were undisputed masters of the South Russian steppes. Some traces of an attempt to repopulate and even to refortify the *gorodishche* at some later period were also found.

These materials are of great importance for the understanding of the settling of the nomads in the southeastern steppes which had begun during the ninth century (cf. yurts with agricultural equipment) and also for uncovering the character of the colonizing movement of the Russian Slavic tribes to the southeast, which was begun with the breaking up of the Khazar Kaganate during the tenth century.

VOLGA REGION

Novo-Akkermanovka Cemetery

The Archeological Expedition from Orsk, organized by G. Podgaetskii [19] for the Marr Academy of the History of Material Culture and the Museum of Regional Studies at Orenburg, studied during 1936 a Bronze Age cemetery situated 27 kilometers west of Orsk near the village of Novo-Akkermanovka.

The tombs were indicated on the surface by 19 stone boulders arranged in a circle and belonging to 13 burials found at a depth of 0.3-1.0 m. In two cases it was possible to determine the limit of the graves: No. 4 was 0.6 x 1.6 m., and No. 13 was 1.3 x 1.8 m.

The skeletons were lying on the right or left sides with legs and arms flexed and the skull facing west. Nos. 4 and 8 were double burials. The unnatural position of skeleton B, which was that of a

---

[19] Podgaetskii, G., in Materialy i Issledovaniia po Arkheologii SSSR, No. 1, p. 82, Moscow, 1940. Résumé in French.

woman, placed beside male skeleton A in Burial No. 4 suggests the idea of immolation in situ.

On the pillow of the deceased had been placed one or two clay vessels. The remainder of the grave furniture consisted of a small copper rod, a sculptured shell, phalanges of horses and sheep (No. 13), 16 sheep astragals and 1 shell from No. 4, recalling bone rings with two openings from Bronze Age burials north of the Black Sea. In addition, in No. 5 were several horse bones, the remains of food placed in the grave.

The character of the grave furniture and the form of the vessels attributed this cemetery to those of Andronovo type whose area extended during the second half of the second millennium before our era across the steppes stretching from the Yenisei to the Urals. In the southern Urals cemeteries of this type present a series of peculiar traits indicating the impact of Western and Eastern cultures.

Kochergino Cemetery

During 1929-1930 this burial site, situated near Kochergino (Dubrovno) on the Nemda River in the Sovetskii District of the Kirov region, was excavated.[20] Five burials were unearthed. Grave No. 3 contained the skeleton of a young man, 25 to 30 years of age, and No. 5 was that of a child 4 to 6 years old. In graves Nos. 1-2 there were traces of incineration; No. 4 contained no bones. The uniformity of the material provided by the different burials permits no chronological subdivisions. These burials were made within a 50-year interval during the period from the ninth to the twelfth century—in order to be more precise, to the end of the tenth or the beginning of the eleventh century of our era.

Upper Volga

According to Tretiakov, from 1933-1937 extensive archeological work was carried out in the region of the Upper Volga. As a result, it became possible to trace a picture of the historical evolution of the region during the first millennium. The explorations encompassed both banks of the Volga for a stretch of more than 350 kilometers, from the mouth of the Dubna (Ivanikovo) to that of the Kotorosli (IAroslav) and the banks of its affluents, including those of Mologa and Seksna, whose valleys were explored for a distance of 100-120 kilometers upstream.

---

[20] Talitskii, M., Le Cimetière de Kocergino, in Materialy i Issledovaniia po Arkheologii SSSR, No. 1, p. 168, Moscow, 1940. Résumé in French.

These explorations led to the discovery of more than 200 sites of varying degrees at antiquity. Remains of Epipaleolithic and Neolithic sites were found, as were *gorodishches* and *selishches* of the first millennium B. C. and the first millennium A. D., and dwelling places and cemeteries of the second millennium. Large-scale excavations were carried out on more than 25 of the sites. Several of them were entirely uncovered.

Before the first millennium B. C.—Tretiakov outlines briefly the early history of the Upper Volga Valley, remarking on its recent, postglacial age. He mentions the Epipaleolithic sites of a higher Sviderskian character, found near Sobolevo and Skniatino. During the Neolithic period the population was concentrated in three low plains: (a) near Kalinin; (b) along the lower reaches of the Mologa and the Seksna; and (c) along the lower reach of the Kostroma. In all these three areas, numerous Neolithic stations are known, as are sites of the Bronze Age. Outside of these low plains, other stations occur on the shores of large lakes as, for example, Nero, Pleshcheevo, Galic, and Cuchloma.

At the end of the second and at the beginning of the first millennium B. C., the inhabitants of the Upper Volga region emigrated from the low plains to higher ground. This migration was in accordance with modifications which had occurred in the economic sphere, when there was a transition from the hunter-fisher economy to that of agriculturist-livestock raiser.

The character of the dwelling sites was also soon modified. Instead of open sites, the population began to construct small fortresses (*gorodishches*). All these changes in the culture of the early inhabitants of the Upper Volga region were connected closely with the changes that were occurring in the social order, exemplified by the transition from matriarchy to patriarchy.

The first fortified sites appeared in the Upper Volga region toward the middle of the first millennium B. C. The materials found in the earliest *gorodishche* were completely in accordance with those of the earliest Bronze Age sites, thus proving the existence of a genetic link between the former and the latter. The three earliest *gorodishches* were: (a) near the village of Gorodisce, in the suburbs of the city of Kaliazin; (b) near the village of Gorodok, downstream from the town of Myskin; and (c) at the mouth of the Nerlia, upstream from Kaliazin. *Gorodishches* dating from the end of the first millennium B. C. have been found in many places. In this group are the Toporok *gorodishche* and one in the outskirts of Borok, etc. Their antiquity has been determined as a result of the repeated finding of bronze

7

objects similar to those from cemeteries in the Kama region of the higher and lower Pianobor types.

The *gorodishches* of the first millennium B. C. were of limited size. The dwellings were built on the ground. Among the inventory, apart from sherds and bone objects, were stone and metal implements and some ornaments. Remains found in even the oldest *gorodishche* establish the complete ascendance of animal raising over hunting. The horse and the pig were the principal domestic animals. Numerous hand mills confirmed the existence of agriculture.

The Upper Volga *gorodishche* can be somewhat distinguished from those of the Kostroma section of the Volga by the form of the dwellings and the pottery. This suggests the existence of two separate tribal groups. Moreover, exploration in this region has shown that a considerable length of the Volga, from the mouth of the Mologa to that of the Kotorosli and the section which lies between the sites of the two tribal groups, was uninhabited at that time.

At the beginning of the first millennium A. D.—Some of the inhabited sites of the first centuries of our era have been excavated. An examination of all these sites, together with their chronological classification, permits the following conclusions to be drawn:

(a) That sites dating from the first centuries A. D. are represented mainly by the remains of fortified sites (*gorodishches*). Many sites of this type are even older (first millennium B. C.).

(b) From the second and third centuries, open sites (*selishches*) were found.

(c) Both types were distributed on the banks of the Volga and its tributaries in compact groups of two to four, which indicates clan grouping and consequently denotes the existence of clan territories. Tretiakov brings ethnographic examples to the support of this theory.

Each locality belonged to a definite patriarchal community whose primitive economy, while multiform, also had a collective character. The main branches of production were the raising of livestock and cultivation in clearings. Hunting and fishing were also carried out. In nearly every *gorodishche* and *selishche* were found traces of iron founding and copper smelting. Commercial relations were barely developed at that period, either between localities or more distant areas.

Tretiakov again comments on the presence of certain distinctions between the population of the Upper Volga and that of the Kostroma sector of the Volga.

A fourth-fifth century gorodische on the Sonochta River.—In 1903 A. A. Spitsyn discovered a *gorodishche* at the mouth of the Sonochta

River, which flows into the Volga 20 kilometers downstream from Rybinsk. This site was destroyed by fire, and it is for this reason that its archeological strata preserved a rich fund of material as well as the remains of burnt construction. This site, which covered an area of more than 2,000 square meters, has been completely excavated.

This *gorodishche* was built on a small eminence of the Sonochta alluvial terrace. Its irregular triangular surface was surrounded by a wooden wall and earthen defense works. In the center there arose a wooden house (5 x 8 m.) which was apparently a public building. Around it six dwellings were distributed. These dwellings were small log cabins (3 x 5.4 x 6 m.) with hearths near the rear walls. The left side of each house was reserved for the men, and there the axes, arrows, fishing tackle, harness, and similar articles were kept. The right side was for the women, and during excavation, pottery and knives were uncovered.

Near the central house, there was a small building without a hearth which was used as granary and mill. Hand mills were also found here. Next to it was a forge which consisted of a solid shed with an enormous hearth in the center. In addition, a quantity of iron fragments and several dozen iron ingots, which had been smelted with bellows, were found.

Opposite the main house there was another shed with a small hearth in one corner. Both this shed and the one already described were probably surrounded by light wattle walls. This latter shed was reserved for use by the women, indicated by the finding of numerous slate distaffs, iron bodkins, a needle, and stones used as pressing irons.

The last of the buildings was a mortuary which gives a very clear insight into the funeral practices of the inhabitants. When a member of the community died, he was cremated elsewhere. The calcified bones were then collected and deposited in the wooden mortuary (2.25 x 2.25 m.), which was located opposite the communal house. Excavations among the ruins brought to light a quantity of calcified bones of adults and children, both male and female, and also five iron axes, knives, arrowheads, and iron and bronze rings and ornaments.

The excellent state of preservation and the richness of the remains, since only bone objects disintegrated, revealed a graphic picture, which is probably typical of all the other Upper Volga sites of the first half of the first millennium. The material found gave a relatively complete picture of the life and activities of the inhabitants. The Sonochta *gorodishche* can be assigned definitely to the fourth-fifth centuries as a result of finding enameled objects of the same type as those from the Riazan cemeteries, and a characteristic clasp in the form of a crossbow which probably originated in the south of the Baltic region.

Middle and second half of the first millennium A. D.—Tretiakov describes several sites contemporary with that on the Sonochta and others of a later date. Toward the middle of the first millennium, the open site, without fortification, became the dominant type. Simultaneously with the change in form the layout of the sites was modified, and they were no longer grouped as before.

All this would indicate a social change in the Upper Volga region after the middle of the first millennium. This was probably connected with the disintegration of the ancient social order based on the patriarchal clan. It would appear that it was at this time that the clan territories began to disappear. The considerable increase, often threefold or even fourfold, in the area of the sites indicated that by the sixth-seventh centuries the localities were no longer inhabited by a single patriarchal community.

Important excavations have been made at: (a) a fourth-fifth century site near the Krasnyi-Cholm Rest Home; (b) a fifth-sixth century site at the mouth of the Iti River, near Uste; and (c) a sixth-seventh century site on the outskirts of Kilino.

These excavations have given a more factual picture of the historical progression during the middle and second half of the first millennium; certain characteristics having already been given above.

At the beginning the inhabitants of every locality worked iron and copper to make themselves tools and ornaments. After the middle of the first millennium there were certain localities engaged in mass production, destined not only for internal use but for purposes of exchange. For example, the inhabitants of the Sonochta *gorodishche* worked iron on a large scale and in the Krasnyi-Cholm *selishche* numerous traces of copper working have been found. On the other hand, the inhabitants of other sites appear to have been consumers.

A second important characteristic of this period was the appearance of agriculture on previously cultivated land, which replaced the former system of cultivating only virgin territory. This is indicated by the increase in the size of the localities and by changes that took place in the methods of livestock raising which show the use of horse traction in agriculture. Finally, there were changes even in shape and size of the implements and tools bearing on agriculture, particularly in the appearance of very large hand mills. This transition led to the rise of a type of allotment economy. The development of trade with neighboring and remoter regions also played a certain role in the historical progression. This is shown by numerous imported articles, such as enameled articles from the middle section of the Dnieper and articles from the central stretch of the Oka.

The evolution of the funeral rites gives an equal insight into the decline of the clan society. Instead of the clan burial grounds, of the type exemplified by the "burial house" of Berezniaki, after the sixth century A. D., we find funeral monuments in the Upper Volga in the form of elongated kurgans. These are also found along the Upper Dnieper and Upper Dvina and, as a result of recent study, are said to belong to the Slavic Krivichi [Crivici] tribe.

This would indicate that the prehistoric inhabitants of the Upper Volga, as well as those of the Dnieper region, were the ancestors of the eastern Slavs.

During the ninth-tenth centuries, instead of elongated kurgans containing several sepulchers of cremated remains, individual funeral monuments were found. These round kurgans contained the remains of a single person with identical cremation procedure.

Inhabitants of the region around Lakes Nero and Pleshcheevo during the middle and second half of the first millennium.—The previously mentioned distinctions between the cultural character of the Upper Volga region and the neighboring regions of Lake Nero and Lake Pleshcheevo and the Kostroma sector of the Volga are very clearly defined in the sites dating from the middle and second half of the first millennium. The existence at this time of two different tribal groups is proved by the following:

(a) In the first region, the houses are built on the ground, while those of the latter are half underground.

(b) In the former region, the dead were cremated; in the latter they were interred in the same manner as along the Oka, the central Volga, and the Kama Rivers.

Beside Lake Nero, along the Kostroma sector of the Volga and along the upper stretches of the Kliazma, occur several cemeteries which contain flat tombs. The most important, which dates from the eighth-tenth centuries, lies near the Sarskoe *gorodishche,* in the outskirts of Diabol.

(c) Certain variations may be noted in the type of pottery, ornaments, and other objects.

The inhabitants of the first region belonged to the eastern branch of the Krivichi; the latter to Merian tribes, related to the eastern Finnish tribes of the Volga region.

However, the fundamental characteristics of the historical progression in all these regions were the same. From a detailed analysis of the objects in the Sarskoe *gorodishche,* this was the first town with artisans. Its existence was a result of the progressive development of the social division in labor and the increasing separation of the crafts from agriculture.

PREVIOUS RESEARCH IN THE UPPER VOLGA REGION

Gorodishche near Kaliazin.—The *gorodishche,* located on a headland on the left bank of the Upper Volga between two deep ravines, is protected by two vallums. It covers an area of approximately 1,500 square meters. The site is of interest because its archeological stratum, which is 3.0 m. deep at certain points, contains the cultural remains of different epochs dating from the middle of the first millennium B. C. to the third-fourth centuries A. D. The upper layers of the *gorodishche* were unfortunately destroyed by a cemetery that existed during the twelfth-thirteenth centuries. Small excavations were made during 1935.

Gorodok gorodishche.—This covers an extensive headland junction of the Gorodetski stream with the right bank of the Upper Volga. Its elevation is separated from the plateau by two ditches. The sides have been heavily eroded by the river. The cultural stratum, which was 30-40 cm. in depth, was completely excavated during 1936. In the lower levels, there were objects dating from the middle of the first millennium B. C.; in the upper levels were articles belonging to the first centuries of our era.

Vladimirskie Khutora selishche.—This site on the right bank of the Mologa River, about 50 kilometers from its mouth, was located on the edge of the first terrace, and is today heavily flooded by the spring waters. The cultural stratum, which lay at a depth of 20-30 cm., was excavated in 1936. Only a few objects were found, mainly pottery dating from the first centuries A. D.

Krugletsy gorodishche.—During 1933 on the right bank of the Volga near Ochotin, about 2 kilometers downstream from Myskin, some traces of this *gorodishche,* which had been almost entirely destroyed by the Volga, were found. The 10 square meters remaining were excavated in 1936. This revealed that the site had been occupied during the first centuries A. D. Typical pottery and some iron articles were found.'

Grechov gorodishche.—This site was located on a promontory on the right bank of the Upper Volga, at the mouth of the Grechov, 7 kilometers upstream from Uglie. Its platform has been almost entirely destroyed by the river. At the side of the platform, the remains of two vallums and a ditch can be seen. All the remaining part of the platform was excavated in 1935. Traces of a charred wooden wall surrounding the *gorodishche* were found, as were holes from the pillars of buildings built above ground. The cultural stratum, which was 50-80 cm. deep, yielded articles which dated from the second-fourth centuries. In the upper level, a large bronze buckle encrusted with red enamel was found.

Sonochta gorodishche.—Excavations during 1934-1935 covered this entire site. The cultural stratum, which never exceeded 35.0 cm., contained remains of buildings in the form of charred beams, pits left by supports, broken stone hearths and the remains of a wooden wall which had surrounded the *gorodishche*. It was possible to reconstruct the character of the defense works as a result of the satisfactory degree of preservation of the wattling which supported them.

Uste selishche.—During 1934 this site, located on the right bank of the Volga at the junction of the Iti, near Uste, 12 kilometers upstream from IAroslav, was examined. Built on a small promontory arising from the flood terrace of the Volga, it had been heavily eroded by the river, to a point where hardly any trace remained. Excavation of the remainder uncovered a stratum, 80 cm. in depth, which contained the remains of a wooden house destroyed by fire. The house had a hearth which had been dug out of the ground. From articles found, this *selishche* was attributed to the fifth-sixth centuries A. D.

Kilino selishche.—During 1936 studies were made on the remains of a site located on the right bank of the Volga near Kilino, about 25 kilometers downstream from Myskin. Built on the bank of the river barely above the water line, it had been heavily eroded by flood waters. The cultural stratum, 50-80 cm. deep, yielded but a limited number of objects dating from the seventh-eighth centuries of our era.

CENTRAL ASIA

UZBEK S.S.R., 1937-1939 [21]

Archeological investigations were carried out mainly by the Uzbekistan Committee for the Preservation and Study of Ancient Monuments (UZKOMSTARIS) with the collaboration of the All-Union and local organizations.

Termez Expedition.—This expedition conducted excavations among the ruins of the Old City of Termez and the ancient site of Airtam, which is situated 17 kilometers east of Termez, on the right bank of

---

[21] Received by Henry Field from VOKS on February 3, 1941. World War II delayed publication. Minor editorial revisions have been made.

the Amu-Darya River. Ancient written sources do not mention this place, but judging by the facts that the ruins cover an extensive area and that the artifacts unearthed here are of skilled workmanship, this must have been a settlement of considerable size. The site comprises an elevated portion (250 x 100 m.), bounded on three sides by D-shaped, clay walls; the fourth side is contiguous with the steep bank of the Amu-Darya. The ruins of the settlement, also enclosed by walls, are directly adjacent to this elevated portion of the site.

The excavations were concentrated on the southwestern part of the elevated portion of the site. Several buildings, belonging to a single edifice, constructed of large, unburnt bricks were unearthed here. Those chambers in which a sculptured cornice, fragments of reliquaries, and of an alabaster statue of Buddha were found during the first excavations on the site undoubtedly served for cult purposes.

The adjacent premises, with several hearths and large clay pots (khumi) for storing food and water, constituted in all probability the sanctuary kitchen. Two floors, dating from different periods, were unearthed in this sanctuary. Parts of the walls between the two floors were covered with a fine layer of alabaster plastering, differing greatly from the rough clay plaster still preserved above the upper floor.

Thus, two different periods have been established for this building, the first of which was dated by a bronze coin of an unnamed ruler, referring to the first century of our era. Excavations carried on at a still greater depth beneath the lower floor brought to light cultural strata attributed to the latest centuries before our era, in which thin-walled pottery of dark-rose clay coated in red engobé, fired-clay tiles, one of which is stamped with a picture of a deer, were found.

The excavations and the material raised to the surface at Airtam yielded a large number of fragments of clay vessels; thick-walled khumi, fired-clay kettles for boiling food, jugs, plates, bowls, saucers, conical vessels for lampions, and other forms. The prevailing type was engobé pottery of brown, cream, and red tones, for the most part without ornament, often superbly burnished and made of a thin mass of clay; there were also specimens of colored, varnished pottery.

The ornaments found on the pottery fall into five categories: stamped, molded, burnished, painted, and incised. The majority of the vessels had been made on a potter's wheel. In several parts of this site were unearthed fragments of pottery-firing ovens and a large mass of clay slag, testifying to the extensive development of local pottery manufacture.

In addition to a rich collection of pottery fragments, the investigations here have furnished a large number of terra cotta figurines of animals and people, objects of a cult nature, statuettes of marly limestone, and architectural fragments of the same material.

The different periods represented in the cultural strata found on this site, the lower of which should be referred to the last centuries before our era and the upper to the first centuries of our era, point to the fact that Airtam existed for a long period of time.

Excavations were conducted at several points among the ruins of Old Termez. An ancient Buddhist monastery, consisting of a large number of artificial caves and of above-ground chambers was found on the Kara-Tepe elevation. The structures above ground were built of unburnt brick and partly faced in stone. The floor was also of the same brick, coated with clay; the walls had an undercoating of clay covered with alabaster, on which traces of varicolored fresco paintings were preserved. The walls of one of the excavated premises, for example, were bordered in red. A picture showing the lower part of a human figure was still preserved above the border; traces of the feet encased in red footgear and parts of varicolored garments could still be discerned. The painting resembles Bamian art in type. ·

The caves, dug out at different levels in the sandstone layers of the mounds, were connected by staircases, while caves situated on one level communicated through corridors. The caves consisted of rectangular chambers (7-12 sq. m. in area) encircled on all sides by passageways about 3 m. wide and 13-16 m. long. The height of the corridors and the caves was 1.5-2.0 m. Benches were hewn along the walls of the caves and shallow niches occurred in the walls of the caves and corridors. Arabic inscriptions were found here and there on the walls, which bespeak the fact that the Arabs visited and possibly used these caves for a considerable time after their conquest of Termez. The excavations brought to light several caves of large dimensions, probably intended for public purposes, and other smaller caves evidently for individual use. Coins, pottery, and other finds discovered in Kara-Tepe date from the last centuries B. C. to the first centuries A. D.

The investigations of a suburban palace of the Termez rulers of the eleventh and twelfth centuries consisted in clearing the eastern facade, which made is possible to establish the plan of this building. These excavations also unearthed a water reservoir (70 sq. m. in area and 2.0 m. deep) constructed in the courtyard of this palace complex.

The walls were faced with burnt bricks, which were also used for · the base, where there were three steps in each corner. Earthenware pipes with a brick trough running parallel, came to light in the northeastern corner. Water apparently flowed into the reservoir both through pipes and trough.

In clearing the northern lateral pavilion of the palace, alabaster was found, together with pieces of colored glass, parts of an alabaster grating, and decorative, oval-shaped glass medallions (5-7 cm. in diameter and 2-5 mm. in thickness) molded from green or reddish glass. The pictures in relief on the obverse of these medallions refer to eight different subjects:

1. An eight-petaled rosette in a double circle, consisting of a center and a row of closely set pearls.

2. A medallion with a Kufic inscription, with floral ornament around the letters and at the edges, the faint inscription reading either "king" or "kingdom."

3. The figure of an animal shown running to the left, encircled by an Arabic inscription which reads "for the most high Sultan Abdul Muzafar Bahram Shah"; this inscription may refer either to the ruler of Ghazni, Emin Addaula Bahram Shah or Masaud ibn Ibrahim (1118-1157), or to Bahram Shah, the son of Imad ad-Dinam, ruler of Termez in 1205.

4. A bird of prey clawing some small animal to pieces.

5. A bird of prey holding an animal in its claws.

6. A lion in a circle.

7. A woman standing beside a horse.

8. A rider mounted on a horse, holding the reins in his right hand, and with a hunting bird on his left hand; the rider wears a crown surrounded by a halo.

Several of these depictions—the bird of prey clawing an animal, the bird holding its prey in its claws, and the rider with a hunting bird—are akin in subject to the pictures on ancient eastern metalware found in the vicinity of the Urals.

One of the groups of the Termez Expedition was entrusted with the task of making preliminary investigations on that part of the site where piles of metal and ash promised interesting finds. The results led to the surmise that this was an artisans' quarter, most probably that of the metal craftsmen of Old Termez. Situated 550 paces from the northeastern corner of the citadel, the metalcraftsmen's quarter occupied an area of 8 hectares, on which there were traces of buildings of unburnt brick, streets, squares, and water reservoirs. Two streets could be traced, one along the eastern and the other along the southern boundary of the quarter. The street to the east divided the quarter from the other section of the site, where the excavations produced a large amount of clay slag, sherds, and pottery-making tools, all of which indicated that this was a potters' quarter.

Excavations in the metallists' quarter were begun at several different levels. The cultural strata reached a thickness of 5.0 m. The upper layers, at a depth up to 1.5 m., were attributed to the eleventh-thirteenth centuries of our era, judging by the pottery and other finds, while the lower strata belonged to the period of the Kushans. Many more or less regularly formed, palm-shaped pieces of metal weighing from 500 grams to 5 kilograms have been found both on the surface and in the excavated portions. Investigations have shown that pieces of pig iron served as raw material for the metalcraftsmen of Old Termez. The discovery, in the upper strata, of fragments of crucibles (which do not relate to iron production), pieces of alloy, and poly-metallic ores, as well as fragments of copperware, all point to the existence of copper fashioning as well as forges.

The presence of jewelers' shops in this quarter has also been proved by the discovery of special furnaces used in this craft. Several buildings were unearthed during the excavations, three of which were evidently used for trading, since they were open to the street on one side; their dimensions were 2.0-2.5 square meters. Behind these premises were located the manufactory buildings, where remains of furnaces, odds and ends of ironware, etc., were found.

Other rooms connecting with the shops served for living quarters, not, apparently, for the shop owner and his family, a fact which would have been inconsistent with the seclusion of family life, but for the apprentices and workers. Fragments of an arch (*tazar*), con-structed of burnt bricks, came to light beneath these trading premises.

Judging by the pottery and other finds, all these buildings belonged to the eleventh and twelfth centuries of our era. In the lower strata, about 1.5 m. beneath the surface, were found pottery, coins, and other articles attributed to the first centuries of our era, and in addi-tion to these, the very same type of iron moldings as were found in the upper layers, of similar palmlike shape and of varying weight.

The material obtained here indicates that manufacturing existed on the site under investigation during a long period lasting from 1,000 to 1,200 years and that pottery making, the jeweler's craft, glass and copper work flourished in Termez during the eleventh and twelfth centuries.

A separate group of the Termez Expedition investigated the ancient irrigation system along the Surkhan-Darya River within the pre-cincts of the Termez district. Of the right bank of the river were found remains of ancient head structures and canals, one of which, taking its start evidently from Salavat, irrigated the territory of Old Termez. On the left bank, in the middle reaches of the Surkhan-Darya, traces have been found of very large irrigation canals leading to the southeast, i.e., to the site of Airtam. These canals carried water to Airtam, where traces have also been found of an irrigation canal leading to the north-northwest to join, as it would seem, the canals which have their source in the Surkhan-Darya. It must be observed that the pottery collected on the left bank is very similar to that found in the oldest levels of Old Termez and to the objects from Airtam. These included thin-walled, engobé pottery, fragments of gobletlike vessels, painted *khumi*, etc. The results of the investigations of this section and at Airtam give reason to affirm that the irrigation structures on the left bank of the Surkhan-Darya River, requiring large-scale organized labor for their preservation and upkeep, fell into a state of disrepair and neglect about the middle of the first millennium of our era, a fact which brought about a decline in the life of Airtam and other populated points on the left bank of the river.

Surkhan-Darya Expedition.—This expedition carried out archeological investigations in the Baisun district. During 1938 excavations were made in the Teshik-Tash grotto at a distance of 18 kilometers northwest of the district center, near Machai. A Paleolithic settlement with artifacts of the classic Mousterian period was unearthed here. The grave of an 8- or 9-year-old Neanderthaloid child was also found here. The exceptional scientific interest of this discovery has already been presented in numerous articles and reports and we shall dwell on the 1939 work. The expedition made some preliminary surveys in the vicinity of Baisun, which resulted in the discovery of new artifacts, including some pertaining to the Stone Age. Two corridorlike caves were found near Baisun in Kaflan-Dara and Dulta-Khan, with large accumulations of bones of wild and domesticated animals. Fragments of ancient vessels were found in one of the caves. These caves evidently served large beasts of prey as places of refuge, and the bones are the remains of their quarry.

In the Ob-Angor grotto remains of ancient metalwork shops have been unearthed including slag and a smelting furnace in the form of a vessel 2.0 m. in height with openings in the sides for forced draft. This site also produced fragments of tenth- and eleventh-century pottery. Two cultural levels were found buried under stones in a cave situated in the Kurgan-Darya gorge; these strata contained coal-ash accumulations, remains of animals, and worked flints of Paleolithic type. Excavations were conducted in an area of 40 sq. km. near Machai in the Amir-Temir grotto, resulting in the discovery of three cultural strata. The upper stratum belonged to the later Iron Age, the middle to the Neolithic, and the lowest to the Paleolithic period.

Typical Mousterian remains have been found in the lower levels, closely resembling the Teshik-Tash implements—a hand cleaver, a discoidal nucleus, a scraper, and others. Investigations begun in the Teshik-Tash cave during 1938 have been finished and, like the preceding investigations, these brought to the surface typical Mousterian remains. Of particular interest were the flint points, which resemble those from the Palestine caves. To the east of Baisun in the gorge which leads from the mountain river Temir-Ulde, traces have been found of a Stone Age settlement where evidences of stone implement making and the bones of wild animals have been established.

Zarafshan Expedition.—This expedition engaged in reconnoitering investigations and excavations to the northwest of Bukhara in the Kizil-Kum Desert. The plot of land under investigation, about 500 sq. km. in area, abounds in the ruins of ancient settlements, castles, the remains of ramparts and irrigation channels, and a large amount of buried material. The ruins of settlements and castles, built of unburnt brick (*pakhs*), at the present time give the appearance of mounds (*tepe*) of various forms, which have been rendered shapeless by the action of precipitation, wind, and the shifting sands that have covered a large part of this locality. Several of these mounds (Besh-Tepe, Aiak-Tepe, and others), irrigation channels, and the shapeless remains of clay structures are to be found at the extreme western point of the investigated area, situated in the desert about 40 km. from the boundary of the oasis. Here, as in the rest of the investigated territory, much material was discovered, distinguished, however, by features pointing to a greater antiquity than that procured from the sites located closer to the modern boundary of Bukhara Oasis.

In the district of Besh-Tepe and Aiak-Tepe thin-walled pottery was encountered, finished on a potter's wheel and made of finely powdered clay, hard-fired and frequently coated with red engobé, containing traces of complete or partial burnishing and sometimes with a stamped ornament. In addition to such pottery, the expedition found bronze triple-faceted arrowheads of Scythian type.

The mounds situated closer to the oasis (Dingil-Tepe, Katta, Khudzha-Ishan, Varakhsha, and others) yielded material relating to the period from the eighth to the twelfth centuries of our era, and some mounds which are directly adjacent to the oasis were attributed to the sixteenth-eighteenth centuries.

Excavations were begun on the site of Varakhsha, which was one of the residences of the country's rulers, the Bukhar-Khudats, situated in the desert 12 km. west of the modern oasis. Excavations were concentrated on the ruins of a large building located on the western side of the citadel which was attributed to the fourth and fifth centuries of our era. This building was constructed of large unburnt bricks. Six rooms were cleared. A number of fragments of stucco carving, marked by various ornamental motifs and diverse methods of execution, were found in the piles of building rubbish which filled one of the rooms. In general, these are carvings in low relief, consisting of geometric and stylized floral ornament, including meanders, rosettes, palmettes of rhombics and crosses, in a geometric pattern. There were also some high-relief carvings, which often merged into sculpture proper. This method was used for depicting different themes and for realistic treatment, such as birds, fish, fantastic beings, a winged horse, a bird with a female head and breast, a male torso, fragments of human figures, trunks of large trees with branches and carved leaves.

A large room with wide clay benches was unearthed in the central part of the building. Traces of a unique distemper painting on clay plaster were found on one of the walls of this room. The wall was divided into two horizontal parts by a cornice. Above the cornice on a vivid red-ocherous background were figures of animals shown moving toward the left: deer, tiger, panther, and horse. The upper part of the picture has not been preserved. Hunting scenes were depicted on the portion beneath the cornice: first come the drivers dressed in short breeches and cloaks, mounted on white elephants; following them are hunters armed with spears and bows. The elephants are sumptuously outfitted in colored saddlecloths and harness. One of the scenes depicts a hunter hurling his lance at a lion who has leapt at him with fangs bared. In another episode a hunter has loosed his arrow at a griffin. The lion is painted in orange-yellow and the griffin in white colors. The contours of the figures are outlined in black and brown; shadow planes and perspective are lacking but the firm painting and the bold strokes reveal the touch of an experienced master. The colors have preserved their freshness, although many portions of the human figures were obliterated as far back as ancient times.

This building, lavishly decorated in stucco work and paintings, is identified with the palace of the Bukhar-Khudats, described by Muhammad Narshakhi, a tenth-century historian, who wrote that this palace, built more than a thousand years before his time, had been repeatedly demolished and restored.

Simultaneously with the excavations of the palace, the expedition carried out some trial trenches, the lower strata of which yielded pottery and other finds dating approximately to the eve of our era, resembling the material of Besh-Tepe and Aiak-Tepe. These discoveries, including artificial irrigation structures, give reason to assert that the territory investigated was a very populous area even before the beginning of our era, and that on the extreme western portions of the site ancient culture began to die out near the beginning of our era, while the more eastern parts which lay higher in regard to the irrigation systems and closer to the water supply—the Zarafshan River—continued to exist up to the eighth-twelfth centuries.

The reasons for this decline can be found in the upheavals brought about by the dissolution of the slave-owning society, the new feudal aspects of social relations and the resultant neglect of the important irrigation system, all of which was supplemented by the intensive advance of the sands of Kizil-Kum on the Bukhara Oasis.

IAngi-IUl Expedition.—This expedition continued investigations at Kaunchi-Tepe and also began excavations of the tumuli located nearby. This group of barrows, consisting of about 1,000 burials, spreads over a distance of several kilometers on the watershed between the Chirchik and Boz-Su Rivers. The barrows are of various sizes, from 0.4 to 5.0 m. in height and 8 to 30 m. in diameter. Twelve barrows were cleared, all of which, judging by the grave furniture, refer to three epochs.

A typical flexed burial was found in one of the cleared barrows, about 0.5 m. in height and 8.0 m. in diameter. A child's body was found at a depth of 0.8 m. in an oval-shaped pit, the head pointing east-southeast. The skeleton was lying on its right side, arms bent at the elbows, the wrists placed under the head; traces of violet-colored paint were found on the soles of the feet. At the head of the skeleton there was a flat-bottomed, wide-necked vessel, hand-made and very slightly fired, 12 cm. high, 13.5 cm. in diameter at the neck, and 9 cm. at the base. The burial ritual and the modeling and form of the vessel date the barrow in the late Bronze Age. Tumuli of this type are well known in the southern part of the R.S.F.S.R. and in the Ukraine, but this was the first example of Uzbekistan.

Another type of burial was represented in one of the barrows, where a group interment was found. The skeletons were lying a tergo, arms extended along the body, and legs thrown widely apart. Pottery, differing both in form and decoration from that found in the first barrow, was found near the skeletons. Narrow-necked vessels with a single handle or none at all, flat plates and jugs almost pear-shaped in form, were discovered here. The jug handles were often fashioned in the form of cowslips. None of these vessels was made on the potter's wheel, but they were all hard-fired. Several of them, for example, the jugs, were coated on the outside with red engobé. This type of pottery was often met in large numbers on the Kaunchi-Tepe site, in those strata which G. V. Grigorev refers to the middle of the first millennium before our era.

The remaining excavated barrows all refer to a single culture. The burials were placed in catacombs, the floor of which was from 2.5 to 3.5 m. below the surface. The average dimensions of the catacombs were: length, 2.5 m.; width, 1.5 m.; and height, 1.5 m.

The catacombs were rectangular with vaulted ceilings. A dromos from 3.85 to 5.0 m. long, and 1.5 to 1.9 m. wide in its upper part, led down from the surface to the catacombs. At a depth of approximately 1.5 m., two or three stepped projections from 0.4 to 0.7 m. wide were found along the main and sometimes along the end walls of the dromos, which correspondingly diminished in size. An opening at the lower end of the dromos led to the catacombs. This opening was about 0.8 m. high, 1.0 m. wide and about 0.5 m. deep. Sometimes the opening was closed with unburnt bricks. Most of the burials in the catacombs contained male and female figures. The skeletons lay stretched out on their backs with the heads pointing north. The grave furniture included the following weapons:

(a) Straight, double-edged iron swords, with narrow shafts at the end for wooden hilts, the length of the blade being about 0.8 or 0.9 m., the shaft for the hilt from 0.1 to 0.13 m. long, and the width of the sword about 4 cm.

(b) Double-edged iron daggers, very massive, from 15 to 20 cm. long and about 4 cm. wide, the remains of wooden scabbards to be found on the swords and daggers.

(c) Triple-faceted iron arrows with shafts, and bone facings of bows.

Lying alongside the female skeletons were found a bronze mirror with a handle sheath at the side, the bone top of a back-comb decorated with small carved heads, a bronze arbalest-shaped fibula ring, a bronze bell, bronze wire earrings, a round bead of blue glass, and other objects.

Among the domestic articles the following may be noted: small iron knives with thick butts 8 to 10 cm. in size; earthenware pottery pitchers with a single handle or without handles; and saddle flasks, flat on one side. The pottery had been fashioned on a potter's wheel, hard-fired, and traces of purplish-red paint could be seen on the flasks.

These tumuli were attributed to the third and fourth centuries of our era.

Ferghana Expedition.—This expedition was undertaken in 1939 and had as its objective archeological supervision of the construction site of the Stalin Great Ferghana Canal. Ferghana, the wealth of which was well known to ancient Chinese writers who knew it under the name of Davin, had never been investigated. In view of the extremely sparse archeological data on the Ferghana region, the organization of work on a large scale promised to be of great interest. Archeological supervision was established over the entire 270-kilometer course of the canal, which intersects the Ferghana region from end to end, from Uch-Kurgan to Kani-badam. Numerous trips were made through the territory lying off the main course of the canal, and in this way a large part of the region was covered by a compact network of scouting parties. Excavation work during the building of the canal unearthed several ancient settlements and tribal sites, burials, and artifacts.

Much material was gathered by the reconnaissance parties. These finds for the most part precede the Arab conquest. Among the coins, some hitherto unknown, was a copper coin of the Greek-Bactrian ruler Heliocles dating to the middle of the second century before our era. The scientific purport of these coins is especially great in that they directly coincide with archeological complexes and with definite geographical points. Among the mass of artifacts of various strata, the ancient complex is especially striking since it is found on the entire territory investigated and should be referred to the second half of the first millennium before our era.

Grain grinders were found in this complex, crude hand-fashioned pottery, pitcherlike vessels, flat dishes, jugs with handles in the form of cowslips coated in red engobé, burnished pottery with incised ornament, stone pestles and mortars. The dense distribution of archeological remains throughout the investigated territory and the great extent of the cultural strata of the ancient settlements make them worthy of particular study. In addition to the sites found directly on the course of the canal, 92 adjacent sites were registered. An unbroken cultural stratum stretches for a distance of 8 kilometers from Lugumbek to the settlement of Tiuiachi.

These facts confirm the evidence of ancient Chinese sources concerning the wealth and highly developed agriculture of Davin, which characterize it as a region with a large agricultural population, famous for its splendid horses, wine distilleries, rice and wheat crops, and numerous cities.

Parties following special routes to the north of the canal into the sands of Kuduk-Kum, lying in the center of the Ferghana region,

8

found numerous remains of ancient settlements, the material from which can be dated to the end of the first millennium before our era and the first centuries of our era.

SOGHDIANA

Grigorev [22] has summarized the results of excavations since 1936 of a series of Soghdian sites in the Zarafshan Valley. The exploration by Grigorev and I. A. Sukharev in the Samarkand area, which covered an area of 200 square kilometers between Samarkand and Zarafshan, disclosed the remains of several dozen ancient settlements. The sites of the most ancient period are in the form of a square surrounded by buildings, with a high central hill in the middle of the square. All these settlements were located in a now waterless steppe on the banks of dry streams. The most extensive excavations were carried on during 1936-1939 at Tali Barzu, now identified with ancient Riwdad. At this site six cultural strata, from the second quarter of the first millennium B. C. to the beginning of the eighth century A. D., have been identified.

The earliest stratum, referred to as Tali Barzu I, contained pottery of the type known from various sites in Iran and Turkestan at the beginning of the third millennium B. C. This refers mainly to the stemmed red matte engobé vases from Tepe Hissar and Anau. Other finds included skewer rests ornamented with ram's heads and archaic female figurines dressed in long robes, trousers, high boots, and with "Scythian" caps (probably *bnahita*).

Tali Barzu II, attributed to the fifth-sixth centuries B. C., was connected with the large fortified building occupying the entire area of the site, or building complex, containing at least 500 rooms. The outer rooms of the apartment served as the city wall. The corners were fortified with multiple towers. A citadel with loopholes was in the center of the complex.

Pottery with ribbon ornament and also with handles depicting animals appears for the first time. Of particular interest were the numerous figurines, some dressed in the typical "Scythian" costume, others in mantles with false sleeves flung over the shoulders (cf. *kuseu* in Afghanistan), and finally in the costume of the Medes (cf. figurines of a king or satrap in crenelated crown and long robe, reminiscent of the Achemenid kings depicted on the seals in the De Clercq collection).

The later periods of Tali Barzu were not as rich in finds. Tali

---

[22] Grigorev, G. V., in Kratkie Soobshcheniia, No. 6, pp. 24-34.

Barzu III belongs to the period following Alexander's conquest, and includes objects showing Greek influence and Greco-Bactrian coins, replacing those with Achemenid influence.

Tali Barzu IV, attributed to the period from the first century B. C. to the second century A. D., is associated with the invasions of the nomads from western China and Yuechi in the northern part of Central Asia. The few finds are of significance because of the lack of any written sources regarding Soghdiana during this period.

Totally different building techniques were used during reconstruction of the large Achemenid buildings. Of special interest were several Buddhist images, an inscribed sherd reported to be the earliest known sample of Soghdian writing, the effigy of an equestrian deity, and a hoard of 20 silver coins resembling those attributed to the reign of Antiochus by Allotte de la Fouye, but with a Soghdian legend on the obverse and probably struck in Soghdiana at the end of the first century B. C.

The settlement was destroyed during the period of the Ephthalite domination, third-fifth centuries A. D., but came back to life during the Turkish conquest in the sixth century (Tali Barzu V). A thick city wall was constructed during this period, and a building of very large slabs of clay was erected upon the central mound. The finds, characterized by Sasanian types of ornamentation both in metal and clay, are much better illustrated from two other sites, Kafiz-Kala and Varakhsh. In the former many coins of Chinese type with square perforation but with Soghdian inscriptions have also been found. The latter, in Bukhara Oasis, contained the ruins of a palace decorated with a magnificent alabaster frieze depicting human beings, plants, animals, birds, and fishes. Subsequent excavations at Varakhsh have disclosed a fresco upon the wall of a palace or temple depicting a procession of animals and a hunting scene [23] with an Indian [?] king hunting elephants and griffins. The type of painting, like that of the sculpture at Varakhsh, is more closely reminiscent of Indian than of Persian art.

Tali Barzu VI (end of seventh—beginning of eighth century A. D.) is contemporaneous with the famous Mount site, discovered by Freimann. Glazed pottery appears for the first time during this period of Arabian conquest, and several coins of the Soghdian King Tarkhun (ante A. D. 710).

Bernshtam [24] summarizes the results of recent excavations by the

---

[23] Cf. frescoes in a villa near Ctesiphon (Iraq) described by Ammianus Marcellinus.

[24] From a report by A. N. Bernshtam in Kratkie Soobshcheniia, No. 6, pp. 34-42.

IIMK jointly with the Scientific Committee of the Kirghiz Republic and the Kazakhstan Branch of the Academy of Sciences in this area to the west of Chinese Turkestan. This area of the ancient nomads, home of the animal style, was not mentioned in the documents collected by Sir Aurel Stein and translated by H. Qeichelt, yet it is known that the main caravan route from the west to Chinese Turkestan crossed the Jetty-Su (Seven Rivers) area and that consequently some important results might be expected here.

The earliest influences from the west described from this area were those from the Achemenid Empire (sixth-fourth centuries B. C.). Bronze altars and lamps in the Hermitage Museum found in 1937 near Issyk-Kul, but as yet unpublished, belong to this period.

In the following period (fourth-second centuries B. C.) for a short time there appear in the art of the nomads of the northern Tien Shan foothills some elements of Greco-Bactrian art.[25] However, these did not affect permanently the art of the nomads, in which the ancient "animal style" soon came back into its own. The Greeks did not penetrate this area, notwithstanding W. Tarn's claims to the contrary, and Greek influence was felt only by the way of commercial relations. During the beginning of the present era new influences from closer at hand replace those of the more distant areas.

A polished wheel-made ware, totally different from the pottery of the nomads, appears (cf. Kenkol and Berkkarin burial grounds), but it is still impossible to decide whether or not it came from Soghdiana or from the oases of eastern Turkestan. More significant, however, are the finds from the various *gorodishches* of this area.

Soghdian inventories are found in the lowest strata of Taraz (Dzhambul) and Krasnaia Rechka. The finds include, associated with pottery and terra cottas, a barbarian imitation of an eastern Roman solidus of the fourth-fifth centuries. While it is still impossible to date the finds from these strata, they definitely belong to the period between the third and fifth centuries. Together with the typical traits of the Soghdian culture, still retaining a strong influence of Greco-Bactrian tradition, these objects also reveal the influences of the style of eastern Turkestan.

In Soghdian tradition were a figurine of Anakhit (forming the handle of a pot) from Taraz, and an oinochoe of Central Asian type. A modeling mold for a masculine head had a Grecian profile and a general resemblance to Gandharan art; the only known analogy to it are the heads of rulers on Greco-Bactrian coins.

---

[25] Cf. Wusun burials described by M. Voevodskii and M. P. Griaznov, Vestnik Drevnei Istorii, No. 2, p. 3, 1938.

The first agrarian settlements in this area (Krasnaia Rechka site) are isolated fortified houses of unbaked brick, two or three stories high, of long parallel apartments (1.5 x 2.0 x 8.0 m.) with flat roofs. These are attributed to the period before the seventh century. At Krasnaia Rechka these buildings were ruined and upon them were Zoroastrian burials, of the seventh-eighth centuries. Bernshtam, who disagrees with the first-century B. C. dating for comparable Soghdian finds from eastern Turkestan by Sir Aurel Stein, attributes them to the fifth or sixth century. According to Bernshtam the colonization activities of Soghdiana were not begun until the period of the third-fifth centuries ("the first period of Soghdian colonization in the Jetty-Su"). During this period Soghdian colonies were still isolated culturally and economically in the midst of the Jetty-Su nomads.

From the end of the seventh century the cultural influence of Soghdiana increased both in volume and significance, in crafts as well as in fine arts. A Soghdian version of the favorite Sasanian decorative motif, a dotted circle filled with either a pictorial or ornamental subject, is encountered in a series of sites, in Mongolia (Tola), Kirghizia (Ak Peshin), and Altai (Katanda). One of the examples combined the Sasanian dotted circle with a Chinese ornamental lotus in the center. Quite possibly the imitations of Sasanian platters, obtained by the Saian-Altai Expedition near Yenisei should be attributed to the Soghdian craftsmen living among the nomads.

Soghdian influences on the pottery of this period from Kazakhstan and Kirghizia have been described by Bernshtam (Vestnik Drevnei Istorii, No. 4, 1939).

A contributing factor here may have been a second mass migration of the Soghdians, particularly from Bukhara, during the seventh century. To this period belongs the founding of the typical Mawerannahran towns with citadel, *shahristan* and *rabat,* in the valleys of the Chu and Talas Rivers in the northern foothills of the Tien Shan. This movement continued during the Arabian conquest of the Jetty-Su during the first half of the eighth century.

To this period belongs the spread of Soghdian writing in this area, and its use for the local Turkish dialect. The oldest examples of Uigurian writing, in Soghdian characters, are the so-called Turgesh coins of the eighth century.

During the ninth century Soghdian culture begins to disappear, and in the Jetty-Su area it become a component part of the culture of Turkish nomads, after the assimilation of Soghdians by the Turkish population. According to Muhammad of Kashgar, the Soghdians adopted the clothes and manners of the Turks, from Balasagun to

Ispindzhab the inhabitants spoke both Soghdian and Turkish, and there were left no people who spoke only Soghdian.

Summary.—Period I (third-sixth centuries) did not result in the assimilation of the Soghdians by the local Turkish populations. The Soghdians engaged in commercial relations with the Turks, but there was no organic intertwining of the Soghdian culture with that of the local nomads.

Period II (from the end of the sixth century) is connected with the emigrations from Bukhara. At the same time this was a period of assimilation of the Soghdians with the Turkish nomads, resulting in complete dissolution of Soghdian culture in the culture of the nomads. This process was completed by the end of the ninth century. Most recent archeological investigations reveal that the second wave of colonization was less "pure" than the first.

Together with the Soghdians in this colonization participated Christian Syrians.[26]

KIRGHIZ S.S.R.[27]

In Frunze [formerly Pishpek] the Kirghiz Museum of National Culture is under construction. Designed by V. Variuzhskii in the shape of a large yurt, the building will be decorated with white marble, majolica work, wood and marble carvings, and colorful national ornaments. The exhibits will trace the history of Kirghizia and will include cultural memorials and works of art. About 3,000 persons will be able to visit the Museum at the same time.

A windowless effect is attained by covering the exterior with a protruding diagonal latticework into whose diamond-shaped openings panes of glass are set. Thus, with the circular glass cupola sufficient light filters through into the building.

SIBERIA

KHAKASS A.S.S.R.

During 1940 while a highway was under construction a slice was cut off a small hill near the Power Collective Farm, 8 kilometers from Abakan, revealing the ruins of a house. On closer study the find proved to be the remains of an ancient Chinese house dating back to the period of the Han Dynasty, approximately the first century B. C.

---

[26] Borisov, A. IA., Syrian inscriptions from Taraz. Izvestia of Kazakhstan Branch of the Academy of Sciences. [In press.]

[27] This summary is based on an article by Nina Riazantseva in the Moscow News, June 1, 1946.

Excavations started in 1941 by an expedition sponsored jointly by the State Museum of History, the Institute of the History of Material Culture (IIMK), and the Khakass Language and Literature Research Institute, were interrupted by the war. Resumed during 1945 under the supervision of Lydia Evtiukhova, with Sergei Kiselev, Barbara Levasheva, archeologist of the Minusinsk Museum, and other scientists participating, the excavations have yielded some interesting results. Parts of the adobe walls of the building up to 2.0 m. high are still intact. Under the floor run the flues of a central hot-air heating system in the form of channels lined and covered with stone slabs. Although the central heating system serviced the entire building, it was evidently not always adequate in the rigorous Siberian winter conditions, for traces of braziers are still visible on the adobe floors of several of the rooms.

The building was roofed with thick rectangular tiles alternating with narrow curved strips covering the gaps between, giving an undulating effect.

The strips jutted out beyond the eaves, terminating in circular ends bearing inscriptions in Chinese. Translated by Academician Alekseev from stamped impressions made on moist clay, these inscriptions read: "To the son of heaven (i.e., the Emperor) 10,000 years of peace, and to her (i.e., the Empress) whom we wish 1,000 autumns of unclouded happiness."

On the outside the walls of the buildings were faced with square bricks decorated with a fir-tree design.

After 2 years of excavations it has at last been possible to reconstruct the plan of this interesting building. In the center was a large hall with a floor space of 140 sq. m. from which smaller rooms, 28 to 30 sq. m. in size, opened. On the northern and southern sides the rooms were laid out in two rows, and on the eastern and western sides, in one row. Before the building is completely excavated it is hard to say exactly how many of these rooms there were, but in all probability there were about 20 of them.

The plan of the house and the character of the ancient Chinese architecture make it possible to establish that the building was covered by a triple roof with an extra tier over the tallest part of the building, above the central hall.

Hollows are still visible within the walls in each room where columns stood that supported the heavy tile roof.

In the course of excavation, frames from the doors between the rooms were discovered: Beside three doors inside the central hall were found massive bronze handles in the shape of fantastic horned genii—the guardians of the entrance—with human faces but animal ears and bovine horns, side whiskers and curled whiskers, and mustaches. Through the nostrils of the hooked noses passed the ring which served as the door handle. The facial features of the gargoyles are of European cast suggesting local workmanship.

Other finds included iron axes, spears, clamps, jade pendants and a jade saucer, a gold earring, bronze buckles, clasps, fragments of a pot, and diverse other objects and ornaments.

The plan of the building itself and the finds brought to light among its ruins indicate that Chinese craftsmen built the structure and that Chinese undoubtedly lived in it. All that remains to be established about this building that differs so markedly from all the other dwellings of the time situated on the territory of the Minusinsk basin is to whom it belonged. It is possible that these are the remains of a trading post of Chinese merchants who in the Han epoch penetrated deep into the land of the "northern barbarians."

There is, however, one detail in the history of ancient Khakassia mentioned by Chinese chroniclers that evokes special interest in connection with these ruins.

In the year 99 B. C. during the fierce battles that marked the period of energetic expansion of the Han empire at the end of the second and beginning of the first century B. C., Li Hwan-li, a renowned Chinese general, suffered a defeat in battle against the nomadic tribes in the north. Surrounded by superior enemy forces he lost some 7,000 in killed and was forced to flee. His grandson Li-Ling, famed for his skill in archery, came to his assistance with 5,000 infantrymen, but he also had to retreat after a bloody engagement. Seeing that further resistance was useless, Li-Ling ordered his men to save themselves, while he himself surrendered. His captors treated Li-Ling with the respect due to his rank and gave him land in the "khyagas" estate inhabited by the ancestors of the present Khakass. He settled in these parts and eventually married the daughter of the nomad chieftain.

Up to the ninth century A. D., according to Chinese chronicles, the Khakass deferred to the descendants of Li-Ling.

Since it is unlikely that the Chinese general would have made his abode in a local yurt or modest wooden dwelling and since there were sufficient Chinese laborers to be found among the refugees and war prisoners, it is quite probable that he built himself a palatial dwelling in Chinese style.

During 1946 Soviet archeologists continued excavation of the ruins of the Chinese palace.

V. MISCELLANEA ANTHROPOLOGICA

INTRODUCTION

This report, which has been delayed by World War II, is based on results obtained by Soviet physical anthropologists together with observations recorded in the Soviet Union during September and October, 1934, by Henry Field, while leader of the Field Museum Anthropological Expedition to the Near East, financed by Marshall Field.

At the conclusion of the compilation of anthropometric data in Iraq and Iran the members of this expedition, then reduced to the leader and Richard A. Martin, later Curator of Near Eastern Archaeology at Field Museum of Natural History,[1] crossed the Caspian Sea to enter the Union of Soviet Socialists Republics at Baku on September 13, 1934.

Their journey took them by train to Tbilisi [formerly Tiflis] ; by automobile over the Georgian Military Highway to Daudzikau [formerly Vladikavkaz and Ordzhonikidze] ; by train to Rostov, Kharkov, and Dnieproges ; by automobile to Dnepropetrovsk ; and by train to Kiev, Moscow, and Leningrad.

In order to add a link to the series of anthropometric data from Southwestern Asia, in Tbilisi 50 male Yezidis and in Ordzhonikidze 107 males and 50 females from North Osetia were measured, observed, and photographed. In addition, 20 skulls from a tomb in the Dargavskaia Valley near Koban were measured and photographed. In the Osetian Museum at Ordzhonikidze 19 deformed skulls from a site near Nalchik were also examined.

These data, together with photographs by Mr. Martin, will appear under the title "Contributions to the Anthropology of the Caucasus," by Henry Field.

Before the expedition left Chicago, Wallace Murray, Chief of the Near East Division of the Department of State, had been advised of the proposed itinerary. As a result Ambassador William H. Bullitt in Moscow had requested a special entry permit at Baku. The Academy of Sciences of the U.S.S.R. and the All-Union Society for Cultural Relations with Foreign Countries (VOKS) were also asked to assist them in any manner within their power.

During their visit to branches of the U.S.S.R. Academy of Sciences,

---

[1] In 1943 changed to Chicago Natural History Museum.

museums, and scientific institutions they were accorded every hospitality and facility for the examination and study of collections as well as an opportunity to discuss anthropological and archeological problems with the members of each scientific staff.

After returning to Chicago, Henry Field kept in touch with many of these Soviet scientists, who have forwarded to him, in Russian or in English, summaries of their own research work or that of their colleagues. In collaboration with Eugene Prostov as translator, more than 50 archeological summaries have been published [2] since 1935.

The compilation of summaries of anthropometric data obtained recently by Soviet physical anthropologists has proved a far harder task, but perhaps one that is no less valuable to those who study the ancient and modern racial problems of Asia and their impacts on America, Europe, and Africa.

Soviet literature in the libraries of Field Museum of Natural History and the Oriental Institute of the University of Chicago was examined by Eugene Prostov, who selected passages for inclusion and supervised the transliterations and the spelling of place names.

Dr. Alexander Sushko, formerly of the University of Chicago, generously assisted with the translation of part of Ginzburg's anthropometric data.

The general arrangement of the articles, each of which must be treated as a separate entity, will be found in the contents.

Throughout the Soviet Union standardized abbreviations for scientific institutions have been introduced and for this reason a list must be appended.

The following abbreviations have been used in this report:

AZH .... Antropologicheskii Zhurnal [Anthropological Journal. Quarterly, edited by M. S. Plisetskii].

GOSSTATISTIKA .... Gosudarstvennoe Statisticheskoe upravlenie, currently Tsentralnoe Statisticheskoe upravlenie [Department of Statistics].

IAE .... Institut Antropologii i Etnografii [Institute of Anthropology and Ethnography of the State Academy of Sciences], Leningrad.

IIMK .... Institut Istorii Materialnoi Kultury, Akademiia Nauk [Historical Institute of Material Culture of the U.S.S.R., Academy of Sciences, since summer of 1937; formerly GAIMK], Leningrad.

---

[2] In the American Anthropologist, American Journal of Archaeology, American Journal of Physical Anthropology, American Journal of Semitic Languages and Literatures, American Review of the Soviet Union, Antiquity, Ars Islamica, Asia, Gazette des Beaux-Arts, and Southwestern Journal of Anthropology. For references see p. 66, footnotes 1 and 2.

MGU .... Moskovskii Gosudarstvennyi Universitet [State University], Moscow.

UAN .... Ukrainska Akademiia Nauk [Ukrainian Academy of Sciences, formerly VUAN, later ANU], Kiev.

UNKHU .... Upravlenie Nauchnykh i Khudozhertvennykh Upravlenii [Russian S.F.S.R. Bureau of Scientific and Artistic Institutions of the Commissariat of Education].

UZKOMSTARIS .... Uzbekistankii Komitet po Okhrane Pamiatnikov Stariny i Iskusstva [Uzbekistan Committee for the Preservation of Monuments of Antiquity and Art], currently known as Uzbekistanskii Komitet po Okhrane i Izucheniiu Pamiatnikov Materialnoi Kultury [Uzbekistan Committee for the Preservation and Study of Monuments of Material Culture], Tashkent.

SREDAZKOMSTARIS .. Sredne Aziatskii Komitet po Okhrane Pamiatnikov Stariny i Iskusstva [Central Asiatic Committee for the Preservation of Monuments of Antiquity and Art], Tashkent.

VOKS .... Vsesoiuznoe Obshchestvo Kulturnykh Snoshenii [All-Union Society for Cultural Relations with Foreign Countries], Moscow.

While all scientific research is under the supervision of the Academy of Sciences of the U.S.S.R., the greater part of all archeological work is done by IAE, IIMK, UAN, and local governmental bodies for the Study and Preservation of Ancient Monuments, such as UZKOM-STARIS and SREDAZKOMSTARIS.

Physical anthropologists are attached to these museums and institutions. There is assembled under M. Plisetskii, Director of MGU, an excellent staff including G. F. Debets, V. V. Bunak, and, until his death in Turkestan during 1937, A. I. IArkho. In the museum of MGU there are some of the best anthropological exhibits, study collections, and research facilities.

Throughout this report [3] the names of physical anthropologists are given in parentheses to indicate the group with whom they worked, e.g., Uzbeks (Vishnevskii).

All words in brackets have been inserted by the editors in order to elucidate the text.

---

[3] Henry Field attended as a guest the Jubilee Session of the 220th Anniversary of the Academy of Sciences of the U.S.S.R. from June 15–July 6, 1945, in Moscow and Leningrad. He accompanied 15 United States scientists on this mission. During 4 weeks he obtained recent information on Soviet anthropology

ANTHROPOLOGY OF THE WESTERN PAMIRS

Ginzburg [4] undertook to edit unpublished anthropological data collected by N. V. Bogoiavlenskii (d. 1930) during his Central Asian Expedition, 1898-1901, and now in the Moscow University Institute of Anthropology. This report includes some measurements on 554 adult males from the regions of Matcha, Karategin, Darvaz, and the western Pamirs (Rushan, Shugnan, Goran, Ishkashim, and Vakhan). The latter area was formerly part of the Khanate of Bukhara, now a portion of the Mountainous Badakhshan Autonomous Region.

The population of the western Pamirs belongs to the eastern branch of the Iranian peoples, and is subdivided into a number of isolated ethnic groups living in narrow mountain valleys and gorges. In addition to their native tongues, these people use the Tajik [Tadzhik] languages. Their material culture is very close to that of the Mountain Tajiks.

The anthropology of this area was first studied by Maslovskii [5] during 1895-1899. A decade later came Shults,[6] whose measurements were discounted by Ginzburg. Then followed Zarubin,[7] who published only a small part of his data, and Joyce,[8] who published Sir Aurel Stein's figures.

Joyce considers that the Vakhan Tajiks are the "average" type for this region, and that they are "pure representatives of the Alpine type." Ginzburg disagrees with this classification, and points out that Joyce's figures do not correspond with other descriptions of the Alpine type, such as that of Collignon.[9]

L. V. Oshanin, leader of the expedition from the Uzbek Institute

and archeology which will form the basis for summaries to be published later. However, when he left in October 1947 to join the University of California African Expedition, these publications were turned over to Dr. Hallam Movius, Peabody Museum, Harvard.

[4] Ginzburg, V. V., Antropologicheskii sostav naseleniia zapadnogo Pamira [The anthropological composition of the population of the western Pamirs according to N. V. Bogoiavlenskii's data]. AZH, No. 1, 91-114, 1937.

[5] Maslovskii, S., Galcha [Galchas]. AZH, No. 2, pp. 17-32, 1901.

[6] Shults, P., Zur Kentniss der arischen Bevölkerung des Pamirs. Orientalisches Archiv, Leipzig, vol. 11, 1912, and Landeskundliche Forschungen im Pamir, Hamburg, 1916.

[7] Zarubin, I. I., Materialy i Zametki po etnographii gornykh Tadzhikov, Dolina Bartanga [Materials and notes on the ethnography of the Mountain Tajiks, Bartang Valley]. Sbornik, Mus. Anthrop. and Ethnogr. U.S.S.R. Acad. Sci., Leningrad, 1917.

[8] Joyce, T. A., Note on the physical anthropology of the Pamirs and Amu Darya Basin. Journ. Roy. Anthrop. Inst., vol. 56, London, 1926.

[9] Collignon, R., Mem. Soc. d'Anthrop., Paris, 1899.

of Experimental Medicine in 1935, published his report subsequent to Ginzburg's article.

In his preliminary report Bogoiavlenskii [10] distinguishes four anthropological types, usually present as a more or less heterogeneous mixture:

1. The principal type into which the others resolve appears to be closely akin to the Persian. This type is described as being brachycephalic, of medium to tall stature, with straight or convex nose, well-developed beard, and intensive pigmentation.

2. The "Semitic" type is relatively short, with a narrow face, thin lips, a convex nose, and dark pigmentation.

3. This type, which is rarer, is brachycephalic, of medium stature, with a light reddish beard, a straight nose, and light or mixed eyes.

4. This type is characterized by a still darker pigmentation, thick lips, and a very broad nose.

Bogoiavlenskii did not find any Armenoids.

He accounts for these various types not through isolation but as a result of the migration and mixture of various groups, following the theory according to which the Iranian populations were pushed into the mountains by Turkish and Arab tribes.

According to Bogoiavlenskii the basic anthropological type came from Iran; the light type from Badakhshan; and dolichocephalic elements of the southwestern Pamirs are the remains of the Siyakhpush, who once inhabited this region. The population of central Darvaz came from the IAkh-Su River, i.e., from western Darvaz. Bogoiavlenskii bases his conclusions chiefly on the local traditions. His failure to find any "Aryan" elements among the inhabitants of the Pamirs is important.

The following regional variations of physical measurements were recorded by Bogoiavlenskii:

Stature.—Ranges from medium to medium tall with the tallest in Shugnan (168.7) and the shortest in Darvaz (164.52). The distribution in the Darvaz area agrees with the figures given by Joyce: lowest in the Vakhio Valley and in the middle section of Piandzh, increasing southward toward Rushan.

Head length.—Medium; equal in Karategin, Darvaz, and Rushan, decreasing in Shugnan, becoming less in the southwestern Pamirs. These figures also agree with those obtained by Joyce.

Head breadth.—Medium; lowest in Darvaz. Regional variations agree with Stein's measurements, but his figures are slightly lower.

---

[10] Bogoiavlenskii, N. V., Verkhoviak reki Amu Dari [At the headwaters of the Amu Darya]. Zemlevedenie, 1901.

Head height.—Great. No comparison possible, as various methods were used in 1901 and 1898.

Cephalic index.—Ranges from brachycephalic to hyperbrachyce-phalic; decreasing from Karategin to Darvaz; approaching mesoce-phalic in the Piandzh Valley; and increasing southward, from Vanch to the southwestern Pamirs, where it becomes hyperbrachycephalic. This also agrees with figures obtained by Joyce.

Three cephalic index groups were distinguished by Ginzburg; Karategin and the southwestern Pamirs having the largest percentage of hyperbrachycephals; in Darvaz, mesocephaly predominates, the brachycephals being second; in Shugnan and Rushan brachycephals predominate, and are followed by hyperbrachycephals. Dolichocephals are numerically strongest in Darvaz and Rushan (10 percent).

Face height.—Greatest in Karategin; decreases in Darvaz.

Face breadth.—Medium to narrow; least in Karategin.

Facial index.—Varies within the range of leptoprosopy; broadest in Darvaz.

Ginzburg distinguishes four typical regional groups:

1. *Darvaz.*—Short in stature; lowest cephalic index, bordering on mesocephaly (because of sharp decrease of head breadth); low and relatively broad face; shorter and wider nose.

2. *Shugnan.*—Tall in stature; high cephalic index; high, fairly broad face; long, narrow nose.

3. *Southwestern Pamirs* (Goran, Ishkashim, Vakhan).—Stature much less than in Shugnan; highest cephalic index; face and nose long and narrow; pigmentation as in Shugnan.

4. *Karategin* (and, partly, Matcha).—Stature slightly higher than Darvaz; cephalic index as great as in Shugnan because of increase of breadth; high, medium broad face of narrow form; darkest pig-mentation of eyes and hair.

These groups correspond with Ginzburg's other data and those described by Joyce.

Ginzburg does not agree with Joyce's definition of the Rushan type as "the pure original type" and considers it to be a transitional stage between the Mountain Tajiks and the tribes of the western Pamirs.

Bogoiavlenskii also measured some Tajiks and Arabs in the IAkh-Su Valley.

The Tajiks are tall (168.0), with a higher cephalic index than in central Darvaz, a narrow face and a narrow, long nose, and intensive head and beard pigmentation. The Arabs from IAkh-Su Valley have practically become assimilated with the Tajiks both in language and in culture. Physically, they are shorter (165.6), with a longer and narrower face, a broader nose, and more intensive dark pigmentation of the eyes.

Bogoiavlenskii also measured seven Afghans, from the left bank of Piandzh in the Afghan portion of Darvaz. This group is very close to the Tajiks from the right bank of the Piandzh, having an average stature of 160.5 and a cephalic index of 80.0.

Summary.—The population of the western Pamirs is relatively homogeneous, belonging to the short-headed Europeoid type referred to by Bogoiavlenskii as the Pamiro-Europeoid type, to which the Tajiks of Darvaz and Karategin belong.

This anthropological type is characterized by medium stature; brachycephaly with relatively small absolute skull dimensions; a rather long face with a narrow, strongly protruding, nose, dark pigmentation of hair and eyes, and a well-developed beard.

Bogoiavlenskii has found local variations of this type among which the peoples of Darvaz, who are characterized by a lower cephalic index bordering on brachy-mesocephaly, are to be found at one extreme, while the Shugnani, who are taller and possess a higher cephalic index bordering on hyperbrachycephaly, occupy the other.

Local variations depend on concentration of genes, the latter being due to considerable isolation in this district, where but slight contact exists between adjacent regions.

Anthropological data serve to refute the existence of Nordic race elements among the population of the Pamirs.

IRANIAN TRIBES OF THE WESTERN PAMIRS

During the summer of 1935 Oshanin [11] of the Medical Institute in Tashkent obtained anthropometric data on some very small Iranian tribes inhabiting the sources of the Amu-Darya, i.e., the Piandzh and its tributaries the IAzgulem, Bartang, Gunt, and Shakhdara. These Iranian dialects differ so much that the inhabitants of two adjacent valleys cannot understand each other.

Among the tribes of the western Pamirs, often separated from each other by inaccessible mountain ridges, Oshanin measured and examined 231 Shugni of the Shakhdara, Gunt, and Piandzh Valleys, 42 Rushani of the Piandzh Valley, 52 Wakhi from various villages of Wakhan, 13 Bartangi of the Bartang Valley, and a few Ishkashmi and Gorani.

Analysis of the anthropometric data reveals that these Iranian

---

[11] Oshanin, L. V., Iranskie plemena zapadnogo Pamira [Iranian tribes of the western Pamirs], text pp. 1-190, 25 plates, many maps, graphs and tables. Inst. Exp. Med., Tashkent, 1937.

tribes belong to the same racial group which is characterized by brachycephalic brunets of medium stature.

This composite type, however, has probably been formed out of different racial elements. The people of the Pamirs have not lived in isolation. In order to solve the question of the racial structure of these tribes it is therefore necessary to compare them with the surrounding peoples.

During 1923-1934 Oshanin measured and observed 3,317 males in Central Asia. Among some groups the measurements were obtained by assistants under his supervision. Anthropometric data on the following peoples and tribes are therefore directly comparable: 100 Kazakhs of Talas, 100 Kirghiz of the Issyk-Kul region, and 100 Kirghiz of Talas; 1,704 Uzbeks and Tajiks of the Duab; 505 Turkoman tribesmen of the Transcaspian steppes; 433 Karategin Tajiks; 202 Jews, immigrants from Asia anterior in the tenth century; and 53 Iranis (Persians), 56 Azerbaijanis, and 83 Baluchis, all immigrants from adjacent regions of Iran.

Part of the material has been published,[12] the remainder being now in press or in preparation.

Oshanin has identified five racial types in Central Asia:

1. Predominant among the Uzbeks and Tajiks, inhabiting the plains and foothills between the Amu-Darya and the Syr-Darya

---

[12] Oshanin, L. V., Tysiacheletniaia davnost dolikhotsefalii u turkmen (opyt obosnovaniia teorii Skifo-Sarmatskogo proiskhozhdeniia turkmenskogo naroda) [A thousand years of dolichocephaly among the Turkomans; an attempt to establish the foundations of a theory of a Scytho-Sarmatian origin of the Turkoman people], SREDAZKOMSTARIS, Izvestia No. 1, Tashkent, 1926; Kirgizy iuzhnogo poberezhiia Issyk-Kulia [The Kirghiz of the southern shore of the Issyk-Kul], V. V. Bartoldu [to V. V. Barthold], Festschrift published by the Society for the Study of Tajikistan and of the Iranian peoples outside its boundaries, Tashkent, 1927; Uzbeki Khorezma [The Uzbeks of Khwarazm], pts. I-II, Biu. Sredne Aziatskogo Universiteta [Bull. Centr. Asiatic Univ.], No. 17 (1927) and No. 18 (1928); Nekotorye dopolneniia k gipoteze Skifo-Sarmatskogo proiskhozhdeniia turkmen [Some supplementary data toward the hypothesis regarding the Scytho-Sarmatian origin of Turkomans], SREDAZKOMSTARIS, Izvestia No. 4, Tashkent, 1928; k sravnitelnoi antropologii etnicheskikh grupp prishlykh iz Perednei Azii—Evreev i Arabov, i etnicheskikh grupp Uzbekistana—Uzbekov i Tadzhikov [Contributions to the comparative anthropology of the ethnic groups which have come out of Vorderasien—Jews and Arabs, and of the ethnic groups of Uzbekistan—the Uzbeks and the Tajiks], in Oshanin, L. V., and IAsevich, Materialy po antropologii Uzbekistana [Materials for the anthropology of Uzbekistan], No. 1, Tashkent-Samarkand, 1929; Pamirskaia antropologo—fiziologicheskaia ekspeditsiia UZIEM [Physiological and Anthropological Expedition to the Pamirs], Bull. UZIEM, No. 4, (5), Tashkent, 1936.

basins, this type must certainly be regarded as belonging to the great European [18] race (*Homo sapiens indo-europaeus*). This group is characterized by brachycephaly, medium stature, dark color of the eyes and hair (typical brunets), moderate development of body hair, and a rather small nose with a straight or sinuous bridge. In accordance with the center of distribution area of this type Oshanin has called this group "the Central Asiatic Duab" or "*Homo sapiens indoeuropaeus*, var. *oxiano-jaxartensis.*"

IArkho,[14] on the basis of data obtained by him in Central Asia during 1928-1932, described the same racial type but gives it the name "Pamiro-Ferghanic" (*Homo sapiens indo-europaeus*, var. *pamiro-ferghanica*). Such an isolation of one and the same type by two independent investigators confirms the reality of this type.

2. The second European type prevails largely among various Turkoman tribes inhabiting the Transcaspian steppes from the Caspian Sea to Afghanistan and from the Amu-Darya to Khurasan. This type, characterized by tall stature, dolichocephaly, and dark color of the eyes and hair, has been called by Oshanin, after the center of the area it occupies, "the Transcaspian race" (*Homo sapiens indo-europaeus*, var. *transcaspica*).

IArkho, while isolating the same racial type on the basis of his own data, defined its position among the dolichocephalic European races more accurately, considering it as a variety of the Mediterranean race and classing it within Fischer's Oriental race (*Homo sapiens indoeuropaeus*, var. *orientalis* Fisch.).

3. The third European type is prevalent in the ethnic groups that have immigrated into Central Asia from Khurasan and Persian Azerbaijan, i.e., among the Persians, Iranian by their language, and the Azerbaijanis, using Turki language. The characteristics of this type are a medium stature, dolichocephaly, and dark eyes and hair. From the tall dolichocephals of the Transcaspian steppes it differs by much more abundant hair and "Assyroid" [of Western Asia] nasal form. By the morphology of the nose and profusion of the hair growth this type might be included among the Armenoids of Western Asia, but it sharply differs from the latter by its well-pronounced dolichocephaly. IArkho therefore separates it into a distinct type, terming it "the Khurasan race" or "*Homo sapiens indo-europaeus*, var. *khurasanica.*"

---

[18] Throughout this section Oshanin has used the word "Europeoid" which we have generally changed to "European." (H. F.)

[14] IArkho, A. I., Antropologicheskii sostav turetskikh narodnostei Azii. AZH, No. 3, 1933.

9

4. The fourth European type was brought into Central Asia by immigrants from Asia Anterior. This is the Armenoid type (*Homo sapiens indo-europaeus,* var. *armenica*). In its purest form this type occurs among Central Asiatic Jews. The brachycephalic Europeans of Asia Anterior (Armenoids) are distinguished from those of the Central Asiatic Duab region by more abundant hair and the typically "Assyroid" form of the nose.

5. The fifth racial type is represented by typical Mongoloids (*Homo sapiens asiaticus*). The Mongoloid type is markedly prevalent among the Kirghiz and Kazakhs, who live mainly on the steppes and in the Tien Shan to the north of the Syr-Darya. IArkho, basing his conclusions on his own extensive data obtained among Turki tribes of the Saian-Altai mountain system, distinguishes the following two varieties among the Mongoloids: the Central Asiatic (*Homo sapiens asiaticus,* var. *centralis*) and the South Siberian (*Homo sapiens asiaticus* var. *sibirica meridionalis*). According to IArkho the latter is predominant in Central Asia.

According to Oshanin a comparison between the Iranian tribes of the western Pamirs and the peoples of Central Asia, Iran, and Asia Anterior reveals that the former must be reckoned among the typical Europeans of Central Asia. No Mongoloid features could be traced among these Iranian tribes.

The European types inhabiting the Pamirs undoubtedly belong to the brachycephalic Europeans of Central Asia, taking an intermediate position between the Tajiks and Uzbeks and the Jews, immigrants from Western Asia. In certain characters, such as abundant hair and a high, prominent nose, the European types in the Pamirs are more related to the Armenoids than to the inhabitants of the Duab region.

As to the racial types distinguished by Risley in the population of India, the comparison indicates that only the Indo-Afghan race cannot be excluded from the population of the Pamirs, where it does constitute a very insignificant admixture. On the other hand the distribution of the cephalic index in the regions south of the Hindu Kush suggests that the migration of the brachycephalic Europeans of the Pamirs to the south was more intensive than the migration of the Indo-Afghans to the north, across the barrier of the Hindu Kush. The cephalic index, indeed, among the Chitrali and Mastui reaches 80.26-80.56, while the admixture of dolichocephals to the Iranian tribes is the most insignificant.

Within the limits of Tibet, there is, according to Risley and Turner, only one admixture of Europeans among its Mongoloid population, namely that of dolichocephals, particularly in the province of Khams. The population of Tibet did not, therefore, take any part in the formation of the racial structure of the Iranian tribes in the western Pamirs.

In eastern Turkestan, as a result of Sir Aurel Stein's investigations, in addition to a Mongoloid type, there has been recognized a brachycephalic European type closely related to the peoples dwelling in the region of the Duab. This same race also inhabits the Ferghana Valley, which is separated from the western Pamirs by the Altai and Trans-Altai mountain ridges and by the plateau of the eastern Pamirs, which are inhabited by the Kirghiz, typical Mongoloids.

Thus, the comparison between the Iranian tribes of the western Pamirs and the peoples of the surrounding countries proves that this region was populated from the west, from Iran. The connecting link was Afghanistan.

On the basis of the scanty historical information, Oshanin states that the western Pamirs appear to have been populated 1,500 to 2,000 years ago by the Iranians, who from the anthropological point of view take an intermediate position between the brachycephalic [15] Europeans of Central Asia and those of Western Asia.

Oshanin then dwells on certain general anthropological problems of Central Asia and adjacent countries:

1. The distribution of the Armenoids of Western Asia and their differentiation into local types. As stated above, the brachycephalic Europeans of the Pamirs, in certain characters, the most important being hair growth and nose morphology, take an intermediate position between the Armenoids and the peoples of the Central Asiatic Duab. They might possibly be considered as a result of a crossing between the two types named, but on the other hand this intermediate position does not necessarily prove the fact of crossing. It is possible, for example, that the Pamir Europeoids may be but a local variety of the Armenoid of Western Asia. Nor is another possibility excluded of their being a certain transitional stage in the racial evolution, and as our knowledge increases, the number of such intermediary stages linking the brachycephals of Central Asia with those of Western Asia may grow.

Studies reveal that among the peoples of Central Asia there occur certain types undoubtedly maintaining the general Armenoid habitus,

---

[15] On the basis of my measurements in Iran and those compiled from numerous sources the basic element on the Iranian plateau is dolichocephalic. Brachycephaly, however, predominates in the northwestern and northeastern areas of Iran. Cf. Contributions to the anthropology of Iran, Field Museum of Natural History, Chicago, 1939. (H. F.)

but deviating from the classical Armenoid type. Such are the immigrants from Western Asia, the Central Asiatic Jews, who differ by their general Armenoid traits not only from the brachycephalic Europeoids of Central Asia, the Uzbeks and Tajiks, but also from the classical Armenoid type in their rounded occiput, rather low and slightly bulging forehead, and less fleshy nose with its considerably narrower base.

Among other peoples the specific Western Asiatic characters, such as abundant body hair and Armenoid features in the structure of the soft parts of the face, combine with an absolutely non-Armenoid, dolichocephalic skull. Such are the markedly dolichocephalic Iranis (Persians) and Azerbaijanis with their abundant hair growth and typically Armenoid form of nose.

It is only when an anthropometric survey of Western Asia,[16] and more particularly of Iran, has been completed, as well as the excavation of accurately dated crania, that we shall be able to attack the problem of the origin and differentiation into local types of the whole racial complex of Western Asia.

2. The second great problem arising in connection with the study of the Iranian tribes of the Pamirs is the distribution of brachycephalic and dolichocephalic European types throughout Asia. If the data obtained by Oshanin and his colleagues are compared with those from India, Tibet, and eastern Turkestan, the Hindu Kush appears as a geographic barrier. To the south there have expanded dolichocephals represented by the Indo-Afghans, which, according to Turner and Deniker, penetrated into the province of Khams in Tibet, and even to Yunan and Szechwan. On the other hand, to the north of the Pamiro-Altai mountain system there have spread brachycephalic Europeans represented by the above race of the Central Asiatic Duab. To judge from Stein's data, this race has also penetrated deep into eastern Turkestan where it forms the basis of the population in oases bordering the desert of Takla-Makan.

In the narrow gorges of the Piandzh, squeezed between the Pamiro-Altai and the Hindu Kush, the brachycephalic Iranian tribes have settled. Their position intermediate between the Armenoids and the peoples of the Duab has already been mentioned.

3. The third problem is that of the Mediterranean race in Asia. As stated above, to the south of Hindu Kush there has expanded the Indo-Afghan race, of which typical representatives are Sikhs, investi-

---

[16] See publications by Buxton, Coon, Field, Huzayyin, Shevket Aziz Kansu, Keith, Krogman, Pittard, Shanklin, and Bertram Thomas.

gated by von Eickstedt.[17] IArkho, in his work [18] on the Turkomans of Khwarazm noted a similarity between the Turkomans on the one hand and the Sikhs of Punjab and the Rifs [19] of Morocco on the other. Oshanin's tables fully confirm this similarity, and the crania obtained by Pumpelly at Anau in 1904 and studied by Sergi show that the Mediterranean racial complex appeared at a very early date in Central Asia.[20] In conclusion, Oshanin states that this appears to be a tall variety of the Mediterranean race, which is now represented only by the following separated groups: the Rifs of Morocco, the Kabyls, certain Beduin tribes, the Turkomans of the Transcaspian steppes, and the Indo-Afghan race.

According to N. G. Malitskii's theory, which on the basis of anthropological and ethnohistorical data Oshanin developed into a working hypothesis, the dolichocephalic European type, now common among the Turkomans of the Transcaspian steppes, was in the past an element of the Scytho-Sarmatian tribes, or Sacae, of Central Asia.

MOUNTAIN TAJIKS [21]

There is no uniformity in the descriptions of the Tajiks, owing to the subjective approach of the older scholars. Most of the older and many of the current scholars, basing their conclusions on the Indo-European theory of the origin of the languages, accept the Tajiks to be more or less pure descendants of the "Aryans," who, according to some of the adherents of that theory, originated in Central Asia.

In the majority of the descriptions there is a tendency to idealize the Tajik type, to endow it with positive moral and physical characters, and to contrast it with the other peoples of Central Asia.

Scholars have been attempting to isolate a specific "Tajik." A typical exponent of this school was Shishlov, according to whom the Tajiks are "the most solid basic Iranian type." Shishlov admits that sometimes it is difficult to distinguish the specific Tajik type from the Persian variety and even from the Central Asian Jews, at the same

[17] von Eickstedt, E., Rassenelemente der Sikh. Zeitschr. Ethnol., pts. 4-5, Berlin, 1931.

[18] IArkho, A. I., Die Alterveranderungen der Rassenmerkmale bei den Erwachsenen. Anthrop. Anz., vol. 12, pt. 2, 1935.

[19] Coon, Carleton, The tribes of the Rif. Harvard African Studies, vol. 9, Peabody Mus. Harvard Univ., Cambridge, Mass., 1931.

[20] Pumpelly, R., Explorations in Turkestan, vol. 2, pp. 445-446, Washington, 1905. Excavation of Anau was recommenced in 1946. (H. F.)

[21] Ginzburg, V. V., Gornye Tadzhiki [The Mountain Tajiks: Materials on the anthropology of the Tajiks of Karategin and Darvaz]. Trudy, IAE, vol. 16, 1937.

TABLE 1.—*Comparison of Shugni and Wakhi with peoples of Eastern Pamirs, Tien Shan, Ferghana Valley, and other Duab Regions*

People	Locality	No.	Glabella-occipital length	Greatest breadth	Cephalic index	Biz. breadth	Observer
Lokai Uzbeks	Duab Region	67	181	155	86.5	144	Oshanin
Karshi Uzbeks	Duab Region	200	181	152	84.11	142	Oshanin
Kermine Uzbeks	Duab Region	95	181	152	84.33	140	Oshanin
Bukhara Tajiks	Duab Region	163	181	151	84.20	138	Oshanin
Kazakhs	Talas Valley	100	188	160	85.20	150	Oshanin
Tajiks	Ferghana Valley	200	185	155	84.04	143	IArkho
Uzbeks (nontribal)	Ferghana Valley	399	183	155	84.68	141	IArkho
Kara-Kalpaks	Ferghana Valley	100	186	156	83.76	143	IArkho
Kipchaks	Ferghana Valley	100	186	156	84.42	144	IArkho
Kirghiz	Ferghana Valley	296	187	157	83.97	144	IArkho
Kirghiz	Tien Shan	784	189	160	85.15	150	IArkho
Kirghiz	Issyk-Kul	100	187	159	84.84	149	Oshanin
Kirghiz	Talas Valley	100	187	159	85.08	149	Oshanin
Kirghiz	Pamirs and Alai	72	187	155	83.34	147	Oshanin
Kirghiz	Alai Valley	35	187	155	83.52	147	Oshanin
Kirghiz	Pamir Plateau	37	187	156	83.15	146	Oshanin
Wakhi	Western Pamir Iranians	52	185	153	85.46	139	Oshanin
Shakhdara Shugni	Western Pamir Iranians	29	184	155	83.83	142	Oshanin
Gunt Shugni	Western Pamir Iranians	64	183	155	84.50	141	Oshanin

TABLE 2.—*Nasal profile*

People	Tribe	No.	Concave	Straight	Wavy	Convex
Shugni	Shakhdara	29	0	65.52	13.79	20.69
Shugni	Gunt	64	7.81	40.62	12.51	39.06
Shugni	Piandzh	138	8.70	50.00	8.70	32.60
Shugni	Total	231	7.36	49.36	10.37	32.91
Other Iranian tribes	Rushani	42	14.29	50.00	9.52	26.19
	Bartangi	13	15.38	46.17	30.76	7.69
	Wakhi	52	9.60	55.78	15.39	19.23
	Ishkashmi	7	0	57.13	14.29	28.58
	Gorani	3	0	66.67	0	33.33

TABLE 3.—*Cephalic index*

People	Tribe	No.	Min.	Max.	Mean	S.D.	C.V.
Shugni	Shakhdara	29	77.5	90.0	83.33 ± 0.76	4.11 ± 0.54	4.90 ± 0.63
Shugni	Gunt	64	77.0	94.0	84.50 ± 0.48	3.84 ± 0.34	4.53 ± 0.40
Shugni	Piandzh	138	74.0	93.5	84.12 ± 0.33	3.92 ± 0.23	4.66 ± 0.28
Shugni	Total	231	74.0	94.0	84.25 ± 0.25	3.94 ± 0.17	4.67 ± 0.21
Other Iranian tribes	Rushani	42	74.0	101.0	84.47 ± 1.00	6.48 ± 0.71	7.55 ± 0.83
	Bartangi	13	79.0	90.5	83.65 ± 0.88	3.18 ± 0.62	3.80 ± 0.74
	Wakhi	52	75.0	93.0	85.46 ± 0.51	3.72 ± 0.36	4.25 ± 0.42
	Ishkashmi	7	82.5	87.0	85.64	....	....
	Gorani	3	...	...	93.5; 83.3; 75.6	....	....

time stressing the importance of ·preserving "this corner-stone [i.e., the Tajik type] for our ethnographical constructions."

Some authors (e.g., Ivanovich) has attempted to identify the Tajiks with the remains of the Nestorian Christians (who lived in Central Asia during the sixth century) or with Slavs, remarking that the Tajiks are blond, have large features, and amiable, frank dispositions.

Other investigators (e.g., Vambery) did not regard the Tajiks as pure representatives of the "Aryans" or of their Iranian branch. Vambery states that it is impossible to consider the Tajiks to be a primary type of the Iranian race; that while their Iranian type is

TABLE 4.—*Grouping according to cephalic index*

Group	Range	No.	Shugni	No.	Rushani	No.	Wakhi
Dolichocephal	x-75.9	3	*1.29*	3	*7.14*	1	*1.92*
Mesocephal	76.0-80.9	34	*14.71*	8	*19.04*	4	*7.69*
Brachycephal	81.0-85.9	94	*40.69*	12	*25.57*	18	*34.61*
Hyperbrachycephal ..	86.0-x	100	*43.31*	19	*45.25*	29	*55.78*
Total		231	*100.0*	42	*100.0*	52	*100.0*

readily apparent to the eyes, their facial characters manifest some alien Turanian traits (broad forehead, wide zygomatic arches, thick nose, and large mouth). Only the inhabitants of Mountainous Badakhshan (Faizabadians) have a more truly pronounced Iranian type.

Danilov does not consider the Tajiks as Iranians. He bases his conclusions partly on the studies of Korsh, who derived the name of Tajiks from the Pehlevi word *tazi,* meaning "Arab," and partly on the brachycephaly of the Tajiks, which Danilov, whose work lay only among the dolichocephalic population of Persia, did not consider an Iranian character.

Other investigators considered the Tajiks to be the resultant mixture of several races. Thus, Virskii considers the Galchas to be a mixed Aryo-Turkish type, preserving certain tribal characters. The Tajiks, according to Virskii, represent a mixture of the Aryan and Turkish races with the Persian and the Jewish types.

Grebenkin, who described the Tajiks of the valleys, states that they do not belong to any established type, but unite in their composition the characters of all the tribes inhabiting the region. "The Tajiks of this region are an amalgam of all the surrounding tribes. . . . This mixture reflects in it the type of Uzbek, Tatar, Hebrew, Gipsy, even Slavic, Arabic, Persian and Indian."

TABLE 5.—*Comparison of Shugni with other Iranian tribes*

People	Tribe	No.	Stature	G. O. L.	G. B.	C. I.	Min. front. diam.	Biz. br.	Big. br.	Total fac. ht.
Shugni	Shakhdara	29	170.53	184	155	83.33	107.8	142.2	108.1	127.0
Shugni	Gunt	64	167.72	183	155	84.50	108.1	141.4	106.3	122.7
Shugni	Piandzh	138	167.14	183	153	84.12	106.0	140.0	106.9	123.3
	Total	231	167.72	183	154	84.25	106.8	140.7	106.9	123.6
Other Iranian tribes........	Rushani	42	166.41	185	154	84.47	105.7	139.9	106.7	121.7
	Bartangi	13	164.29	151	151	83.65	104.8	137.7	102.4	120.7
	Wakhi	52	164.08	180	153	85.46	107.2	138.8	105.8	121.8
	Ishkashmi	7	165.5	178	152	85.64	106.4	141.0	104.6	120.5

TABLE 5a.—*Comparison of Shugni with other Iranian tribes*

People	Tribe	Nas. ht.	Nas. br.	Nas. ind.	Ear ht.	Ear br.	Ear ind.	F. I.	Chest
Shugni	Shakhdara	52.9	34.6	65.55	64.1	35.2	54.93	77.5	88.24
Shugni	Gunt	52.0	34.0	65.44	62.0	34.5	55.90	77.5	86.89
Shugni	Piandzh	51.9	34.5	66.40	65.5	34.4	55.29	76.6	85.53
	Total	52.1	34.3	66.00	63.5	34.4	55.42	77.0	86.25
Other Iranian tribes........	Rushani	51.5	34.2	66.70	61.29	34.0	55.67	77.4	85.83
	Bartangi	50.2	34.3	68.60	58.54	32.8	56.23	77.4	85.46
	Wakhi	52.1	34.3	66.20	60.90	33.8	55.37	77.2	85.62
	Ishkashmi	52.0	35.3	68.00	62.57	34.7	55.64	78.5	83.43

TABLE 6.—*Cephalic index of peoples in the Caucasus* [1]

People	Locality	No.	C. I.	Observer
Turks	Nakhichevan	151	76.1	Anserov
Tatars	Azerbaidzhan	207	77.6	Various
Kurds	Transcaucasia		77.6	Ivanovskii
Tatars	Aralych	16	77.96	Chantre
Azerbaidzhanis	Azerbaidzhan		78.1	Deniker
Persians	Azerbaidzhan		78.4	Deniker
Kurds	Transcaucasia		78.5	Deniker
Circassians (Mokoch tribe)			78.5	Chantre
Tatars	Azerbaidzhan	19	78.83	Chantre
Yezidis	Yerevan district	20	78.90	Field
Tats	Baku	129	79.2	Deniker
Turkomans	North Caucasus	302	79.3	IArkho
Turks	Gandzha, Azerbaidzhan	230	79.3	IArkho
Azerbaidzhanis	Azerbaidzhan		79.4	von Erckert
Tatars	Yerevan	17	80.11	Chantre
Tajiks	Norachaine	14	80.11	Chantre
Chechens	Ingushetia		80.4	Chantre
Osetes		14	80.5	von Erckert
Gurians			80.5	Chantre
Yezidis	Total in Tbilisi	51	80.58	Field
Osetes	Terek		80.7	Chantre
Khevsurs	Khevsuretia		80.7	Chantre
N. Abkhazians (Abaze tribe)			80.7	Chantre
Kumyks		130	80.8	Debets and Trofimova
Imeretians			80.9	Chantre
Kalmyks			80.9	von Erckert
Edishkul Nogais		145	80.9	IArkho
Edissan Nogais		146	81.0	IArkho
Osetes		16	81.1	von Erckert
Karatchais			81.1	Chantre
Osetes (tall)		20	81.3	Gilchenko
Circassians	Adighe		81.4	Deniker
Osetes		16	81.4	von Erckert
Osetes		300	81.5	Riskine
Azerbaidzhanis	Lake Goktcha		81.6	Chantre
Abazes		11	81.6	von Erckert
Kurds			81.6	Chantre
Yezidis	Lake Van district	22	81.75	Field
Osetes		554	81.9	Deniker
Circassians			81.9	von Erckert
Kabardins	Kuban		82.0	Chantre
Circassians		54	82.05	Kappers
Circassians (Shapsug tribe)			82.1	Chantre

[1] Note.—In the compilation of the data on the cephalic index among the peoples of the Caucasus I have used Baschmakoff (1937, pp. 29-31), Rudolf Martin, Gilchenko, IArkho, and the figures quoted in my "Contributions to the Anthropology of Iran." (H. F.)

TABLE 6.—Continued

People	Locality	No.	C. I.	Observer
Circassians (Beslinais tribe)			82.2	Chantre
Osetes		200	82.62	Gilchenko
Osetes			82.7	Deniker
Chechens	Imertia		82.9	Chantre
Circassians	Temergais		83.0	Chantre
Abkhazians	Coastal Abkhazia		83.0	Chantre
Osetes	Terek Valley (7), Koban (10)	17	83.11	Chantre
Mingrelian			83.2	Chantre
Georgians	Georgia	900	83.2	Dzhavahov
Kara-Nogais		188	83.3	IArkho
Embailuk Nogais		176	83.3	IArkho
Georgians	Georgia		83.5	von Erckert
Tatars (Mountain)			83.6	Deniker
Kabardins			83.6	Deniker
Circassians (Natukhai tribe)			83.8	Chantre
Svans			83.8	Deniker
Kumyks			84.0	Chantre
Kara-Nogais	Eastern	156	84.0	Terebinskaia
Nogais	Terek region	108	84.2	Levin
Chechens			84.2	von Erckert
Georgians			84.3	Chantre
Osetes	North Osetia	105	84.60	Field
Balkars		314	84.6	Levin
Lesghians			84.6	Deniker
Kurds (deformed)			84.6	Chantre
Jews		20	84.7	Weissenberg
Osetes	Koban necropolis		84.7	Chantre
Nogais	Khasavyurt region	165	84.8	Terebinskaia
Tats	Daghestan		84.9	Deniker
Nogais			85.0	Chantre
Kumyks			85.0	Chantre
Karachais		211	85.1	Levin
Assyrians		5	85.1	von Erckert
Armenians			85.1	Chantre
Lesghians	Avars		85.1	von Erckert
Jews	Akhaltsikh		85.2	Deniker
Turks	Kakh, Azerbaidzhan	201	85.3	Debets
Turks	Nukha, Azerbaidzhan	301	85.3	IArkho
Lesghians			85.5	von Erckert
Armenians			85.6	Deniker
Armenians (deformed).			85.6	Chantre
Lazes			85.6	Deniker
Nogais			85.8	Deniker
Georgians	Georgia		85.8	Chantre
Jews	Georgia	33	85.9	Weissenberg
Nogais			86.0	Chantre

TABLE 6.—Continued

People	Locality	No.	C. I.	Observer
Azerbaidzhanis	Bayazid		86.0	Chantre
Lesghians			86.2	Deniker
Avars			86.4	Chantre
Nogais			86.4	von Erckert
Mountain Jews	Daghestan		86.7	von Erckert
Lazes			86.8	Deniker
Mountain Jews	Daghestan		87.0	Deniker
Lazes			87.3	Chantre
Lazes (deformed)			87.4	Chantre
Jews		43	87.5	Pantiukhov
Lesghians (Avars)			87.6	von Erckert
Lesghians			87.77	Chantre
Assyrians			88.7	Deniker

TABLE 7.—*Stature of peoples in the Caucasus*

People	Locality	No.	Stature	Observer
Ambailuk Nogais		176	162.5	IArkho
Turks	Nukha, Azerbaidzhan	301	162.7	IArkho
Turks	Kakh, Azerbaidzhan	201	162.9	Debets
Edishkul Nogais........		145	163.0	IArkho
Kara-Nogais	Western	188	163.1	IArkho
Kara-Nogais	Eastern	156	163.3	Terebinskaia
Turkomans	North Caucasus	302	163.5	IArkho
Nogais	Khasavyurt region	165	163.8	Terebinskaia
Turks	Gandzha, Azerbaidzhan	230	164.1	IArkho
Edissan Nogais		146	164.3	IArkho
Nogais	Terek region	108	164.6	Levin
Turks	Nakhichevan	151	165.1	Anserov
Kumyks		130	165.9	Debets and Trofimova
Balkars		314	166.9	Levin
Karachais		211	167.9	Levin

Kuznetsov mentions that this unity of type of the Tajiks is due to their Turkization, the degree of which differs in various localities.

The absence of sufficient data on the anthropology of the Tajiks caused von Eickstedt to group the Tajiks as belonging to the Turanian type. This is due to his migrationistic theories claiming the origin of European racial types from the "Turanids" inhabiting Central Asia.

Many authors admit the presence among the Tajiks of two or more types, obtained as a result of the influence of one or the other ancient race.

Snesarev points out the great difference between the Mountain Tajiks (from Karategin and Darvaz) and the Valley Tajiks (from Kuliab and Baldzhuan). The former have retained the characters

of the original Iranians with occasional admixture of the "blond
Aryan"; the latter are a variation of the Persians with a strong Arabic
admixture.

TABLE 8.—*Head length of peoples in the Caucasus*

People	Locality	No.	Head length	Observer
Turks	Nukha, Azerbaidzhan	301	181.9	IArkho
Nogais	Khasavyurt region	165	182.2	Terebinskaia
Turks	Kakh, Azerbaidzhan	201	183.9	Debets
Kumyks		130	184.6	Debets and Trofimova
Kara-Nogais	Eastern	156	184.7	Terebinskaia
Nogais	Terek region	108	185.8	Levin
Embailuk Nogais		176	186.8	IArkho
Kara-Nogais	Western	188	187.1	IArkho.
Balkars		314	187.7	Levin
Edissan Nogais		146	188.8	IArkho
Karachais		211	189.1	Levin
Edishkul Nogais		145	189.1	IArkho
Turks	Gandzha, Azerbaidzhan	230	189.9	IArkho
Turks	Nakhichevan	151	190.0	Anserov
Turkomans	North Caucasus	302	192.8	IArkho

TABLE 9.—*Head breadth of peoples in the Caucasus*

People	Locality	No.	Head breadth	Observer
Turks	Nakhichevan	151	145.0	Anserov
Turks	Gandzha, Azerbaidzhan	230	150.4	IArkho
Edishkul Nogais		145	152.7	IArkho
Edissan Nogais		146	152.8	IArkho
Turkomans	North Caucasus	302	152.8	IArkho
Nogais	Khasavyurt region	165	154.2	Terebinskaia
Turks	Nukha, Azerbaidzhan	301	155.0	IArkho
Embailuk Nogais		176	155.4	IArkho
Kara-Nogais	Eastern	156	155.6	Terebinskaia
Kara-Nogais	Western	188	155.7	IArkho
Nogais	Terek region	108	156.4	Levin
Turks	Kakh, Azerbaidzhan	201	156.6	Debets
Balkars		314	159.2	Levin
Karachais		211	160.9	Levin
Kumyks		130	161.8	Debets and Trofimova

Grebenkin also distinguishes two groups among the Valley Tajiks:
Uzbek blood predominated in one of the groups; and Jewish and
Persian, with a slight admixture of Uzbek, in the second group.
There are no "pure Tajiks" in the valleys of Central Asia.

Ujfalvy distinguishes three types of Tajiks in Turkestan: Autochthonous Iranians; Persian colonists; and descendants of Persian
slaves.

TABLE 10.—*Eye color of peoples in the Caucasus*

People	Locality	No.	Light	Mixed	Dark	Observer
Turkomans	North Caucasus	302	1.1	21.9	77.0	IArkho
Turks	Gandzha, Azerbaidzhan	230	1.5	54.7	43.8	IArkho
Turks	Nukha, Azerbaidzhan	301	1.0	37.9	61.1	IArkho
Turks	Kakh, Azerbaidzhan	201	1.5	32.0	66.5	Debets
Turks	Nakhichevan	151	0.7	41.3	68.0	Anserov
Kumyks		130	8.5	51.2	40.3	Debets and Trofimova
Karachais		211	11.0	80.0	9.0	Levin
Edissan Nogais		146	2.1	41.9	56.0	IArkho
Balkars		314	8.0	61.0	31.0	Levin
Edishkul Nogais		145	0.7	42.0	57.8	IArkho
Embailuk Nogais		176	0.0	38.4	61.6	IArkho
Kara-Nogais	Western	188	2.2	44.3	53.5	IArkho

TABLE 11.—*Bizygomatic breadth of peoples in the Caucasus*

People	Locality	No.	Biz. br.	Observer
Turks	Nakhichevan	151	136.0	Anserov
Turks	Nukha, Azerbaidzhan	301	139.1	IArkho
Turks	Gandzha, Azerbaidzhan	230	139.7	IArkho
Turks	Kakh, Azerbaidzhan	201	140.5	Debets
Kara-Nogais	Eastern	156	142.3	Terebinskaia
Nogais	Khasavyurt region	165	143.9	Terebinskaia
Nogais	Terek region	108	145.1	Levin
Edissan Nogais		146	145.4	IArkho
Turkomans	North Caucasus	302	145.5	IArkho
Kumyks		130	145.7	Debets and Trofimova
Edishkul Nogais		145	145.8	IArkho
Balkars		314	146.0	Levin
Embailuk Nogais		176	147.4	IArkho
Kara-Nogais	Western	188	147.5	IArkho
Karachais		211	147.6	Levin

The groups differ greatly in their physical characteristics. Among
the "Persian slaves" there are no blonds with blue eyes, but they do
occur occasionally among the second group.

Among the autochthonous Iranian group blonds are fairly common,
and brown-haired individuals outnumber brunets. Ujfalvy designates
the autochthonous Tajiks as the Mountain Tajiks, as different from

the Persian colonists whom he calls Valley Tajiks, although he admits that these divisions are not absolute and not always exact.

It is worth remarking that Ujfalvy, who represents the French

TABLE 12.—*Cephalic index of peoples in the Volga Region*

People	Locality	No.	C. I.	Observer
Mishari Tatars	Christopol region	122	79.5	Trofimova and Debets
Tatars Proper	Christopol region	109	80 2	Trofimova and Debets
Teptiars		112	80.3	Baronov
Kriashen Tatars	Christopol region	121	80.7	Trofimova and Debets
Mishari Tatars	Birsk region	149	80.7	Baronov
Tatars Proper	Elabuga region	146	81.1	Trofimova and Debets
Bashkirs	Birsk region	123	81.4	Baronov
Kriashen Tatars	Elabuga region	103	81.9	Trofimova and Debets
Tatars Proper	Kasimov region	196	82.2	Trofimova and Debets
Tatars Proper	Arsk region	160	82.3	Trofimova and Debets
Bashkirs	Argaiash region	131	83.0	Baronov
Karagash Tatars	Astrakhan region	158	83.6	Trofimova and Debets
Mishari Tatars	Narovchatsk region	175	86.0	Trofimova

TABLE 13.—*Cephalic index of peoples in the Crimea*

People	Locality	No.	C. I.	Observer
Karaims	Crimea	93	82.9	Adler
Mountain Tatars	Crimea	180	84.1	Nasov
Steppe Tatars	Crimea	200	84.8	Terebinskaia
Mountain Tatars	Crimea	300	84.8	Terebinskaia
South Coast Tatars	Crimea	200	85.3	Terebinskaia

TABLE 14.—*Cephalic index of peoples in the Tannu-Tuva Region*

People	Locality	No.	C. I.	Observer
Kemchik	Tannu-Tuva	124	80.5	IArkho
Seldzhek	Tannu-Tuva	40	83.1	Bunak
Tosingal	Tannu-Tuva	67	83.2	Bunak
Todzha	Tannu-Tuva	57	84.2	Bunak

school, describes the Mountain Tajiks, who, according to him, were the remnants of true Aryans, as the best-preserved, dark pigmented, . most brachycephalic type. Ujfalvy states that he encountered many blond Tajiks in the southeastern part of Ferghana Valley, where

TABLE 15.—*Cephalic index of peoples in Siberia*

People	Locality	No.	C. I.	Observer
Beltir	Khakass	119	79.2	I Arkho
Koibal	Khakass	41	79.8	I Arkho
Shortsi	Khakass	119	80.3	I Arkho
Kumandin	Oirot	99	80.3	I Arkho
Yakuts	Siberia	440	80.6	Schreiber
Kyzyl	Khakass	128	80.8	I Arkho
Teleut	Oirot	56	81.0	I Arkho
Sagai	Khakass	106	82.0	I Arkho
Maimalar	Oirot	125	82.0	I Arkho
Kachin	Khakass	207	82.1	I Arkho
Tubalar	Oirot	203	82.4	I Arkho
Telengit	Oirot	227	84.4	I Arkho
Altai-Kizhi	Oirot	200	84.5	I Arkho

TABLE 16.—*Cephalic index of peoples in Soviet Central Asia*

People	Locality	No.	C. I.	Observer
Iomud Turkomans	Khwarazm	107	75.2	I Arkho
Chaudyr Turkomans	Khwarazm	200	77.2	I Arkho
Mangyt Uzbeks	Khwarazm	80	80.7	I Arkho and Libman
Barlas Uzbeks	Turks	100	82.2	Belkina
Kaltai Uzbeks	Turks	100	83.4	Belkina
Uzbeks	Khwarazm	100	83.5	I Arkho and Libman
Kara-Kalpaks	Ferghana	100	83.8	I Arkho and Libman
Kirghiz	Ferghana	292	84.0	I Arkho
Uzbeks	Karshi town	200	84.1	Oshanin
Kara-Kalpaks	Kara-Kalpak A.S.S.R.	303	84.2	I Arkho and Libman
Kipchak Uzbeks	Ferghana	100	84.4	I Arkho
Uzbeks (tribal)	Ferghana	399	84.7	I Arkho
Astrakhan	Kazakhstan	105	84.9	Timofeeva and Debets
Kirghiz	Tien Shan	784	85.2	I Arkho
Bukhtarma	Kazakhstan	482	85.3	Baronov
Uzbeks	Shakhraziab town	200	85.3	Oshanin
Chuisk	Kazakhstan	120	85.4	I Arkho
Malaia	Kazakhstan	466	85.9	Rudenko
Kurama Uzbeks	Ferghana	672	85.9	I Arkho
Uigurs		450	87.1	I Arkho

chestnut-haired individuals predominate, and he explains their presence by the mixture of the local population with the original blond element, the Usuns [Wusuns], and partly with the blond Galchas.

Kuznetsov discerns three types of Tajiks:

1. Those with an Indo-European outline of the face, with regular features. Many individuals of this type have prominent ears, nose, and lips; dark, brown, or black eyes of medium size; and abundant dark hair on the face.

2. Strongly reminiscent of the Jewish type, thin skin on the face, large black almond-shaped eyes, aquiline nose; long, wavy, pitch-black beard.

3. A very rare type with light hair and eyes.

Shishlov agrees that the blond mixture came from the outside, but in the distant past, which is borne out by its absence among the modern Persians. The dark type, according to him, is the only typical Tajik type.

Tsimmerman distinguishes two types among the Tajiks of the Pskem Valley:

1. Tall, pale pink skin on the face, which does not become dark brown with sunburn; slender waist, broad shoulders, and, probably, light hair and eyes. (Less numerous.)

2. Not as tall, more darkly pigmented, more rugged build, and dark hair and eyes. (More numerous.)

Many other authors think that Tajiks belong to a firmly established and defined type.

Thus Middendorff (quoted from Shishlov) thinks that the Tajiks have a completely defined, sharply expressed, independent type, and does not agree with the opinion that the Valley Tajiks are a mixture of Persian, Arabic, Uzbek, and even Kirghiz blood.

He describes the Tajiks as very brachycephalic, with dark hair and eyes, with high and large cranium, rounded domed sinciput, noble, broad, and high forehead, protruding browridges, elevated glabella, deep nasal furrow, thick, protruberant, aquiline ("humped") nose, European eyes, and very thick, dark or light chestnut or red beard. Tajiks have large noses, medium-size hands and feet, and thin calves.

Maslovskii thinks that "Tajik" is a collective term. At first this term may have meant a group of various peoples united by a bond of religion who later were amalgamated into a new general type, represented by a clearly defined tribe known as the Tajiks. Maslovskii does not believe that it is possible to determine by means of anthropological measurements the original elements entering into the composition of the Tajik people.

10

He does not agree with the authors who think that only one people, by mixing with incoming tribes, produced the type known as Tajik, and that this type is represented by the Mountain Tajiks. Together with Barthold, Maslovskii thinks that in the mountains are found not the pure type of Tajiks, but only the various elements, which, mixing in the valley, produced the current tribe of Tajiks.

Maslovskii discerns five such elements, including the Arab, Jewish, Slavic, Armenian, and eastern Iranian types. The last group belongs to the "Alpine" race; according to Maslovskii this group had the greatest share in forming the Tajik type. Maslovskii's data exemplify the metaphysical method of constructing a scheme of the formation of a type: on one side he admits that it is impossible to discern the constituent elements of the type; on the other, he finds them in the mountains, even delineating their geographical boundaries.

1. *Arab type.*—Fan gorge; Samarkand region; Taghana; Hissar region; IAkh-Su River region. These are Arabs who have partly embraced Tajik culture.

2. *Jewish type.*—Widely spread. According to Maslovskii, Afghans belong to this group. Isolated communities of this type are found in the Zarafshan Mountains, in the Hissar and Karategin. This type is particularly pure in the upper course of the Zarafshan River, and in the lower course of the IAzgülem River. A strong admixture of this type is also found in Rushan and Badakhshan, and, partly, in Shugnan. On the basis of philological study, Ginzburg considers that it is impossible to suspect them of Semitic origin.

3. *Slavic type.*—To this type belong tribes of northern Karategin and Darvaz, and a group of mountaineers of Vakhan.

4. *Armenian type.*—On the left bank of the IAgnob River and in the northern section of Hissar and Karategin.

5. *Eastern Iranian type.*—Right bank of IAgnob, Hissar, and Karategin, and along the Darvaz River, from Kalai-Khuban to Vanch. This type forms the basis of the Tajik race.

According to Bogoiavlenskii, representatives of several types are found in each *kishlak* (hamlet). In its basic traits, the population is brachycephalic, and resembles the Persian type. The following are the characteristics of this dominant type: medium to tall stature, brachycephalic brown eyes; long, wavy (sometimes slightly curly) black beard, and a straight (sometimes aquiline) nose.

Another common type, to which belong the majority of some of the settlements, is the "Semitic type," which is characterized by fairly low stature, exceptionally thin lips, brown eyes, aquiline nose, narrow face, and a slightly curly black beard.

A third rarer type resembles Russian peasants with a light reddish beard, medium stature, greenish, sometimes light blue, eyes, and a straight nose.

A fourth type, having a more darkly pigmented body skin, very wide nose, thick lips, widely set eyes, differs greatly from the first three types.

T. A. Joyce, who published the materials collected by Sir Aurel Stein, illustrates the mechanistic approach toward the study of the variegated characters of the Tajiks. Together with Stein, Joyce believes that the best-preserved autochthonous type of Tajiks is found among the inhabitants of Rushan. Under the influence of the other types (wide- and narrow-nosed Turko-Mongol types) this type has changed to the north and south of Rushan.

Ginzburg criticizes this because the geographically central location is taken as the sole reason for considering Rushan as the original type. This type, according to Ginzburg, is also a result of a definite set of changes, and cannot be taken as the ancestral type.

Most of the remaining descriptions of Tajiks have been summarized by Shishlov.

The authors who have studied the Tajiks of various regions point out the difference between the Plains and Mountain Tajiks. Thus, according to Ujfalvy the Mountain Tajiks were more brachycephalic than the Plains Tajiks.[22]

According to several authors, Mountain Tajiks are more homogeneous in type than the Plains Tajiks. Thus, Arendarenko states that the types of the Karategin and the Darvaz Tajiks are similar. According to his descriptions, the Tajiks of these regions have swarthy skin; straight, thick hair, black, red, or chestnut; black and light brown eyes; regular, expressive faces; broad, steep, or low forehead, and bold nose.

The variation in the descriptions of Tajiks is due to the fact that the population of different regions was studied. Sometimes the descriptions were affected by the tendentiousness of authors, some of whom (Biddulph and Grebenkin) wanted to represent them as weak, undeveloped, and lacking in endurance, or those who described them as strong, broad-shouldered, and sturdy (Pokatilo).

Even some of the older explorers were known to point out the social, as well as historical and geographical, reasons for the variations of the types of Tajiks. Thus, Biddulph states that in certain localities the "higher classes" show best the admixture of "Aryan" blood.

---

[22] According to Ginzburg this was discovered to be wrong.

According to Grebenkin, the villagers prevailingly belong to his first group (with a greater admixture of Uzbek characters). The author of an anonymous old description of Tajiks states that rich Tajiks differ greatly from poor Tajiks in type, and that the richer they are, the greater admixture of Persian and Jewish blood they seem to have.

Shults points out the considerable difference between the "fine" type of the members of the noble families, most of whom derive from ancient military leaders, and the coarse type of the rest of the population.[23]

History of anthropological study of the Tajiks.—Probably the earliest measurements are those taken by A. I. Fedchenko in 1869, who measured 33 individuals, including four Tajiks from Zarafshan Valley. He also brought out several skulls. These materials were published by Bogdanov, who gave a detailed characterization of Turkestan crania, and noted their extreme brachycephaly. The crania studied by Bogdanov were characterized by exceptional height. It is interesting to record that at that time European anthropologists (Topinard and Girard de Rialle) thought that Central Asian Tajiks were dolichocephalic, probably basing their figures on de Khanikhov's materials on the Persian Tajiks. At a later date Topinard studied the crania brought back by Fedchenko,[24] and had more correct information regarding Mountain Tajiks.

Ujfalvy measured 58 Tajiks from Koghistan (upper Zarafshan Valley) whom he called "Galchas," 31 Tajiks from Ferghana, 29 from Samarkand, and 10 from Hissar.[25]

In 1890 Troll published brief data regarding 148 Central Asians, including 6 Tajiks.

In 1894 IAvorskii, who was particularly interested in Turkomans, measured 16 Tajik women. During 1895-1899 Maslovskii measured 583 individuals, of whom 381 were Plains Tajiks (no specified locality), 42 individuals from IAgnob and Darvaz, 21 from IAngulem, and 34 from Matchin. On the basis of his published figures it is impossible to justify his division of Tajik tribes into five types.

---

[23] Ginzburg states that such judgments, based on superficial observations, are typical for the adherents of the Indo-Aryan theory.

[24] Cf. Crânes Galtchas. Bull. Soc. d'Anthrop., p. 247, Paris, 1878.

[25] Ginzburg observes that these materials are too diffuse: great geographical range and differences of age; his claims regarding the common occurrence of light elements among the population have not been substantiated; his methods make it impossible to compare his figures with those obtained by more recent explorers.

In 1898 and 1901 N. V. Bogoiavlenskii made two trips along the upper course of the Amu, together with Bobrinskii and Smirnov.

The object of his trip was the study of the contemporary inhabitants of the Pamirs with a view to finding out whether they were autochthonous, and, if so, of what race; and, if immigrants, their origin. Bogoiavlenskii concluded that Tajiks of the Darvaz are of the Persian (Iranian) race, with a certain admixture of alien blood, and that their ancestors did not live in the mountains, but came from the valley of IAkh-Su under the pressure of invaders.

Bogoiavlenskii measured approximately 600 Tajiks from the valleys of Karategin, Darvaz, and the western Pamirs. Unfortunately, the death of Bogoiavlenskii prevented the conclusion of his labors on the publication of these data.[26]

The crania from Makshevat caves, brought back by Bogoiavlenskii, were studied by Zograf, who pointed out their extreme brachycephaly.

In 1912 Blagoveshchenskii published brief anthropometric data on 21 Tajiks (15 from Ferghana, 4 from Karategin and Darvaz, and 1 each from Afghanistan and Persia) whom he measured in the Eye Clinic at Marghellan.

Shults collected anthropological materials in the Pamirs during 1911-1912. He thinks that the Tajiks of the western Pamirs belong to an "Aryan" people who came from the west. According to Shults, Pamirian Tajiks are slender, of medium-tall structure, with elongated extremities, small feet and hands, and thin calves. Their faces are elongated, with prominent noses, deep-set, dark, usually brown, green, gray, rarely blue, eyes. Their hair is dark or brown, sometimes light. Skin color is brownish. Yet even a superficial examination discloses later admixtures of alien blood. Thus, the Afghan type manifests itself in a broader face; the Uzbek ("Sart") type in their straight noses and thicker lips; the Hindu type in the occasional strikingly narrow face; the Kirghiz type in high cheek bones. Sometimes the influence of the Jewish and Russian types was observed.

In one of his papers Shults gives the table of individual measurements of 35 individuals from Khorog, yet there was some confusion in the publication of the figures, and it is not possible to use them. Ginzburg's conclusions are obviously based on subjective observations and generalizations.

Sir Aurel Stein, who visited the Pamirs in 1915, states briefly that

---

[26] They were studied and systematized by Ginzburg in 1936, with the permission of the State Institute of Anthropology of the Moscow State University; the anthropometric data do not correspond with the preliminary conclusions reached by Bogoiavlenskii.

the inhabitants of the western Pamirs have best retained their original ancient type. This is particularly true of Rushan where, because of the extreme isolation of the region the purest type of *Homo alpinus* is represented among the Galchas. To the north of IAngulem and Vanch the Turkish element begins to be felt, both in the physical type and in the culture. The material collected by Stein includes 55 individuals from Vakhan, 34 from Shikashim, 40 from Shugnan, 58 from Rushan, 20 from IAngulem, 23 from Vanch, 25 from Darvaz, 26 from Karategin, and 16 Plains Tajiks from the oases of Bukhara.

This material was published by T. A. Joyce, who comes to the conclusion that it is possible to divide the Tajiks from the western Pamirs into two groups:

1. *Northern and northwesterly.*—IAngulem, Vanch, Darvaz. and Karategin: characterized by relative dolichocephaly, narrow noses, euryprosopy, and small stature.

2. *Southern and southeasterly.*—Shugnan, Ishkashim, and Vakhan: relatively brachycephalic, long-nosed, leptoprosopic, and tall.

The Tajiks from Rushan stand between the two types, forming the connecting link. This is explained by the fact that they represent the best-preserved type of the original inhabitant of the region, *Homo alpinus,* which was changed to the north and the south under the influence of the broad-nosed and the narrow-nosed Turko-Mongolian type. Plains Tajiks are also basically *Homo alpinus,* transformed under the influence of a wide-nosed Mongolian type (represented by the Kirghiz). In using the term "Alpine type" Joyce specifies that it does not imply the presence of any sort of kinship between the Pamirians and Alpines, but only a similarity of physical characteristics.

The nasal and facial measurements recorded by Joyce are much smaller than any other, probably owing to the fact that Stein and Joyce were not using the standard methods for this measurement. Joyce's method of mechanically summarizing the coefficients of racial similarity in the presence of small samples may lead to erroneous conclusions.

Several investigators, including Shishlov, Kapusto, and Shirokova-Divaeva, have studied the physical development of school children. Attention is also being paid to the study of blood groups of various peoples of Central Asia (IAsevich, IArkho, Vishnevskii, Petrov, and others). Unfortunately much of the material collected has not been published.

Chronologically, the study of the Tajiks since the Revolution has progressed as follows:

1. In 1925 V. V. Bunak studied the blood groups of the students of the various nationalities represented at the Institute of Oriental Peoples in Moscow. Among these were 25 Tajiks.

2. L. V. Oshanin, in the period between 1925-1927, investigated 433 Tajiks from Karategin employed in seasonal labor in Tashkent. The materials have not yet been published.

3. In 1926 Oshanin examined 100 Tajiks from Bukhara, and published detailed data regarding their racial composition.

According to Oshanin's conclusions, Tajiks belong to an independent "autochthonous" type which he calls *Homo sapiens indo-europaeus* var. *turkestanica centralis,* subsp. *iranoides brachycephalica,* with the focus of habitation within the Central Asian interfluvial region (between the basins of the Amu-Darya and Syr-Darya Rivers). Oshanin believes that this type does not differ from the ethnic groups, but admits the possibility of local variations.

Constitutionally, the majority of Bukharan Tajiks are asthenic, and only a small percentage are pycnic, which, according to Oshanin, points to the paratypical nature of the phenomenon. The general conclusion regarding constitutions is that the types found among the native population are no less real than those of some Europeans.

4. S. Tsimmerman studied, in 1925, 100 Tajiks aged 20 to 80 years, 73 of whom were from Pskem Valley near Tashkent, 19 from Mountainous Bukhara, and 8 from the Samarkand region. Tsimmerman distinguishes at least two types among the Tajiks, and thinks that the Tajik type is very near to that of the Uzbeks (having in view "Sarts" studied by Shishlov in Tashkent). Tsimmerman's materials were taken summarily, and it is possible that the types which he distinguishes came from various districts.

5. In 1926 the Academy of Sciences sent a large expedition into Central Asia under the leadership of Barthold. B. N. Vishnevskii, who was in charge of the anthropological work of the expedition, measured 279 Tajiks aged 16 to 61, from the Pendzhikent region. Blood groups were studied in addition to other physical characters. According to Vishnevskii, the Tajiks of the region are, anthropologically speaking, a variegated group. Among them were observed several Mongolian types. Blue-eyed, fair-skinned individuals were also found along with the ordinary brunets.

According to Vishnevskii, various types are found among the Tajiks, while the most prominent type is that of *Homo tauricus* (O. Reche). Of the individuals studied, 85 percent were mesosomic, 10 percent leptosomic, and 8 percent eurisomic. Unfortunately, the complete account of Vishnevskii's study has not yet been published.

In 1926 M. I. Gagaeva-Vishnevskaia collected anthropological materials on the women of Central Asia, among them 158 Tajiks. The only published results consist of a brief note by Vishnevskii stating that 20 percent belong to the leptosomic type, 75 percent to the meso-somic, 5 percent to eurisomic.

In 1927 G. G. Petrov measured 629 Tajiks from Ura-Tiube and Shakhristan regions and from Samarkand and vicinity. On the basis of the blood group distribution he concludes that the Plains Tajiks have been greatly mixed with the neighboring peoples. Petrov has also published a paper on the muscular strength of Tajiks from the vicinity of Ura-Tiube, and some other materials on Tajiks have been published by him. The bulk of his materials remains unpublished.

A. I. IArkho was in charge of the anthropological work of the Society for the Study of Soviet Asia, from 1928-1931. In 1929 he studied 200 Tajiks from Khasan (Ferghana region). He thought that the Tajiks were Europeoids, and, admitting that the type *Homo sapiens indo-europaeus* is not homogeneous in Central Asia, classifies them as the Pamiro-Ferghan subtype. "This is a brachycephalic type, with a short skull, straight forehead, hair development above medium, straight or slightly convex nose. . . . It is doubtful whether this type stands alone in the European groups. It is probable that it is connected with the short-headed population of Vorderasien and the non-Armenoid population of the Caucasus."

IArkho noticed some variations among the tribal and territorial groups. According to him, the mestization between the Europeoid and Mongoloid types in Central Asia has progressed to such an extent that even the most Europeoid and Mongoloid groups are not lacking characters of the opposite type.

The expeditions led by IArkho have also collected materials bear-ing on the physical development of the populations of Central Asia. Very little of this material has been published.

Korovnikov, who in 1928 participated in an expedition for the study of endemic goiter in the region of the Vanch River, measured 80 individuals who were not greatly afflicted by endocrine disorders. He recorded data bearing on racial and constitutional characters. With Oshanin, Korovnikov classifies the Tajiks of the Vanch area as *Homo sapiens indo-europaeus* var. *brachymorphus* (Giuffrida-Rug-gieri) with pronounced traits of the Iranic type. The eastern Iranian type of Vanch mountaineers, classed as Alpines, is the connecting link between the mountaineers of Europe and Asia.

V. K. IAsevich measured in detail 150 Karategin Tajiks (Garm) and 202 Tajiks from Matcha during an expedition in 1930. This material, cited after a report of Oshanin at the December 1932 meeting of the anthropological section of the IAE, is not known. We have also learned that at the end of 1932 IAsevich investigated the blood groups of 831 Tajiks from Karategin, 1,570 Tajiks from Isfara, and 309 Tajiks from Matcha.

Other yet unpublished anthropological material is known to have been collected by P. K. Arkhibaev in the Kurgan Tiubin and the Kuliab regions of the Tajik S.S.R.

Head length (M = 182.80) is medium, with regular distribution of variants, and slight preponderance of greater lengths.

Greatest length is found in Karategin; shortest in southwestern Darvaz. There is little difference between Plains and Mountain Tajiks in this respect.

A comparable length is observed among Ferghana (IArkho) and Angren (IArkho) and Tashkent (Shishlov) Uzbeks; also among Shakhrasiab and Karshi Uzbeks (Oshanin). The greatest deviation from this length is found among the Mangyt clan of Uzbeks and the Uzbeks from Khwarazm (Khoresm). Samarkand and Karshi Arabs have a similar head length, as well as Central Asian Jews (Oshanin and Weissenberg). Pamir Kirghiz (Joyce) have a similar length, probably because of geographical proximity. The Issyk-Kul, Ferghana, and Tien Shan Kirghiz have a much greater length.

Turkomans have a much greater length, and this is their most pronounced difference from Tajiks. Persians have also greater length. A similar and, occasionally, greatly exceeding length is found among Afghans and Hindus (Risley).

Head breadth (M = 152.55) is also medium, although greater breadth is found much more frequently than greater length. Karategin region gives a greater breadth than Darvaz. Mountain Tajiks' breadth is less than that of Ferghana Tajiks (IArkho) and Plains Tajiks (Joyce), with the exception of Karategin and Muminabad Tajiks. Bukhara and Pskem Valley Tajiks vary within the same range. Tajiks from western Pamirs also have smaller breadth.

The head breadth of the Tajiks approaches that of Jews, Khwarazm Uzbeks, Shakhrasiab, and Karshi Uzbeks (Oshanin), Tashkent Uzbeks ("Sarts") (Shishlov), and Mangyt clan (IArkho). Ferghana and Angren Uzbeks (IArkho) have greater breadth. Pamir Kirghiz have similar breadth, while those of Ferghana, Tien Shan, and Issyk-Kul have greater breadth. Arabs (Samarkand) have similar or greater breadth than Mountain Tajiks. Variety of breadth, greater and smaller than that of Mountain Tajiks, is found in Afghanistan. Turkomans, Persians, and Hindus have smaller breadth than Tajiks.

Bregma-tragion diameter (M=127.55) is great; large deviations occur. This height is greater in Darvaz than in Karategin. It is similar to the height of Bukhara and Pskem Tajiks, less than that of Ferghana.

The head height of Karategin Tajiks approaches that of Central Asian Jews and Shakhrasiab Uzbeks; of southwestern Darvaz, approaches that of Uzbeks, Kirghiz, and Turkomans (IArkho). Hindus (Risley) vary within the same range, being occasionally greater.

Tsimmerman's [27] claim that the Tajiks' head height stands on the border between medium and small sizes cannot be accepted, as Bunak's scheme is not applicable in Central Asia; according to this scheme, head height is very high, and not medium, if one compares all the available figures from Central Asia.

Cephalic index (M=83.5) is brachycephalic with a tendency toward hyperbrachycephaly; only a few dolichocephals have been found. The variations are small, the highest being found in southwestern Darvaz where the head form approaches hyperbrachycephaly. Lowest is found in central and eastern Darvaz. The cephalic index of the Mountain Tajiks equals that of Ferghana, Pendzhikent, and Bukharan Tajiks, and with the population of the western Pamirs (except Ishkashim and Vakhan, where it is higher).

The cephalic index of Mountain Tajiks (Karategin and southwestern Darvaz) approaches that of Kirghiz, Uzbek (except Mangyt) Jews, and Arabs, and differs greatly from that of Turkomans, Persians, Hindus, and some Afghan tribes.

This similarity of cephalic index of Tajiks with other Central Asian peoples (except Turkomans), even with the highly mongolized Kirghiz, forced Ginzburg to join Oshanin and IArkho in their opinion that in Central Asia absolute measurements of the head permit a better differentiation of racial types than the cephalic indices.

Height-length index (M=69.77) agrees with the other characterizations of the extremely high head of Mountain Tajiks. Orthocephalics are few; chamaecephalics are practically absent.

Occipital deformation was found in 69 percent of cases, in Darvaz more frequently than in Karategin. This deformation was usually asymmetrical.[28] Asymmetrical deformity is usually due to the influence of the position of the infant's head in the cradle.

---

[27] Following Bunak's method.

[28] Ginzburg differentiated the naturally flat occiput from the deformed "flattened" occiput.

According to Oshanin, Bukharan Tajiks had a flattened occiput in 20 percent of the cases; deformed occiput in 70 percent of the cases. A flat occiput is more common among Jews. In the case of Uzbeks, percentages vary. Among Uzbeks ("Sarts") from Tashkent, Shishlov found 70.3 percent of deformed occiputs; 41.2 percent of cranial asymmetry. Among Vanch Tajiks Korovnikov found 34.7 percent occipital deformation.

Within the range of probable error, the correlation between breadth and length in the entire material (without taking into consideration the degree of occipital deformation) is so little as to be practically absent. The correlation calculated for certain groups having varying degrees of deformation shows that the correlation is positive where deformation is absent, the correlation is lessened where deformation is slight, and negative where deformation is strong. The validity of this observation is proved by the fact that the coefficient of correlation greatly exceeds its probable error.

Stature.—Mountain Tajiks are of medium stature $(M = 165.83)$, with a preponderance of medium-tall and tall individuals.

Considerably lower stature is found in central and eastern Darvaz. The lowest stature has been observed in Vakhio (eastern portion of Tavil Darya region) and in the Kalai Khumb region (Piandzh coastal region).

A comparison of stature disclosed that the Ferghana and Plains Tajiks have in general greater stature than the Mountain Tajiks. The stature increases in the western Pamirs, except for Tajiks and Jews measured in Bukhara by Oshanin.

The stature of other people of Central Asia varies greatly, so that this measurement is of little value for general diagnostic characterization of the group.

The population of central Darvaz, because of their lower stature, have a smaller trunk length and a correspondingly larger relative sitting-height index. This is also true of the population along Piandzh and in the Tavil Darya region.

Bukharan and Pskem Valley Tajiks do not differ from Mountain Tajiks in their relative sitting-height index. Vanch Tajiks differ in this respect (probably because of the technique used by Korovnikov). Jews from Bukhara and Kernini have the same index as Mountain Tajiks, and slightly lower than Bukharan Tajiks.

Uzbeks of Shakhrasiab and Khwarazm have a higher, those of Tashkent a much lower, relative sitting-height index. While the variations of this index among the Uzbeks parallel those of Tajiks, in general the former are slightly more brachyskelic.

TABLE 17.—*Head size and cephalic index under varying degrees of occipital deformation* (24-50 years old)

Region	No deformation				Adjusted for deformation								Unadjusted for deformation			
					Slight deformation				Medium and strong deformation							
	No.	L.	B.	C.I.	No.	L.	B.	C.I.	No.	L.	B.	C.I.	No.	L.	B.	C.I.
Karategin	99	185.40	152.34	82.0	56	183.11	156.11	85.3	19	180.22	156.21	86.7	174	184.10	153.90	83.5
Central and eastern Darvaz	17	186.17	150.92	80.7	93	183.59	151.49	82.5	22	183.40	156.12	85.3	150	183.70	152.0	83.5
Southwestern Darvaz	28	183.44	151.55	82.7	97	181.42	150.71	83.0	33	177.74	155.07	87.2	184	180.90	151.60	84.0
Totals	144	185.05	153.03	82.7	246	182.62	152.22	83.3	74	179.98	155.66	86.5	508	182.80	152.55	83.5

TABLE 18.—*Correlation between head length and head breadth* (24-50 years old)

Region	Undeformed			Adjusted for deformation						Unadjusted for deformation		
				Slightly deformed			Medium and strong deformation					
	No.	R.	M_r	No.	R.	M_r	No.	R.	M_r	No.	R.	M_r
Karategin	99	0.134	0.083	56	0.083	0.133	19	−0.073	0.228	174	+0.032	0.075
Central and eastern Darvaz	17	0.126	0.22	93	0.052	0.133	22	0.102	0.191	150	+0.054	0.081
Southwestern Darvaz	28	0.279	0.04	97	0.059	0.10	33	−0.318	0.157	184	−0.097	0.073
Totals	144	0.125	0.013	246	0.0875	0.015	74	−0.102	0.012	508	−0.0208	0.044

TABLE 19.—*Head height*

TURKESTAN

People	No.	Mean	Author
Bukhara	163	128.0	Oshanin
Pskem Valley [1]	100	127.07	
Ferghana	200	132.35	IArkho
Teke	51	129.0	IAvorskii
Chaudyrs	200	129.13	IArkho
Iomuds	107	132.33	IArkho
Arabs	29	155.0	Maslovskii
Arabs	17	155.0	Maslovskii

AFGHANISTAN

Afghans	18	153.0	Matseevskii

[1] And Mountainous Bukhara.

TABLE 20.—*Height-length index*

TURKESTAN

People	No.	Mean	Author
Bukhara	163	70.82	Oshanin
Pskem Valley [1]	100	71.33	
Ferghana	200	71.47	IArkho
Chaudyrs	200	66.88	IArkho
Iomuds	107	68.40	IArkho

AFGHANISTAN

Afghans	18	74.43	Matseevskii

[1] And Mountainous Bukhara.

TABLE 21.—*Physiognomic height*

TURKESTAN

People	No.	Mean	Author
Ferghana	200	186.92	IArkho
Teke	51	186.0	IAvorskii
Chaudyrs	200	184.87	IArkho
Iomuds	107	184.28	IArkho

IRAN

Iranians	50	191.0	Maslovskii

AFGHANISTAN

Afghans	18	198.0	Matseevskii
Afghans	18	190.0	Poiarkov

[1] And Mountainous Bukhara.

The Kirghiz are the most brachyskelic people of Central Asia according to all available literature, and invariably possess higher relative sitting-height indexes.

Average data for stature and cephalic-index correlations was tabulated for other Central Asian groups, and an apparently reverse phenomenon was observed—i.e., greater stature was accompanied by lesser cephalic index. In order to investigate this contradiction, a small group of brachycephalic peoples was taken (Kirghiz, Uzbek, Kara-Kalpak, Jews, and Arabs of Central Asia), and the coefficient of correlation was calculated for the group. This was insignificant but negative ($R = -0.076 \pm 0.199$), and typical for intertribal correlation of stature and cephalic index pointed out by Pearson.

The positive correlation among the Tajiks seemed to indicate the intratribal character of the difference, which would seem to strengthen

TABLE 22.—*Correlation between stature and cephalic index of Tajiks aged 24 to 50*

Region	Deformed occiput			Undeformed occiput		
	N.	R.	M_r	N.	R.	M_r
Karategin	74	+ 0.0203	0.068	28	− 0.141	0.081
Central and eastern Darvaz.	111	+ 0.006	0.095	18	− 0.32	0.215
Southwestern Darvaz	129	+ 0.081	0.031	27	− 0.031	0.19
Totals	314	+ 0.094	0.006	143	− 0.120	0.071

Ginzburg's premise that the Tajiks belong to a single group, fairly homogeneous in character.

An attempt was made to verify this conclusion by calculating the individual correlation data for the entire group and for the regions.

Cranial deformation was found to be a significant factor. In the presence of occipital deformation the correlation was found to be insignificant but invariably positive.

In the presence of undeformed occipita the correlation is negative, and the coefficient of correlation is fairly sizable. Thus, it is clearly seen that the cephalic index decreases with the increase of stature, but that occipital deformation entirely obscures these relationships.

In comparing cephalic index with stature it may be seen that the decrease of cephalic index progresses until tall medium stature is reached, but that in the presence of high (170.0 cm.) stature cephalic index increases both in the case of deformed and undeformed occipita.

The problem of interdependence of cephalic index and stature is an independently important problem of ontogenetic development, of particular interest in connection with the study of deformed occipita.

Facial dimensions and indices.—Morphological face height (nasion-gnathion) ($M = 126.92$) is great, but in comparison with the facial height of other Central Asian peoples is medium. High faces predominate. In Karategin face height (M = 129.34) is greater than in Darvaz (M = 125.67, 125.35). The comparison of data with the results obtained by various authorities is difficult and sometimes impossible because of techniques employed. Oshanin and IArkho accepted as nasion the lower end of the eyebrows. Korovnikov measured from the deepest point of the bridge as did Tsimmerman and Stein.

According to Stein (Joyce) Darvaz facial height is also less than in Karategin. In Vanch his measurements agreed with those of Korovnikov, disclosing a greater height than in Darvaz and comparable to facial height in Karategin. Ginzburg and others found, however, that facial height in Vanch is less than that of Karategin.

It is still more difficult to compare the facial height of Tajiks with that of other peoples. Uzbeks and Jews have varying facial height, sometimes greater and sometimes less than that of Tajiks. The same phenomenon prevails among Turkomans, the Iomuds equaling that of the Tajiks, the Chaudyrs being greater. Arabs and Kirghiz have greater facial height than Tajiks.

Morphological face height, while valuable for characterizations of various groups within a people, is, in many cases, not indicative of differences between various peoples.

Physiognomic face height (M = 182.52) is medium, with a preponderance of greater sizes. In general, it varies by regions comparably to the morphological face heights. It is easier to compare face height with the figures disclosed by various authors. IArkho's Ferghana Tajiks have somewhat greater face height than Mountain Tajiks. Kirghiz have greater face height; Uzbeks vary, giving smaller and greater values, although the latter prevail. The Turkomans range between that of Ferghana and Mountain Tajiks.

The bizygomatic breadth (M = 140.66) is medium, compared to the European facial breadth, but rather low for Central Asia. The distribution of broader and narrower faces is regular. In Karategin facial height is greater than in Darvaz. Facial breadth in southwestern Darvaz is somewhat less than in central Darvaz. The methods of measurements vary greatly. Karategin Tajiks approach IArkho's and Maslov's Ferghana and Plains Tajiks. Pskem Valley and Bukharan Tajiks have narrower faces and are comparable to central Darvaz Tajiks. Korovnikov's data from Vanch cannot be utilized for comparative purposes because of difference of method used. Joyce's data show greater figures for Karategin than for Darvaz.

Kirghiz have greater facial breadth than Tajiks. Uzbeks and Turkomans vary comparably to Tajiks in Karategin and Darvaz respectively. Arab facial breadth approaches that of Karategin Tajiks. Smallest bizygomatic breadth is found in the Jews who are comparable to southwestern Darvaz Tajiks.

Frontal height (M = 55.5) is medium, but varies by regions. The greatest is found in southwestern Darvaz (M = 56.21); Karategin (M = 55.04) has the intermediate place, while lowest frontal height is found in central and eastern Darvaz (M = 53.06).

Minimum frontal diameter (M = 107.51) is of average size for Central Asia, and does not vary greatly in different regions, being greater in Karategin and lesser in southwestern Darvaz than in central and eastern Darvaz.

Frontal-zygomatic index varies to a greater degree because of greater intensivity of the decrease of zygomatic diameter in various regions.

Tajiks from Ferghana, Turkomans, and Chaudyrs have a similar index; Kirghiz and Uzbeks, somewhat greater; Iomuds, much smaller.

Bigonial breadth is small and varies: Karategin 108.23; central and eastern Darvaz 107.89; and southwestern Darvaz 106.36. Ferghana Tajiks and Kirghiz have greater breadth, Uzbeks and Turkomans the same or greater.

Morphological face index (M = 90.17) is leptoprosopic. There are more hyperleptoprosopic individuals than mesoprosopic. Euryprosopics were very rare and hypereuryprosopic individuals were practically absent. Morphological face index does not vary by region, greatest deviation being in Vanch region, with a lower index prevailing as a result of generally lower morphological height.

Because of variation of method, it is impossible to compare the morphological face index of the Mountain Tajiks with most of the other peoples measured. Ferghana (IArkho), Pendzhikent (Vishnevskii), and Bukhara (Oshanin) Tajiks have a similar index as do the Kirghiz, Uzbeks, and Jews; Turkomans have a slightly higher index.

Physiognomic face index (M = 77.55) is of medium size, with preponderance of lower values. The variations are not great and, in general, correspond to those of the morphological face index.

The physiognomic face index of southwestern Darvaz and Surkh Oba Valley Tajiks is similar to that of Ferghana Tajiks. The index of Kirghiz, Uzbeks, and Turkomans varies within the same range as that of Mountain Tajiks.

Thus it may be stated that in Central Asia facial indices are better suited for the characterization of subdivisions within a group than for comparison of larger groups ("intro-group" rather than "inter-group").

Vertical face profile.—Straight in the majority of cases (85.62 percent); slightly prominent in 13.7 percent of cases; prognathism rare (1.31 percent), usually among Karategins.

Straight profile most prevalent in southwestern Darvaz (97.48 percent). Because of discrepancy of methods the data cannot be compared with those of other recorders; yet it appears from Oshanin's figure that the profile of both Uzbeks and Jews is more prominent than that of Mountain Tajiks.

General form of face is ovoid in 40.08 percent. Breadth of mouth medium. Lip thickness medium, 47.27 percent, and thick, 34.42 percent. Chin prominent, 89.76 percent.

TABLE 23.—*Position of eyeball*

Group	Locality	Deepest Percent	Medium Percent	Protuberant Percent	Author
Tajiks	Darvaz II	40.26	58.49	1.26	Ginzburg
Tajiks	Bukhara	5.0	62.0	33.0	Oshanin
Uzbeks	Shakhrasiab	4.9	85.0	10.2	Oshanin
Jews	Bukhara	8.0	65 0	27.0	Oshanin
Jews	Shakhrasiab	7.8	79.4	12.8	Oshanin

Thus the face of Mountain Tajiks may be characterized as narrow, of medium height, with medium or weakly expressed cheek bones, medium or strong cross section, and straight vertical profile.

In general, Karategin Tajiks have greater absolute dimensions of face than the Tajiks of Darvaz.

External eye.—Eye opening spindle-shaped in 98.70 percent; rare cases of almond-shaped eyes are mostly from Karategin and are more common among Bukharan Tajiks and still more common among Bukharan Jews (Oshanin). However, he remarks that this does not present valid enough difference between Tajiks, Uzbeks, and Jews. The majority of Kirghiz have almond-shaped eyes. Vanch Tajiks (Korovnikov) cannot be compared with the present series because of variations in methods of measurement. Eye width (distance between inner and outer corners) was medium in 48.27 percent. Narrow eyes are more common in Karategin; wide eyes in southwestern Darvaz.

Eyes deep-set, 40.26 percent; medium (southwestern Darvaz only), 58.49 percent. Protuberant eyeballs observed only in Shuroabad and Muminabad regions (1.26 percent).

Mongoloid fold of upper eyelid found only in 3.68 percent, and is usually not strongly expressed. Ginzburg did not record one fully developed Mongoloid fold among adults (24 to 50). Mongoloid fold was most frequent in Karategin (Surkh Oba Valley), and most rare in central and eastern Darvaz.

Mongoloid fold is much more common among nonadult individuals. In a young group (18 to 23) it was absent in 78.34 percent, weakly developed in 19.11 percent, strongly expressed and medium in 1.27 percent of cases. In this age group, Mongoloid fold was most commonly present in southwestern Darvaz.

Mongoloid fold is as rarely observed among Bukharan Tajiks (Oshanin), Pendzhikent Tajiks (Vishnevskii), and Ferghana Tajiks (IArkho). Tsimmerman observed a Mongoloid fold more frequently in Pskem Valley. However, the ages were not differentiated in comparative data.

Mongoloid fold is rarely observed among the Jews; among Turkomans (IArkho) percentages vary in groups, and the same is true of Uzbeks although here it is more clearly expressed than among Tajiks. The same is true of Kirghiz with the exception of the Issyk-Kul group, where it was found in the majority of cases. This variation may be due to difference of recording method.

In contrast to the Mongoloid fold the upper eye fold among Mountain Tajiks was absent in 36.15 percent. It was weakly developed in 25.97 percent, medium in 25.32 percent, and strong in 12.56 percent of all individuals.

The upper fold is more common in Darvaz than in Karategin; in southwestern Darvaz it is better expressed than in central and eastern Darvaz. Comparative study of upper fold discloses that it is somewhat better expressed among Pendzhikent Tajiks (Vishnevskii) to a degree similar to that observable in southwestern Darvaz. Various degrees of development of upper fold are found among Uzbeks and Jews. In general, Jews have less-developed upper fold than the Tajiks, and much less-developed than the Uzbeks.

Thus, it may be concluded that the Mongoloid traits in the structure of the eye are but slightly expressed among the Mountain Tajiks, but that Mongoloid influence is undoubtedly felt. This may be seen through the study of the younger individuals, and also from the relatively high percentage of strongly and less strongly expressed fold of the upper lid. This influence is most strongly felt in southwestern Darvaz, then in Karategin, and, least of all, in central and eastern Darvaz.

Nose structure.—The nose is usually of medium size (54.33 percent). Large noses appear in 39.18 percent, small in 6.49 percent.

TABLE 24.—*Comparative table on upper eyelid*

People	Locality	Mongol fold Percent	Upper fold Percent	Author
Tajiks	Bukhara	5.2	...	Oshanin
Tajiks	Pskem Valley	11.0	...	Tsimmerman
Tajiks	Pendzhikent	4.3	89.6	Vishnevskii
Tajiks	Ferghana	5.0	...	IArkho
Tajiks	Karategin	5.26	55.55	Ginzburg
Tajiks	C. and E. Darvaz	2.26	58.33	Ginzburg
Tajiks	S. W. Darvaz	3.14	77.36	Ginzburg
Uzbeks	Khwarazm	25.0	...	Oshanin
Uzbeks	Shakhrasiab	10.1	72.4	Oshanin
Uzbeks	Karshi	22.5	...	Oshanin
Uzbeks	Samarkand	24.2	98.1	Vishnevskii
Uzbeks	Ferghana	7.1	...	IArkho
Uzbeks	Angren	7.5	...	IArkho
Uzbek Kipchaks	Ferghana	23.0	...	IArkho
Uzbek Mangyt	Ferghana	35.4	...	IArkho
Jews	Bukhara	0.0	...	Oshanin
Jews	Shakhrasiab	1.0	21.6	Oshanin
Jews	Samarkand	0.0	87.3	Vishnevskii
Turkomans (Chaudyrs)..		24.6	80.3	IArkho
Turkomans (Iomuds)...		6.6	67.0	IArkho
Kirghiz	Issyk-Kul	86.0	...	Oshanin
Kirghiz	Tien Shan	24.0	95.0	IArkho
Kirghiz	Ferghana	19.4	...	IArkho

TABLE 25.—*Comparative table of development of upper eye fold*

People	Locality	No.	None Percent	Light Percent	Medium Percent	Strong Percent	Author
Tajiks...	Karategin	171	44.45	20.46	25.73	9.36	Ginzburg
Tajiks...	Darvaz I	132	41.67	35.60	16.67	6.06	Ginzburg
Tajiks...	Darvaz II	159	22.64	23.90	32.08	21.39	Ginzburg
Tajiks...	Pendzhikent	279	10.4	25.0	43.9	19.8	Vishnevskii
Uzbeks (tribesmen)		...	1.9	10.2	65.0	22.9	Vishnevskii
Uzbeks ..	Shakhrasiab	190	27.5	44.0	25.5	2.9	Oshanin
Jews	Samarkand	143	12.7	31.4	50.8	5.1	Vishnevskii
Jews	Shakhrasiab	101	78.4	17.0	4.6	....	Oshanin
Kirghiz..	Tien Shan and Ferghana	...	5.0	....	....	....	IArkho

Straight profile is most common (40.47 percent). Wavy nose, 24.03 percent; convex, 17.75 percent; concave, 11.47 percent; "with a break," 6.28 percent. For convenience, these forms have been grouped in three classes:

1. Concave, 11.47 percent.
2. Straight (straight and "wavy" concavo-convex), 64.50 percent.
3. Convex (convex and "with break"), 25.03 percent.

Concave noses are more common in Darvaz, especially in the central and eastern portions, than in Karategin, while convex ones are more common in Karategin. Concave noses are least common among Bukharan Tajiks. Pendzhikent Tajiks do not differ from the Mountain Tajiks from Darvaz. Korovnikov's Vanch Tajiks have an unusually large percentage of concave noses (32.5 percent). It is probable that his figures are affected by age range represented.

Comparison with other data discloses that Uzbeks have nearly the same distribution of variations. Jews and Arabs have fewer concave and more convex forms. The Kirghiz of Issyk-Kul have a much greater percent of concave forms, which cannot be said of Tien Shan Kirghiz.

The profile of the bony and the cartilaginous structure of the nose was observed only in southwestern Darvaz. No significant difference was observed between this character of Tajiks and of other peoples of Central Asia (IArkho's data), so that it was found difficult to utilize them for racial criteria.

General protuberance of the nasal ridge was observed only in Darvaz. Medium protuberance was observed in the majority of cases. Strong protuberance was next numerous; least numerous were the cases of slight protuberance. In central and eastern Darvaz very prominent noses were more common than in southwestern Darvaz, with the exception of the Muminabad region.

In Central Asia this is a very typical trait, differentiating the Mongolized Kirghiz and some other Mongolized tribes much better than the profile of the bony and cartilaginous structure.

According to Oshanin the Jews have even more prominent nose ridges than the Tajiks.

The bridge height of Tajiks was usually medium (55.41 percent) less commonly great (42.21 percent). Low nose bridge was observed only in 2.38 percent.

Small nasal bridges were much fewer in central and eastern Darvaz than in all other regions. There were exceptionally few individuals with high nasal bridges in Vanch.

Mountain Tajiks have the highest nasal bridge in Central Asia with the exception of the Jews, who have a still higher percentage. Bukharan Tajiks, like Mountain Tajiks, have high nasal bridges. Ferghana Tajiks approach the Uzbeks. Kirghiz, Kara-Kalpaks, Mangyt Uzbeks, and Chaudyr Turkomans have greater percentages of individuals with low nasal bridges and smaller percentages of

TABLE 26.—*Comparative table of nasal profile*

People	Locality	Concave Percent	Straight or concavo-convex Percent	Convex or aquiline Percent	Author
Tajiks	Pendzhikent	17.7	63.3	23.1	Vishnevskii
Tajiks	Bukhara	5.0	51.0	44.0	Oshanin
Tajiks	Pskem Valley	12.0	42.0	46.0	Tsimmerman
Tajiks	Vanch	32.5	52.5	15.0	Korovnikov
Tajiks	Ferghana	...	...	19.6	IArkho
Uzbeks	Khwarazm	16.0	58.0	26.0	Oshanin
Uzbeks	Shakhrasiab	13.2	67.3	19.5	Oshanin
Uzbeks	Karshi	22.5	57.5	20.0	Oshanin
Uzbeks (clansmen)....		20.4	72.9	6.08	Vishnevskii
Uzbeks (clansmen)....	Ferghana	7.3	64.9	28.8	IArkho
Uzbeks (clansmen)....	Angren	...	...	28.1	IArkho
Uzbeks Kipchaks		9.1	62.6	28.3	IArkho
Uzbeks Mangyts		2.5	95.0	2.5	IArkho
Jews	Bukhara	5.0	27.0	68.0	Oshanin
Jews	Shakhrasiab	2.9	32.0	65.0	Oshanin
Jews	Samarkand	7.0	51.2	41.7	Vishnevskii
Arabs	Karshi	3.0	48.0	49.0	Oshanin
Turkomans Chaudyrs..	Khwarazm	8.6	70.7	20.7	IArkho
Turkomans Iomuds ...	Khwarazm	2.8	71.1	27.1	IArkho
Kirghiz	Issyk-Kul	48.0	52.0	...	Oshanin
Kirghiz	Tien Shan	12.2	67.6	20.2	IArkho
Kirghiz	Ferghana	13.0	64.3	22.7	IArkho
Kara-Kalpaks	Kara-Kalpak A.S.S.R.	5.0	82.3	12.7	IArkho
Kara-Kalpaks	Ferghana	10.1	69.7	20.2	IArkho

individuals with higher nasal bridges. This observation is also valid for differentiating the anthropological types of Central Asia. Breadth of nasal bridge is usually medium (51.51 percent); small breadth is found in 34.85 percent, and great in 13.64 percent of cases. Broad-bridged individuals were more common in Karategin than in Darvaz.

Comparing the Tajik's nasal bridge with that of other peoples, we see that they stand in this respect nearest to Jews. Among Uzbeks and Arabs there are few individuals with narrow bridges.

TABLE 27.—*Comparative table of nasal bridge height*

People	Locality	No.	Low Percent	Medium Percent	High Percent	Author
Tajiks ....Bukhara		100	3.0	68.0	29.0	Oshanin
Tajiks ....Ferghana		199	13.1	70.8	16.1	IArkho
Tajiks ....Karategin		171	2.34	50.87	46.78	Ginzburg
Tajiks ....Darvaz I		132	2.27	68.94	28.79	Ginzburg
Tajiks ....Darvaz II		159	2.52	49.06	48.43	Ginzburg
Uzbeks ....Shakhrasiab		190	7.9	84.2	7.9	Oshanin
Uzbeks ....Karshi		198	14.1	79.3	6.6	Oshanin
Uzbeks Mangyts		78	46.1	51.3	2.6	IArkho
Uzbeks ....Khiva		100	10.0	80.0	10.0	IArkho
Uzbeks (*not* clans)..Ferghana		386	10.1	68.4	21.5	IArkho
Uzbeks Kipchaks		99	21.2	68.7	10.1	IArkho
Uzbeks ....Angren		82	15.9	70.7	13.4	IArkho
Uzbeks ....Khwarazm		100	7.0	64.0	29.0	Oshanin
Kara-Kalpaks ....Kara-Kalpak A.S.S.R.		299	43.2	56.5	0.3	IArkho
Kara-Kalpaks ....Ferghana		99	28.3	64.7	7.1	IArkho
Turkomans Chaudyrs.Khwarazm		198	28.3	66.2	5.5	IArkho
Turkomans Iomuds ..Khwarazm		107	7.5	68.2	24.3	IArkho
Kirghiz ....Issyk-Kul		100	67.0	27.0	6.0	Oshanin
Kirghiz ....Tien Shan		769	30.0	65.6	4.4	IArkho
Kirghiz ....Ferghana		154	26.6	68.8	4.6	IArkho
Jews ....Bukhara		100	2.0	36.0	62.0	Oshanin
Jews ....Shakhrasiab		103	1.0	25.2	73.8	Oshanin
Arabs ....Karshi		100	2.0	68.0	30.0	Oshanin

TABLE 28.—*Comparative table of nasal bridge breadth*

People	Locality	Narrow Percent	Medium Percent	Broad Percent	Author
Tajiks ....Karategin		35.67	46.78	17.54	Ginzburg
Tajiks ....Darvaz I		31.82	53.79	14.4	Ginzburg
Tajiks ....Darvaz II		36.48	54.71	8.81	Ginzburg
Tajiks ....Bukhara		26.0	66.0	8.0	Oshanin
Uzbeks ....Khwarazm		19.0	61.0	20.0	Oshanin
Uzbeks ....Shakhrasiab		4.7	88.4	6.9	Oshanin
Uzbeks ....Karshi		4.5	83.0	12.5	Oshanin
Jews ....Shakhrasiab		33.7	66.3	...	Oshanin
Jews ....Bukhara		34.0	58.0	7.0	Oshanin
Arabs ....Karshi		6.0	75.0	19.0	Oshanin

The nasal tip is most commonly rounded (55.85 percent) ; a sharp nose is found in 35.72 percent of cases. Angular tip was found in 6.53 percent, blunt tip in 2.82 percent. Rounded tip was slightly less common in Darvaz than in Karategin. Sharp tip was most common in southwestern Darvaz. Angular and blunt forms were found most commonly in central and eastern Darvaz. With regard to the form of the tip, the Mountain Tajiks stand midway between the Jews (among whom a sharp form is more common) and Uzbeks (among whom sharp form is rarer, but rounded and blunt forms are more common, according to Oshanin).

The inclination of the nasal tip is more commonly horizontal (51.51 percent) or pointing downward (42.21 percent). The deviations from the horizontal are usually slight. There is no great difference between regional degrees of nasal inclination. A slightly higher percentage of raised tips is found only in the Kalai Khumb region along the Piandzh River and in Vanch. From a comparison of our data with those obtained by IArkho and Oshanin, it was observed that Mountain Tajiks differ in this respect from the other groups of Central Asia, having the highest nasal index (i.e., having the smallest percentage of raised noses). Shakhrasiab Jews are nearest to them in this respect. Ferghana Tajiks and Angren Uzbeks are the next nearest. Tien Shan and Kuram Kirghiz are slightly more snub-nosed.

The inclination of the base of the nose was examined only in southwestern Darvaz; a relatively large percentage of individuals with upward trend was found in Shuroabad region, and a relatively small percentage of such individuals occurred in the Muminabad region.

According to IArkho's figures only Angren Uzbeks are comparable to Shuroabad Tajiks in this regard. All other groups, including Ferghana Tajiks, give a much lower percentage. Jews (Oshanin) also give a slightly larger percentage of raised, and lower percentage of lowered, noses. Bukharan Tajiks give a slightly lesser percentage of lowered forms.

The height of nasal wings is most often medium (42.42 percent) or small (40.02 percent). Great height was observed only in 17.53 percent. A greater percentage of high nasal wings was observed in Darvaz and lower in Karategin. Particularly great wing height was observed in Vanch. Smallest wing height was observed in Karategin and southwestern Darvaz. In comparison with IArkho's figure, measurements in Darvaz were very low. Only in Darvaz is wing height comparable to that of other Central Asian groups. Great wing height is commonest among Mangyt Uzbeks and Ferghana Kara-Kalpaks.

Ferghana Tajiks in this respect approach the Tajiks of southwestern Darvaz. Bukharan Tajiks (Oshanin) have an exceedingly low percentage of low wings, and heavy preponderance of medium. High wings predominate among the Jews.

The flare of alae is usually small (58.02 percent) or low (38.09 percent). Strong flaring was observed in 3.89 percent. The degree of flaring was found higher in Karategin than in Darvaz.

The percentage of highly flaring wings among Bukharan Tajiks was like that in Karategin. The Jews approached the percentage observed in Darvaz. Uzbeks have a much greater percentage of greatly flaring wings, while the Arabs stand in the middle (Oshanin).

The nasal furrows were usually medium (47.40 percent) or slight (35.93 percent). Highly developed furrows were found in 16.67 percent. More highly expressed furrows were found in Karategin, less so in Darvaz. In this respect, the Tajiks of Bukhara and Ferghana approach Mountain Tajiks. Tien Shan Kirghiz and Khiva Uzbeks are nearer the Karategin Tajiks. Shakhrasiab Jews have much less pronounced furrows, while Bukharan Jews approach Bukharan Tajiks. Uzbeks generally have much less developed furrows than Tajiks.

The size of nostrils is: Small 15.40 percent; medium, 56.28 percent; and large, 29.23 percent. Small nostrils are more common in Karategin than in Darvaz. The largest nostrils are found among the Jews and the Arabs; Tajiks and Uzbeks are next. The Kirghiz have a predominance of small nostrils.

Form of nostrils.—Oval, 92.64 percent; round, 5.84 percent; and triangular, 1.52 percent. Higher percentage of oval nostrils in Darvaz than in Karategin.

The percentage of oval nostrils is higher among the Jews, and similar to that of Arabs. Among the Uzbeks the rounded form is slightly more common. The Kirghiz have a slightly greater percentage of round nostrils than the other groups.

The direction of maximal diameter of nostrils was diagonal, 53.25 percent; sagittal, 42.21 percent; crosswise, 4.55 percent. Sagittal direction is slightly less common in Darvaz than in Karategin. It is slightly more common among the Jews. Uzbeks are like Tajiks, having smaller percentages of sagittal diameters. Sagittal direction is still less common among Kirghiz.

Nasal length (nasion-subnasale) is large (M=58.14). Shorter noses are more common in southwestern Darvaz (except in Muminabad and Tavil Darya regions where the maximum length is observed). Jews and Uzbeks have comparable nose length, the latter with a slightly greater percentage of long noses. Nasal length of Kirghiz varies by regions, being greater than that of Tajiks in Tien Shan; equal, in Ferghana; less, in Issyk-Kul and Pamirs.

Nasal breadth (M = 34.40) is medium to small. It is slightly greater in Karategin, smaller in southwestern Darvaz than in central and eastern Darvaz. As an exception, widest nostrils have been observed in Vanch.

Among the Jews, nasal breadth is generally less than in Karategin and eastern and central Darvaz; it approaches that of southwestern Darvaz. Uzbeks have similar, or greater, nasal breadth, Turkomans have greater; the greatest nasal breadth has been observed among the Kirghiz.

Nasal index is fairly low (M=59.44). Tajiks are mostly leptorrhine (65.80 percent); hyperleptorrhines are 25.97 percent; mesorrhines, 8.01 percent.

The highest nasal indices were found in extreme southwestern Darvaz, although in general little variation was found between Karategin and Darvaz.

Owing to differences of method, it has not been possible to compare the data with those obtained by other investigators. However, it is possible to state that the Kirghiz have the highest, and Jews the lowest, nasal indices.

Ear measurements (L=61.07, B=33.20, Index=65.51). Form: oval, 60.09 percent; elliptical, 15.42 percent; pear-shaped, 13.60 percent; triangular and heart-shaped, 7.94 percent. Ear lobe, medium; adhering lobe more common in southwestern Darvaz.

PEOPLES OF UZBEKISTAN

Oshanin [29] observed that in 1923 a large portion of the population of Khwarazm called themselves "Sarts" and considered themselves distinct from the Uzbeks. Originally this term signified traders or merchants. At the present time both groups, the Uzbeks and the "Sarts," are called Uzbeks.[30] While no attempt has been made in this study to describe the differences of physical type between the Khwarazmian "Uzbeks" and the Tashkent "Sarts," Oshanin states that the modern settled Khwarazmians, known as "Uzbeks," do not differ

---

[29] Oshanin, L. V., Tysiadieletniia davnost dolichotsefalii u turkmen i vosnio-zhyne puti ee proiskhozhdeniia. Izvestia, SREDAZKOMSTARIS, No. 1, pp. 131-132, 1926.

[30] The most recent invaders of this area were the Turko-Mongol conquerors during the sixteenth century.

from the denizens of Tashkent who were formerly known as "Sarts" and are now called "Uzbeks."

The data on 119 Sarts used by Oshanin had been collected and published by A. P. Shishlov. Both the Khiva Uzbeks and the "Uzbeks" of Tashkent are in equal degree representatives of the ancient Indo-European [81] type, i.e., of the Iranian physical type which once inhabited the entire area of Turkestan, and was but sightly Mongolized by subsequent stratifications, in the course of centuries, of the Turko-Mongolian tribes. The Uzbeks of Khiva have a somewhat greater admixture of this Mongolian element, yet among them the traits of the Indo-European type are much more clearly expressed.

Accordingly, both terms "Sart" and "Uzbek" will be used in this work to denote the Iranian populations of Turkestan in general and Khwarazm in particular, who had become completely Turkized as to the language, but have remained until this day but very slightly Mongolized as to racial type.

During the study of historical sources Oshanin came across an item of information of anthropological character, from the tenth century A. D., which drew attention to the Turkomans.

The entire factual information regarding the Turkomans used in this work is that of IAvorskii based on a very small series of only 59 males. Consequently, the theories herein proposed are presented as a provisional working hypothesis subject to change on the basis of additional data. This hypothesis is based entirely on the cephalic index.[82] The extreme dolichocephaly of the Turkomans stands out amid the brachycephaly of all other peoples of Turkestan. The remaining Indo-European traits of the Turkomans (stature, nasal index, pigmentation) are given at the end of this article on the basis of IAvorskii's data.

K. L. Inostrantsev, in his work on the pre-Muslim culture of the Khiva Oasis, quotes Al-Mukkadisi to the effect that the settled Khwarazmians, whose Indo-European nature has been universally accepted in the interior of the irrigated Khiva Oasis, had become so similar to the Turks, who were wandering on the periphery of the oasis, that when Khwarazmians happened to go to one of the neighboring Muslim countries (Mawerannahr,[88] Persia, or Arabia) they were mistaken for Turks, and as such sold into slavery.

---

[81] In the sense of *Homo sapiens indo-europaeus* of Giuffrida-Ruggieri.

[82] Boas and Fleming notwithstanding, but with the support of Pearson and Dixon. (L. V. O.)

[83] By this name the Arabs understood the area between Oxus and Jaxartes, with the exception of the Khiva Oasis.

From an anthropological point of view this fact of the similarity between the Aryans and the nomadic Turks is paradoxical. Present-day settled Khwarazmians, both "Sarts" and "Uzbeks," are undoubtedly less similar to the nomadic Turkish peoples than one could conclude from the words of Al-Mukkadisi. This is easy to understand since during the four centuries following Sheibani's conquests the Uzbeks, who were (originally) a motley conglomeration of Turkish tribes and clans subject to the Golden Horde, wandering in the Dasht-i-Kipchak (to the west and north of the Aral Sea), having absorbed the fragments of tribes which were wandering in Mawerannahr, managed to become settled, to become mixed with the ancient Indo-European population of Turkestan, and to lose all degree of purity of their Mongol traits.

Consequently, the modern population of Khwarazm, whether "Uzbek" or "Sart," does not differ in the main from the other populations of Turkestan which are predominantly Indo-European with a small admixture of the "Asiatic," [34] Mongoloid element. However, it would be natural that during a millennium the degree of Mongolization of the native Indo-European types should increase [35] rather than decrease.

According to Al-Mukkadisi the measures taken by the Khwarazmian government in order to change the outward appearance of its subjects, and to make them look less like the nomadic Turks, were, according to Inostrantsev (p. 304) : "Khwarazmian women were ordered to tie bags filled with sand on both sides of the heads of newborn babies, in order to make their heads wider." In another place Al-Mukkadisi [36] states that the Khwarazmians tried to cause the heads of the newborn to become broader and shorter in order to distinguish them from the surrounding nomad Turks.

Al-Mukkadisi's testimony is corroborated by another authority, Yakut ibn-Abdullah, who wrote, at the beginning of the thirteenth century, that among the Khwarazmians broad heads and foreheads were due to the custom of artificial cranial deformation. [37]

These data regarding brachycephaly also sound paradoxical. The

---

[34] After Giuffrida-Ruggieri.

[35] Mongol tribes were the masters; cf. language, conquest, etc.

[36] Oshanin admits that he does not know whether Inostrantsev quotes Al-Mukkadisi verbatim or gives a free rendition of the general sense. (E. P.)

[37] Barthold checked the references from Al-Mukkadisi (Arabic text in Biblioth. Geograph. Araborum) and found the rendition of the sense "correct." He thought that Yakut ibn-Abdullah's reference may have been copied by Yakut from Al-Mukkadisi.

modern settled population of Khiva Oasis are in this respect very closely related to the "Sarts" with a tendency toward subbrachy-cephaly. Oshanin states that this brachycephaly is not due to the modern practice of artificial cranial deformation. While occipital flattening, due to the type of cradle, is found among both "Sarts" and "Uzbeks," this type of flattening does not affect the cephalic index to such a high degree. Flattening had been observed equally among dolichocephalic and brachycephalic individuals. Consequently, the brachycephaly of the "Sarts" and "Uzbeks" can be considered to be innate. Al-Mukkadisi also states that dolichocephaly was acquired by Khwarazmians from the surrounding Turkish nomads. Thus, the nomadic Turki tribes of Khwarazm were dolichocephalic. However, we know that the many peoples united by philologists [38] under the term "Turki" belong to the Mongol group, whose representatives are distinguished by extreme brachycephaly. Turki nomads of modern Turkestan, the Kara-Kirghiz [39] and the Kirghiz-Karakhs [40] are not exempt from this brachycephaly.

The Turkomans alone are dolichocephalic in predominantly brachy-cephalic Turkestan.

With which Turki people were the Khwarazmian of the tenth century in closest relation and with which modern ethnic group of Tur-kestan can they be identified by historians and ethnologists?

N. Veselovskii quotes Arabian travelers and geographers who state that the Khwarazmians were in close contact with nomadic Turki. Arabian authors refer to these nomads as "Guzes."

Yakut writes in his Geographical Dictionary that in the territory adjoining the Turki the contacts between the nomads and the settled peoples were so close that a new language "which was neither Khwarazmian nor Turkish" arose in this area.

Al-Istakhri observed during the thirteenth century: "Khwarazm is a land distinct from Khurasan and Mawerannahr. On all sides it is surrounded by plains; at the same time, to the north and the west its boundaries adjoin the lands [ranges] of the Guzes. The Khwaraz-mians are in great danger from the Guzes and are perpetually forced to keep them at bay."

Al-Masudi states: "Loaded caravans go at all times from Bulgaria to Khwarazm and back. They always have to defend themselves from the nomadic Turki tribes through whose lands lies their route."

Al-Istakhri, describing the wealth of Khwarazm and the prosperity

---

[38] Cf. Fischer's Turk Tatarische Stämme.
[39] The Kirghiz proper. (E. P.)
[40] The Kazakhs. (E. P.)

of its inhabitants, writes: "There are no gold or silves ores here, nor precious stones. The people are rich solely because of the commerce with the Turks . . . the large city of Al-Dzhurdzhania on the southern shore of the Dzheikhun River [the Amu] is the main trading place for the Guzes."

Oshanin does not believe mestization by marriage would take place to any marked degree between settled agricultural people and the nomads. There are no indications that there was mestization with the Turkish troops inside the oases at that early date, although there are definite indications of such mestization at a much later date through captured slaves.

Ethnologists and historians identify the Guzes with the Turkomans for the followng reasons:

1. This is indicated by such trustworthy traits as the cephalic index.

2. A thousand years ago Turkomans were as dolichocephalic as they are now.

3. We must conclude that at one time the settled populations of the Khwarazmian Oasis had a much larger admixture of Turkomans than it does now. However, we have no factual data to explain this.

Tentative explanations include the fact that during the eleventh century the Guzes went farther south, to Persia. They started commerce in Persian captives from Khurasan, who were better slaves than the Turkomans and also had farther to go in order to escape. This custom of recruiting Persian slaves continued after the Turkish conquest. During the Russian conquest of Khwarazm in 1873, thousands of Persian slaves were discovered. The descendants of these slaves still live in Khwarazm and are called *kul* (slaves).

There are no indications that Turkomans practice artificial cranial deformation to elongate their heads. The use of the cradle, which was borrowed by the Turkomans from the Sarts, could only flatten the occiput and not elongate the head.

In order to exclude the possibility of "secondary" elements, the Turkomans are compared with their neighbors, the Khurasanians, who during many centuries were subjected to Turkoman invasions. They called them "Alaman"; many became slaves of Turkoman families.

Masalskii states that in the course of only one century, at least one million Khurasanians were enslaved by the Turkomans. IAvorskii adds that until the Russian invasion all the field labor in Turkmenistan was performed by Persian slaves, while Turkomans engaged in nomadic pursuits. Masalskii also explains the purity of the Indo-European traits among the southern (Teke) Turkomans by mestization with the Persians. Consequently no dolichocephalic influence could have come from Persia, especially since the Turkomans were reported as dolichocephalic during the tenth century and did not come into contact with the Khurasanians until the Seljuk period.

The population of the entire area bounded by Khurasan to the south, the Pamir-Alai and Tien Shan mountain systems to the east, Jetty-Su on the north, and the Caspian Sea and the Aral Sea and the Kirghiz steppes on the west, can be divided into three groups: [41]

1. Pure Aryans (*Homo sapiens indo-europaeus* Giuffrida-Ruggieri), Turkestan Tajiks and Khurasanians.

2. Pure Turko-Mongols (*Homo sapiens asiaticus* (Giuffrida-Ruggieri), or E. Fischer's "Mongolian Race"), Kara-Kirghiz and Kirghiz-Kazakh. For lack of data and because of numerical unimportance, such peoples as the Kara-Kalpaks and the Kipchaks have been omitted.

3. Mixed peoples, resulting from mestization of groups 1 and 2, which we shall call "Eurasian type." These include the Sarts and Taranchis of the Jetty-Su region.

For the following four groups some adquate data are available:

1. Turkomans.[42]
2. Uzbeks of Khwarazm.[43]
3. Sarts of Tashkent.[44]
4. Kara-Kirghiz [45] (i.e., Kirghiz) of the southern shores of Issyk-Kul.

For other groups there exist only averages and percentages of brachycephaly, for Turkestan, from S. I. Rudenko's work on the Bashkirs for Iran, and from Deniker and Roland Dixon.

Let us compare the variational series of the cephalic index of the Turkomans, the mixed group (Sarts and Uzbeks), and the Mongol group (Issyk-Kul Kirghiz).

IAvorskii's group included 59 men aged 15 to 60 measured in Merv; 51 were of the Teke tribe, 4 were of the Saryk tribe, 3 Ersari, and 1 Alieli. No data were available for other groups. Oshanin states that both the Iomud tribe (Turkomans in Khiva) and the Turkomans of Murgab appear to be dolichocephalic.

The mixed group is shown to be between the Mongols and the

---

[41] This is not an attempt to draw a classification for the Turkestan peoples—such an attempt would not be possible on the basis of the available factual data—but is merely a descriptive scheme used for the sake of convenience. (L. V. O.)

[42] IAvorskii's material.

[43] Oshanin's data from 1923.

[44] A. P. Shishlov's measurements.

[45] Based on 100 males measured by Oshanin in 1924.

Turkomans, the former being entirely brachycephalic, the latter dolichocephalic.

The Eurasian type, represented by the Uzbeks of Khiva (C.I. 82.21) and the Sarts of Tashkent (C.I. 82.73), resembled the Mongolians (C.I 84.84), but differed from the Turkomans (C.I. 75.6).

The Turkomans could not derive their dolichocephaly from admixture with the Tajiks, who are also known to be typical brachycephals. They do not differ from northern Persians, whom both Deniker and Dixon class as a dolichocephalic type.

To Oshanin it appears possible that the Kurds are products of mestization of the Assyroid (Central Asian brachycephalic) race with the dolichocephalic Iranian nomadic tribes. Tajik brachycephaly may be linked tentatively to the *Homo sapiens indo-europaeus* var. *brachycephalicus* subvar. *pamirensis* Giuffrida-Ruggieri.

Furthermore, the Persians carried away by the Turkomans to Turkmenistan and Khwarazm from the area adjoining the Turkoman steppes and to the west of Asterabad were the brachycephalic Tajiks. Consequently their importation resulted in the strengthening of the brachycephalic element in Khwarazm.

Because of the isolated position of Turkoman dolichocephaly, the kindred races should be looked for in the more or less distant part of Turkestan and neighboring lands.

In the purely Aryan period of Turkestan, we find in the first millennium B. C. irrigated oases with settled agricultural population forming several organized states, with the warrior nomads occupying unirrigated areas unsuited to cultivation. It is also recognized that both the settled and nomadic groups belonged to the Iranian branch of the Indo-European linguistic family.[46]

The ancient anthropological indications permit us to conclude that both these branches belonged to *Homo sapiens indo-europaeus* Giuffrida-Ruggieri, but to which branch—brachycephalic or dolichocephalic?

The only known craniological material is that from Anau.[47] According to Dixon, crania from the upper strata belong to the third millennium or not later than the beginning of the second millennium B. C. and include both brachycephals and dolichocephals in approxi-

---

[46] Only very scanty anthropological information regarding these peoples appears, partly in Chinese chronicles, partly in the works of Procopius. (Cf. Veselovskii, p. 11).

[47] See also Field, Henry, Contributions to the anthropology of Iran. Chicago, 1939. Soviet archeologists planned to recommence excavations at Anau during 1946-1948.

mately equal quantities. It must be remembered that Anau lies far from the area which was first to become Turkized (Jetty-Su), and that it is 2,000 years earlier than the first Turkish appearance in Turkestan. Accordingly, the brachycephaly of Anau cannot be considered to be related to Turko-Mongols.

Although no information is available regarding the linguistic affinities of Anau, its material culture is related to the so-called Tripolje culture. However, by comparing paleoethnological and historical data with the geographic distributions, Oshanin believes it entirely permissible to attribute dolichocephaly to the nomadic tribes engaged in agriculture living in irrigated oases. Oshanin gives the following categories:

1. Long-headed Khwarazmians were mistaken for Guzes (cf. Al-Mukkadisi) by Iranians. However, brachycephaly was customary among Iranians. During the period of Al-Mukkadisi there were no Iranian nomads in Mawerannahr; Arabs found no nomads there at the beginning of the eighth century.

2. Settled Iranians of Khwarazm, who in the tenth century were most probably closely related to the Iranians of Mawerannahr, were originally brachycephalic and obtained mesocephaly only through becoming mixed with the Guzes.

3. Both Plains and Mountain Tajiks (the latter not having come in contact with Turko-Mongols) represent the remains of the ancient Iranian population and are both brachycephalic (cf. Stein).

A. P. Berezin's collection of photographs made by Shults in Piandzh included specimens having Assyroid traits, probably representing *Homo sapiens indo-europaeus* var. *brachycephalicus* subvar. *armeniensis*. Berezin also found a large admixture of light hair and gray eyes in the Pamirs.

Surprisingly enough, the Sarts and Uzbeks, who were subjected to a greater Turkization, were less brachycephalic than the Tajiks.

REASONS FOR SUPPOSING NOMADS DOLICHOCEPHALIC

During the ancient pre-Turkish period we find in Mawerannahr nomadic tribes bearing such names as Sacae, Massagetae, etc. These tribes were known to the Greek authors under the general name Saka or Scythians. The fact that these people used a language of the Iranian branch [48] is now accepted.

---

[48] V. V. Barthold told Oshanin that this cannot be insisted upon in this categorical form, since the latest investigations of N. Marr indicate the possible Japhetic affinities of the Scythians.

While we have no craniological data regarding the ancient Scythians of Turkestan, we have adequate data regarding the Scytho-Sarmatian tribes of southern European Russia. The idea of connecting Turkomans with the Scythians belongs to N. G. Malitskii. Oshanin first attempted to connect the Turkomans with the Dinlins of the Chinese chronicles. The information regarding Dinlins is contained in Grum-Grzhimailo's work entitled: "On the Blonde Race in Central Asia." The possibility of such a connection was suggested by the Turkoman tradition claiming that the original home of the Turkoman people was on the coast of Lake Issyk-Kul. According to the Chinese chronicles, this area was inhabited by the mysterious, apparently Indo-European people known to them under the name of Wusuns [Usu-Ni or Usuns]. Grum-Grzhimailo considers that the Wusuns were the extreme southwestern branch of the long-headed Dinlin group.

There is a mention of Nshun as a family name of one of the Armenian Turki, who are closely connected with the Turkomans, discovered by Barthold in "The Book of Korkud" in the Dresden Library. Aristov (p. 417) identifies this name with the word Wusun. Finally, Thomson [49] identifies the Uigurs and the Oguzes [50] as one and the same people. Grum-Grzhimailo considered the Uigurs as definitely belonging to the Dinlin groups.

Thus, the Scytho-Sarmatian tribes were linguistically, philologically and culturally closely related to the Iranian peoples. According to Herodotus, the Sarmatians were but a branch of the Scythians and their language was a Scythian dialect. Oshanin places the Scythians proper between the Boristhenes (Dnieper) to the west and Tenaissus (Don River) to the east; to the east and near Tenaissus extended the ranges of the Sarmatians. One of the Sarmatian tribes, the Alani, reached far east, to the Caspian and Arabian steppes adjoining Khiva Oasis. According to Strabo (first century B. C.) the Sarmatians moved farther west, and having occupied the Scythian lands, gave rise to the mixed Scytho-Sarmatian population of the area.

The craniological material was obtained during the 1870's by Samokvasov and Kidalchick from a tumulus near Aksiutenets close to Romny in Poltava *Oblast*, Ukraine.

Ten out of eleven crania published by A. P. Bogdanov were extremely dolichocephalic; the remaining cranium was extremely brachycephalic and was justly considered to belong to some indeterminate group.

According to Herodotus, in Sarmatia Proper, to the east of the

---

[49] Inscriptions de l'Orkhon, p. 148, 1896.
[50] Another name for the Turkomans.

12

Don, lived the Osetes,[51] who use an Iranian language and are considered to be the remains of Sarmatian tribes. Ivanovskii, who excavated ancient Osete burials, discovered that 59.9 percent of the crania were dolichocephalic. Gilchenko supposes that these crania belong to the forefathers of the Osetes, the Sarmatian tribe called the Alani. The present brachycephaly of the Osetes, described by Gilchenko (C.I. 82.16; 7.0 percent dolichocephalic; 16.0 percent mesocephalic), is attributed to subsequent mestization with Caucasian peoples.

In his work, "On the Influence of Turki Blood on the Iranian Type of the Osetes," Kharuzin attributes much of this brachycephaly to mestization with the Turki. Dixon believes that not only the dolichocephaly of the Ukraine and steppes to the north of the Caucasus, but also the admixture of dolichocephaly to the south of the Caucasian range, among the Kurds and Osmanli Turks, are due to the migrations of Scytho-Sarmatian tribes.

The Scytho-Sarmatian world ended at the Caspian and Aralian steppes only because that was the extent of geographical knowledge of the ancient authors. We know from other sources relating to Mawerannahr (Persia) and Asia Minor, that the Sarmatian world extended much farther east, for example, the nomadic Iranian tribes. There are no reasons to consider the "Scythians" or "Sacae" wandering over the steppes of Turkestan as distinct from the Scythians of European Russia.

Thus on the basis of anthropological and paleontological evidence we can, with an adequate degree of certainty, suppose that the Iranian tribes which had once wandered in Mawerannahr were dolichocephalic. From the evidence it is also seen that the sole source of of dolichocephaly among the Turkomans were these nomadic tribes wandering on the periphery of the irrigated oases.

The information regarding these nomadic peoples ceases at an early date. We know that as late as the eighth century the Arabs who occupied Mawerannahr did not find the nomads. It is probable that part of the nomads went farther south and are possibly represented by the modern nomadic Iranian tribes [52] of Afghanistan, Seistan, Baluchistan, and Persia. The present small admixture of dolichocephaly was introduced in later years through the nomadic Iranians. This admixture may have begun as early as the second millennium

---

[51] See Henry Field's forthcoming work, Contributions to the anthropology of the Caucasus.

[52] Data regarding these tribes were not available to Oshanin. Dixon states that the settled Afghans (the "Pathans") were originally pure brachycephals.

B. C. contemporaneously with the invasion of Persia by the same dolichocephalic element. D. D. Bukinich, who led an expedition into Afghanistan in 1924, noticed that the Iranian nomadic tribes [53] to the south of the Hindu Kush were dolichocephalic.

Dixon similarly explains the admixture of dolichocephaly observed in Baluchistan as an influence of nomadic Iranian tribes upon this basically brachycephalic people. Oshanin had no data on the cephalic index of nomadic Baluchis, and none regarding the nomads of Seistan who the Orientalists, according to Barthold, consider to be direct descendants of the Sacae (or Scythians) or of the Se people of the Chinese chronicles, who once wandered through Turkestan.

In modern Persia, there is a great dolichocephalic admixture among the Kurds. Oshanin thinks this is due to mestization of brachycephalic Assyroid (Vorderasiatisch) race with the dolichocephalic Iranian (Scytho-Sarmatian) groups. Dixon (p. 309) states that there is a strong admixture of dolichocephaly among the nomadic Lurs [54] of Luristan. The nomadic Bakhtiaris living between Isfahan and Kermanshah are brachycephalic, but Dixon suggests that the widely practiced artificial cranial deformation may be responsible.

It should be very interesting to investigate thoroughly the abovementioned nomadic Iranian tribes, since they may prove to be the last remnant of the Scytho-Sarmatian tribes which had once wandered in Turkestan.

A portion of the ancient nomads must have settled down and become mixed with the agricultural population of the oases. Traces of this Oshanin found in the large deviation toward subbrachycephaly and mesocephaly, with a few dolichocephals, arising, in the course of Mendelian bifurcation, among the Sarts and the Uzbeks. That these Plains Tajiks, who have become entirely Turkized in language, and have become mestized with Turko-Mongols, are much less shortheaded than the Mountain Tajiks, who escaped mestization with the Turks, Oshanin is inclined to explain by the admixture of the Scytho-Sarmatian dolichocephaly among the Plains Tajiks.

Finally, a large section of Scytho-Sarmatian tribes was very early completely Turkized in language and partly Mongolized in type, yet they preserved in its purity the dolichocephaly of their ancient original types. These people are the modern Turkomans.

---

[53] Oshanin does not know if these were Dzhemshids, and if so, whether the latter are characterized by dolichocephaly. He did not have access to Ujfalvy, who described tribes to the north and south of the Hindu Kush. (H. F.)

[54] Cf. Henry Field, Contributions to the anthropology of Iran. Field Museum of Natural History, 1939.

From this point of view, the nearest blood relations of the Turkomans are the Osetes. These are the two vestigial lakes remaining from the Scytho-Sarmatian ocean, which once occupied the large territory between the Tien Shan and Pamir-Alai mountain systems in the east and the Dnieper steppes in the west.

The connection of the Osetes with the Scytho-Sarmatians is established on the basis of philological evidence. The connection of the Turkomans with the Scytho-Sarmatian group is established only on the basis of craniological evidence derived from the study of various ethnic groups inhabiting Turkestan and neighboring steppes.

It may also be remarked that the southern Turkomans, who were the least mestized with the Turko-Mongols who had come from the north and northeast, have also preserved in greatest purity the traits of the ancient Scytho-Sarmatian Indo-European physical type. Thus, the average height of the "Teke" Turkomans is 1,700 mm., the tallest in Turkestan; only 20.0 percent were in the short category. Their nearest neighbors are another Indo-European people, the Tajiks, with a mean stature of 1,600 mm., including 33.0 percent short individuals according to Maslovskii.

Mixed Eurasian types occupy an intermediate position as shown by the following table:

Group	Stature	Short Percent	Observer
Sarts	168.0	51.0	Maslovskii, Blagoveshchenskii, Poiarkov
Uzbeks	168.0	32.0	Maslovskii, Ujfalvy
Uzbeks (Khiva)	166.71	?	Oshanin
Sarts (Tashkent)	167.6	?	Shishlov

Purely Asiatic peoples are the shortest, for example, the Kazakhs with a mean stature of 164.0 according to Ivanovskii, Ivanov, and Maslovskii.

The Turkomans, who include many individuals with regularly formed noses, possess a nasal index of 66.6, midway between the Tashkent Sarts (63.06±0.69 with 81.9 percent leptorrhine) and the Khiva Uzbeks (68.0±0.57 with 60.0 percent leptorrhine).

While true light-haired individuals are not known, IAvorskii records 14 of 59 individuals (23.8 percent) having gray eyes, which is a high percentage for Turkestan, excluding the Mountain Tajiks. Oshanin wonders if this is not the last remnant of the trait noticed by Ammianus Marcellinus (XXI, 21 (48)) among the Alans; "Crinibus mediocriter flavis."

COMPARISON WITH HISTORICAL, ETHNOLOGICAL, AND PHILOLOGICAL DATA

Data regarding the Turkomans are very scant. The only original source is the manuscript "Genealogy of Turkomans," by Abul Ghazi Bahadur Khan, written in Khiva during 1659-1660, now in the Tashkent Public Library, translated into Russian by A. Tumanskii.

Abul Ghazi does not doubt that the Turkomans are full-blooded Turks. He quotes legends stating that they have come from the "lands of Al-Malik and Issyk-Kul," i.e., the Jetty-Su.

According to the Genealogy, Turk,[55] son of Japheth and grandson of Noah, settled near Issyk-Kul, having sought a suitable place for many years. He had started from the shores of Atel (Volga) and IAik (Ural) where Japheth, son of Noah, had settled after the Flood.

From Issyk-Kul the Turkomans were pushed out by Nainans, Rhatais, and Kanglas, and proceeded to settle on the lower course of the Syr-Darya. From there they were forced out by the "Bedjene" people (identified with the Pechenegs). Then they settled in Mawerannahr where they lost their Turkish type and acquired Indo-European traits.

The Turkomans, who had come to Mawerannahr, were first called Turki by the Tajiks. After five or six generations, they became changed under the influence of the earth and the water . . . they became short, their eyes became large, their faces became small and their noses great. When slaves and merchants, from among those who had come into Turkmenistan and settled there, began appearing in Mawerannahr, the difference was seen between them and the Turki. These latter were then so called by the Tajiks and to the first Turks they gave the name "Turkmanend," meaning "resembling a Turki." The plain people who could not pronounce Turkmanend, said Turk (men). . . .

Oshanin thinks that except for "becoming short," the traits enumerated by Abul demonstrate the purity of the Indo-European traits of the Turkomans, which at once distinguished them from the Turki tribes. The southern (Mawerannahr) Turkomans were the least mestized with the Turks. The role played by mestization with the Persian slaves cannot be determined.

Abul Ghazi treats in his final chapter of the seven legendary women who once ruled over the Turkomans. Oshanin wonders if this is not a memory of the ancient matriarchate of the Sarmatians; all ancient authors connect the legend of the Amazons with the Sarmatians. According to Seredonin the word "Sarmad" may have originated from two Iranian words, "Sai"=king and "Mada"=girl.

Aristov agrees with Abul in considering the Turkomans to be pure-blooded Turki genetically related to the Kanglas, and coming

---

[55] One of the Scytho-Sarmatians tribes was named Tork.

from Issyk-Kul. Anthropologically this theory is not satisfactory, since the Kanglas later became a part of the Kazakh Hordes, the Kazakhs being extremely brachycephalic. Syr-Darya Kirghiz, who also contain a Kangla admixture, are also 100 percent brachycephalic according to Maslovskii.

The tribal names of the Turkomans are of relatively modern origin. The exception is the "Sakar" tribe, the name of which Aristov connects with the Sakarauk or Sacaraul, the Scythian peoples who, according to the Greek and Roman sources, destroyed the Greco-Bactrian state. Guttschmidt in his "Geschichte Irans" identified them with the Kang-gu people mentioned by the Chinese historians. Modern historians, however, think that the Sakarauks were a nomadic Iranian Scythian people, while the Kang-gu are identified with the Kanglas.[56] Chinese sources quoted by Bidurin state that in the second century B. C. the Chinese sent an embassy to Mawerannahr and Khwarazm to obtain aid against the Huns. About the year 129 B. C., the Chinese Ambassador, Djan Tsan, discovered that the lower and middle course of the Syr-Darya was inhabited by a numerous people whom the Chinese called Kang-gu, whom Aristov identified with the Kanglas. This allows at least 800 years for the Turkization of the Turkomans. Kwarazmians, who now consider themselves pure Turks, were using an Iranian language as late as the eleventh century. Only the anthropological analyses of the modern city and country peoples of the Khiva Oasis disclose their Indo-European racial foundations.

LINGUISTIC AND ANTHROPOLOGICAL CHARACTERISTICS OF THE TURKOMANS

F. E. Korsh, in his classification of Turkish tribes on the basis of their language, divides all Turkish languages into two groups, southern and northern. The southern group is subdivided into the eastern, including mainly the dead languages, Orkhonian of the Yenisei inscriptions, Uiguric, Jagatai, and the language of the Polovtsi, and the western branches. The latter includes the Osmanli, Azerbaidzhan, and Turkoman languages. V. V. Radlov also groups the last three languages together as his "southern" group. Korsh suggests the desirability of checking his philological classification with anthropological data. While in the main the data agree, some discrepancies are observable on the basis of materials available to Oshanin. The anthropological data on the Osmanli Turks are very scanty and sometimes contradictory. They are limited to a few measurements of Turkish

---

[56] Oshanin wonders when the Turkomans (Guzes), who used the Turkish language as early as in the tenth century, were first Turkized as to language.

subjects using the Turkish language and inhabiting the Anatolian Plateau. They are characterized by more than medium height and by many (40.0 percent) light-eyed individuals. This admixture is particularly strong among the Bektashi, Kizilbash, and Aizar tribes, all of them living in isolation, according to Arutiunov. Dixon is inclined to attribute this to the admixture of the invaders from the north, the Scythians and Cimmerians. On the other hand, these tribes are not characterized by the dolichocephaly of the Scythians and are, on the contrary, strongly brachycephalic. This may be due to artificial cranial deformation which, according to von Luschan in 1911, is widely practiced among the Takhtadzhis. On the other hand, the dolichocephaly in this case may have been absorbed by the brachycephaly characterizing the peoples of the "Vorderasiatische Rasse." According to Dixon the most brachycephalic group here is the Turkish city population of the Anatolian Plateau; the villagers occupy an intermediary position; the largest admixture of long-headed individuals is found among the nomadic peoples, who Dixon considers to be the descendants of the Turkoman invaders of the eleventh century. However, Eliseev's measurements in 1891, quoted by Dixon in support of this conclusion, do not bear it out.

Eliseev, remarking on the 20.0-percent admixture of dolichocephaly among the Anatolian Turks, shows their craniological heterogeneity. Eliseev states that the greatest percentage of dolichocephaly was found among the city dwellers (32.6 percent), less among the villagers (26.0 percent), and least among the nomads (3.5 percent). Eliseev thought that the Turkomans were typical brachycephals. According to him, the Turkoman nomads in Anatolia have retained the greatest purity of the original brachycephalic Turki types; they do not intermarry with any other tribes. The villagers, and particularly the city dwellers, are less rigorous in this respect. They may have obtained their dolichocephaly from marrying Kurdish and Arabic women.[57]

The question is then raised whether all the Osmanli Turks are related genetically to the Seljuk-Turkomans, and whether there is not present among the Turks of the Anatolian Plateau an admixture of other, later invaders coming, for example, from the north through the Caucasus?

The answer to this question cannot be given until it is known whether all Turkish tribes wandering on the Anatolian Plateau are

---

[57] The opposite phenomenon was to have been expected of the Turkomans who were originally dolichocephalic . . . the purity of dolichocephaly would be best preserved among the nomadic tribes; Turkomans settling in cities would absorb brachycephaly of the "Vorderasiatische Rasse." (L. V. O.)

homogeneous both linguistically and anthropologically. The Azerbaidzhan Turks ("Tatars") are far better known from the anthropological point of view.

Dixon, who uses Chantre's data (1892), considers the Azerbaidzhan Turks to be typical dolichocephals, standing alone among the brachycephalic peoples of the southwestern and southeastern littoral of the Caspian. Dixon, who compares the data from Kurdov (1912), Chantre (1892), and Shchukin (1913), concludes that the southern types of Caucasian Tatars differ sharply from the northern. According to Shchukin, the northern group is related to the Nogai Tatars and to the Kirghiz of the Volga steppes, having a sharply expressed brachycephaly. Chantre's and Kurdov's Tatars to the south of the Caucasian range are much taller and show clearly the domination of the dolichocephalic element. Dixon (p. 331) thinks accordingly that the Azerbaidzhan Tatars are closely related, and regards them as the remains of the dolichocephalic element, originally Indo-European as to the language, which were later "partly Tatarized" as to type and completely Turkized as to the language.

This point of view entirely coincides with that of Oshanin, except that the Azerbaidzhan Tatars should be regarded not as an independently Turkized, long-headed Aryan group, but rather as the direct descendants of the Turkomans.

The coincidence of the anthropological, philological, and historical data will become still more obvious if we remember Eliseev's conclusion regarding the distribution of dolichocephaly on the Anatolian Plateau, namely, that it is in general most stable in the southeast, barely noticeable in the center, and completely lost on the west coast.

Beginning in the eleventh century under the leadership of the Suljuk Sultans, the Turkomans terminated five centuries of their penetration of Persia and Asia Minor by conquering Constantinople. Their northeastern group, the Turkomans [of Khwarazm], have retained to the greatest degree the dolichocephaly of the Scytho-Sarmatians. The intermediate group, the Turks of Azerbaidzhan, have partly lost this dolichocephaly, and the westernmost group, the Osmanlis, have lost it to the largest extent, preserving a slight admixture of dolichocephaly only in their easternmost branch. In this process of replacing the hereditary factors of dolichocephaly by the factors of brachycephaly, an important role was played by the peoples of the "Vorderasiatische Rasse."

It remains to find out to which group of Turkish languages belonged the language of the Kanglas, who had completely Turkized the Scytho-Sarmatian nomads. According to Korsh, the Kirghiz language (the Kirghiz having included the remains of the Kanglas tribes) belongs in the "northern" group of his classification and not the western (Radlov's "southern"), which unites in it the Turkomans, Azerbaidzhans, and Osmanlis. Even in the past, according to Korsh, the Turkoman language was closer to the Jagatai than to the Kirghiz, forming a part of the eastern branch of his southern group. Could this contradiction be eliminated by assuming that the Turkomans embraced the Jagatai dialect only at a later date, when they settled in Mawerannahr?

Polivanov and Korsh demonstrate Iranian elements in the Persian language. According to Polivanov, these elements are distinct from the Persian language proper.

Since this hypothesis, namely that the Turkomans are the remains of the Scytho-Sarmatian peoples, is based on scanty factual materials, it must be considered as provisional.

V. V. Barthold, who examined this work, agrees with it on the main points. He objects, however, to the identification (by Aristov) of the Kanglas with the Kang-gu of the Chinese sources, and states that there is no evidence for this identification other than that of the similarity of the two names. According to Barthold, it is not probable that the Kanglas, like the other Turki tribes, could have come to Turkestan before the sixth century A. D. The Guzes (Oguzes) who, according to Barthold, are correctly thought to be the ancestors of the Turkomans, are Turkish people who had migrated to Turkestan from Mongolia between the sixth and eighth centuries A. D. In the light of this supplementary data, Oshanin is inclined to think that the Guzes became sufficiently intermixed with the Scytho-Sarmatian tribes in the period between the sixth and the tenth centuries to Turkize them completely in language, at the same time acquiring their Indo-European racial type. That such a period of time is sufficient for a loss of an original racial type and for a complete assimilation with another race is seen from the example of the Khwarazmian Uzbeks, who belong to the same physical type as the Tashkent Sarts. In other words they have the anthropological type of the Indo-Europeans (Giuffrida-Ruggieri) with a relatively small admixture of Mongoloid traits.

Another point of view is represented by V. V. Bunak. Having examined this manuscript, Bunak writes that the Turkomans, together with the Kurds, Persian Ajemis (Adzhemis), many Syrians, Arabs, etc., must be considered to belong to the Mediterranean physical type. Anthropologically this is proved by the works of Chantre, von Luschan, and others. According to Bunak's opinion, it is very probable that the Scythians belong to one of the branches of the Mediterranean race. However, these data, unfamiliar to us because of the scarcity of the anthropological literature on Turkestan, do not change the basic tenets. It remains only to state that the dolichocephaly of the Turkomans is the dolichocephaly of that branch of the Mediterranean race which was once represented by the Scytho-Sarmatians.[58]

In the former study Oshanin stated that artificial cranial deformation is not practiced by the Turkomans. However, new data show that the Turkomans themselves explain their dolichocephaly, which is different from the usual head form of their neighbors, by the custom of binding tightly the heads of their newborn children. Data were also forthcoming that this custom is still actually practiced. The Turkomans also state the wearing of tight skullcaps by young children contributes to their eventual dolichocephaly.

In the spring of 1926 the ethnographical expedition of Madame N. V. Briulova-Shaskolskaia, studying the Ersari tribe of the Turkomans on the Amu-Darya between Khodzhambas and Kelif, was joined by Maslov and Fokina who had previously collected anthropological data under Oshanin's guidance in Tashkent.

According to the data collected by Maslov and Fokina during this expedition, the Ersari Turkomans were less long-headed than the Teke Turkomans measured by IAvorskii, yet the Turkomans are still by far the most long-headed people of Central Asia as may be seen from the following table.

People	No.	C. I.	Author	Date
Teke Turkomans	59	75.6	I. L. IAvorskii	1891
Ersari Turkomans	124	77.0	Shaskolskaia Expedition	1926
Khwarazm Uzbeks	100	82.21	Oshanin	1923
Tashkent "Sarts"	119	82.73	A. P. Shishlov	1905
Karategin Tajiks[1]	433	82.77	Central Asian University	1926
Bukharan Central Asian			SREDAZKOMSTARIS	
Jews, Kermine	195	84.45	Expedition	1926
Issyk-Kul Kirghiz	100	84.84	Oshanin	1924

[1] Karategins working in Tashkent.

At the same time it was found out that the Ersari Turkomans always bind tightly the heads of their young children with a folded handkerchief in order, as they themselves state, to make the head as long as possible.

A diagonally folded handkerchief is tied below the occiput in such

---

[58] Oshanin, L. V., Nekotorye dopolnitelnye k gipoteze skifo-sarmatskogo proiskhozhdeniia Turkmen [Some supplementary data to the hypothesis of the Scytho-Sarmatian origin of the Turkomans]. Izvestia, No. 3, pp. 85-97, 1928.

a way that the most prominent part of the back of the head protrudes above the knot. Oshanin considers it possible that such a manner of bandaging may operate to elongate the skull by causing the protrusion of the occipital region above the bandage. This area of the head of adult Turkomans protrudes very sharply.

For a final solution of this problem it is necessary to study the morphology of Turkoman crania. As far as Oshanin was able to discover, this custom is widespread among other Turkoman people. The following queries arise as to whether:

1. Dolichocephaly can still be considered a racial (i.e., innate) trait of Turkomans, regardless of their tendency to elongate children's heads by means of artificial cranial deformation.

2. This custom, of ancient origin, has been practiced by the Scytho-Sarmatian tribes, whom Oshanin is inclined to regard as linguistically Turkized ancestors of the Turkomans.

3. There are many indications that artificial cranial deformation was practiced in ancient times by any other ancient peoples of Central Asia.

No. 1 may be an attempt to perpetuate the ancient dolichocephalic [59] type in spite of mestization with brachycephals. The fact that Khwarazm in the tenth century acquired dolichocephals through mixing with the Guzes, shows that the dolichocephaly of the latter was of a hereditary nature.

K. Z. IAtsuta [60] describes the artificially deformed crania from South Russia. Together with naturally dolichocephalic crania, obviously artificially deformed [61] crania (elongated with a very slant-

---

[59] Arabs mentioned the dolichocephaly of the Guzes in the tenth century. In modern times Basmachi bandits, who included together with the Iomud Turkomans some Uzbeks, were asked when captured during the siege of Khiva in 1823, "watermelon or cantaloupe?" If the captive was a "cantaloupe," i.e., long-headed, he was considered to be a Turkoman and dealt with accordingly.

[60] In Ob iskusstvenno deformirovannykh cherepakh na iugovostoke Rossii. Izvestia Donskogo Gos. Universiteta. [No date.]

[61] This "Hippocrates' macrocephaly" has been attributed by various authors to practically every people inhabiting the area near the Sea of Azov: Sarmatians, Cimmerians, Huns, Avars, Armenians, and "Tatars." Similar crania have also been found beyond the boundaries of the Scythian and Sarmatian world, on the Volga near Samara, in many localities of western Europe, and also in Peru, Mexico, and North America. Consequently, the custom of artificial dolichocephaly was practiced by many peoples bearing no relation to the Scytho-Sarmatians. Hippocrates states that the peoples of the Sea of Azov consider dolichocephaly as a mark of nobility and that they used artificial cranial deformation to intensify their dolichocephaly. He also implies that dolichocephaly is inheritable.

ing forehead and extremely protruding occiput) have been found in ancient burials in the Crimea,[62] in the Don Region, and in the Caucasus.

Kerch crania are attributed to the period from the fourth to the second century B. C. Macrocephalic crania are found in the areas inhabited by Sarmatians, such as Osetia. On the other hand, dolichocephalic crania from Scythian burials and from the ancient burial grounds of Osetia described by Bogdanov[63] and A. A. Ivanovskii[64] do not include artificially deformed crania, so that Scytho-Sarmatian dolichocephaly was of a racial character.

Data regarding other people practicing artificial cranial deformation in Central Asia are found in Chinese sources, which refer to another Scythian people, the Sacae, known to the Chinese sources as Se,[65] and to their eastern neighbors, known in the western sources as Kushes, Kushans, or Tokharians, and to Chinese sources as Yuechi.[66]

In the history of the Tang Dynasty (seventh-tenth centuries A. D.) quoted by Bichurin,[67] the following is told of the people of Kuchi (Chinese Kiu-tsi) of the extreme north of eastern Turkestan: "The head of a [new] born boy is pressed by means of a tree."

The same thing is told of the people of Kya Sha (Kashgar): "The people in general are treacherous and crafty. They also depress the heads of male infants in order to make them flat. These people are of tall stature and have blue eyes."[68]

It is, however, impossible to conclude on the basis of these texts whether the practice was to elongate the heads. Bichurin does not give any direct indications that artificial cranial deformation was practiced by the Yuechi. He only states that this custom was widespread in definite areas during definite periods.

However, by analyzing the anthropological composition of the modern population of eastern Turkestan, we come to the conclusion that it has absorbed some elements of *Homo sapiens indo-europaeus dolichomorphus* Giuffrida-Ruggieri.

Stein found that the Indo-European element[69] predominates in the

---

[62] The so-called "Kerch" and "Chersonesus" crania.

[63] Poltava burials: IOLEAE, 3, 1880.

[64] Osetia: IOLEAE, 21, 1891.

[65] Nothing is known regarding their anthropological type.

[66] After leaving Jetty-Su they divided into two groups: Little Yuechi, who settled in eastern Turkestan, and the Great ("Da") Yuechi, occupying the area of present Uzbekistan.

[67] In Sobranie Svedenii, vol. 3, p. 218.

[68] Loc. cit, p. 244.

[69] Brachycephalic, hypsicephalic, and leptorrhine, i.e., Dixon's Alpine type.

areas closest to the Pamirs (Khotan, Polu, Kok IAr, and possibly in Yarkend and Kashgar). Another Indo-European element still clearly predominates in the Lob Nor area, and east to the Sa Shu area, on the boundary of Kansu Province. However, a large admixture of this dolichocephalic type was found in areas far to the west of this region. So it is that to the east of Khotan [70] Przewalskii had noticed a large number of blonds among the inhabitants of the Kerian Mountains.[71]

Comparing these data, Roland Dixon postulates his hypothesis according to which the dolichocephalic Indo-Europeoid type had once been widespread throughout eastern Turkestan, and was only gradually pushed east by the continuous pressure of brachycephalic Indo-Europeans from the direction of the Pamirs and Mongols from the north and northwest.

The Scythians are regarded by several other anthropologists as an ethnic group carrying with it eastward the elements of *Homo sapiens indo-europaeus dolichomorphus*. Thus, Montandon [72] refers to Haddon's proto-Nordic race as a possible "historical, geographical, and somatological link connecting the modern Ainu with other varieties of *Homo sapiens indo-europaeus*." According to him these proto-Nordics, light-eyed, and above medium stature "aurait été fortement representé par les anciens Scythes."

The western branch, Yuechi-Tokharians, were known to Byzantine historians under the name of "White Huns" or "Ephthalites." Procopius of Caesarea wrote: "Even though the Ephthalites are a people of Hunnish stock, they have not become mixed with the Huns known

---

[70] In the area where the remnants of the Indo-Scythian Tokharian language was discovered.

[71] Grum-Grzhimailo, G. E., Zapadnaia Mongoliia i Uriankhaiskii Krai, vol 2, p. 19. Leningrad, 1926.

[72] In L'Anthropologie, vol. 37, p. 338, 1927, he also refers to the find by A. P. Mostits of two dolichocephalic crania associated with a Scythian cauldron, in Trans-Baikalia (Izv. Tr.-Kiakh. Otd. Russ. Geo. Ob., vol. 3, 1895). A dolichocephalic type is also known in Baltistan, southern Tibet. (Cf. A. H. Keane, A. C. Haddon, and others in Man, Past and Present, p. 167, Cambridge, 1920; Ujfalvy, Les Aryens du Nord et Sud de l'Hindou-Kouch, p. 319, Paris, 1896). Ujfalvy, Keane, and Haddon regard these people as the descendants of the Sacae. The "Balti are not Tibetans or Mongols at all, but descendants of the historical Sacae, although now of Tibetan speech and Moslem faith." Rock paintings in Baltistan resemble Scythian representations of weapons; this was where a portion of the Sacae, invading India from the north in the year 90 B. C., settled down.

to us. Alone of all Huns they are not of repellent countenance and have white bodies."

This testifies to the Indo-European appearance of the Huns. An attempt to discern the dolichocephaly of the Huns from the effigies on their coins has not been successful. M. E. Masson states that it is difficult to attribute certain coins definitely to the Ephthalites. In addition, the head form of the effigies is hidden by the headgear depicted.

Conclusions.—1. Turkomans practice the custom of binding the heads of babies and explain by this custom their own dolichocephaly.

2. Whether this achieves the desired effect cannot be answered definitely until more information regarding the morphology of the Turkoman skull is forthcoming. According to the preliminary studies of Fokina and Maslov, the dolichocephaly of the Turkomans is due mainly to the relatively lesser lateral development of the skull, something which could hardly take place under the influence of the bandage as described.

According to Oshanin's data, the brachycephaly of the Kirghiz is due to the relatively stronger lateral development of skull, and not to the smallness of its length as, for example:

Group	G. O. L.	G. B.	C. I.	Observer
Issyk-Kul Kirghiz	187.0	159.0	84.84	Oshanin
Ersari Turkomans	188.4	145.0	77.0	Fokina and Maslov

3. Even if it should be proved that artificial cranial elongation of the Turkomans actually takes place, this still would not mean that the dolichocephaly of the Turkomans is not inheritable.

4. The racial (inheritable) character of Turkoman dolichocephaly is clearly indicated by the reference to Al-Mukkadisi.

5. On the basis of historical, philological, and anthropological data, Oshanin considers that the Turkomans have received their dolichocephaly through the admixture of the Guze ancestors of the Turkomans with the Scytho-Sarmatians, whose language they Turkized, but whose physical type they changed but slightly.

6. The custom of intensifying dolichocephaly by means of bandages was widely used by Scytho-Sarmatian tribes, definitely in Europe and very probably in Asia down to the boundaries of eastern Turkestan.

7. It is possible that this custom among the Turkomans is a survival of this widespread custom of their ancestors, the Scytho-Sarmatians.

UZBEKS OF KHWARAZM

Oshanin [73] described the anthropological type of the Uzbeks of Khwarazm in the following manner:

Pigmentation.—On this basis these Uzbeks are not homogeneous. Among them clearly predominate darkly pigmented individuals. However, there is a slight admixture of a lighter pigmentation of skin and eyes.

Hair.—Facial and body hair are of medium development. The admixture of individuals with a sparse growth of hair is small.

Face.—The predominating forms are oval and elliptical. The face is of medium height and breadth, with a moderately developed, but not infrequently narrow and low, forehead, more frequently straight and flat than convex and sloping.

Stature.—Medium with a tendency toward tallness.

Facial index.—This varies from euryprosopy to mesoprosopy.

Cephalic index.—Although the mean is subbrachycephalic, there is considerable admixture of both brachycephals and dolichocephals.

Nose.—Medium size predominates. However, there is a small group with low, broad noses. On the other hand, persons with high, narrow noses are frequently encountered. The nasal profile is either straight or convex; concave noses are rarely found. The nasal index is leptorrhine with a strong tendency toward mesorrhiny.

Mongolian fold.—This feature occurs not infrequently.

Summary.—In general, the Uzbeks of Khwarazm may be characterized as representatives of the brachycephalic variety of *Homo sapiens indo-europaeus* of Central Asia, with a significant admixture of Type I (Asiatic type) and a lesser admixture of Type II (dolichocephalic variety of *Homo sapiens indo-europaeus* of Central Asia). This is seen, for example, in the fact that while in all tables of measurements the Uzbeks of Khwarazm occupy an intermediate position between the Tashkent Tajiks and the Uzbeks (i.e., Turkized Iranians) on one side and the Kirghiz on the other, in all basic characters they stand much closer to the Tajiks. The admixture of the dolichocephalic variety of *Homo sapiens indo-europaeus* is expressed in the increased stature and the decreased cephalic indices of the Uzbeks of Khwarazm.

The undoubted, and fairly significant, admixture of Mongoloid traits among the Uzbeks of Khwarazm must be attributed to the preservation of elements of the original Mongoloid Uzbek type which had become dissolved in the autochthonous Indo-European population of Khwarazm.

---

[73] Oshanin, L. V., in Sred. Az. Univ. Bull. No. 17, pp. 97-101. Selected from summary.

This point of view is supported by the fact that in comparison with the Uzbeks of Khwarazm the native population of Tashkent is much less Mongolized. However, the opposite was to be expected from both historical and geographical considerations. The admixture of "Asiatic" inheritable traits among the settled peoples of the oasis was introduced largely by Uzbeks who settled mainly in Khwarazm and Mawerannahr; Tashkent received a relatively smaller admixture of Uzbeks.

KAZAKHS OF THE ALTAI

IArkho [74] measured 120 individuals of the Naiman, Kirei, and Kara-Kirei tribes of the Middle Horde Kazakhs, in the Chuiskaia steppes of the southeastern Altai. This is one of the easternmost Kazakh groups. The Chuiskaia steppe is populated by 2,175 Kazakhs ("Kirghiz") who are Moslems, 1,500 Telengets (who represent the ancient Turkish stratum, being an Altaic tribe practicing Shamanism), a few Russians, Tannu-Tuvans (Soiots), and Mongols. The last two are Buddhist groups. Because of religious differences, no mestization is practiced between the Kazakhs and these other peoples.

From the statistical tables the following conclusions have been drawn:

1. The Kazakhs are a strongly brachycephalic (medium-long), and broad-headed euryprosopic (long- and broad-faced), leptorrhine (narrow-nosed) group.

2. These peculiarities differentiate them from many peoples of Asia and the world.

3. This complex of traits places them close to certain tribes of Asia, e.g., the Telengets (in Altai), Buriats, Tannu-Tuvans, Torguts, and possibly the Yakuts.

4. By comparing their morphological peculiarities with those of other brachycephals of Europe and Asia Anterior it is discovered that a significant difference is observed not only in the structure of the facial skeleton, but also in the cranial structure. Thus, the brachycephaly of the Dinaric and Armenoid types (as well as that of some other Asiatic and North American tribes) is determined, to a great extent, by the decrease in head length.

5. Comparison of our data with that of other authors does not show any significant discrepancies. Thus, the analysis of head and facial measurements of the Kazakhs puts them close to certain other

[74] IArkho, A. I., Kazaki Russkogo Altaia: Rasovye tipy Altae-Saianskogo Nagoria. Severnaia Aziia, Nos. 1-2, pp. 76-99, 1930.

Turko-Mongolian tribes. A particularly close resemblance is found between the Kazakhs and the Buriats.

The following morphological characters were recorded:

PIGMENTATION

The highest percentage of light and mixed eyes was found in the western part of Tavil-Darya region and in the southern part of Dasht-i-Dzhum region. The darkest pigmentation was found in the Kalai Khumb (Piandzh Valley) and the Muminabad regions.

In order to find out whether the blue-eyed Tajiks represented a special type, Ginzburg measured separately a group of adults having eyes of this color (Nos. 12, 14-16 on Martin's scale). It was discovered that in the range of variations of absolute measurements, head and body proportions and indices, and of the descriptive characters of head and face, the blue-eyed group did not differ from all other Tajiks. The only difference was a lighter pigmentation of hair and beard in this group, which consisted of eight subjects. Among the Tajiks from the other regions the darkest-pigmented eyes were found among the Bukharan Tajiks.

The Ferghana Tajiks were but slightly more darkly pigmented than the Mountain Tajiks. Joyce's materials show that the Tajiks of Darvaz are more strongly pigmented than the Tajiks from Karategin. The lightest pigmentation was found in the southwestern Pamirs.

While the Jews, measured by Oshanin, have a larger percentage of mixed eyes than the Tajiks, the former are in general more darkly pigmented than the latter and have a much larger percentage of the darker shades of brown eyes.

The pigmentation of the eyes is darker in the younger age groups, while for the group 24 to 50 years old the commonest shade is No. 4, followed by No. 3; for the ages 18 to 23 the most common shade is No. 3, followed by No. 4 (Martin's scale). The mean shade for the 24- to 50-year-old group was 4.83; for the 18- to 23-year-olds, 3.96.

Turkomans and Kara-Kalpaks are more highly pigmented than the Mountain Tajiks, and less pigmented than the Bukharan Tajiks. In general, the Uzbeks are more strongly pigmented than the Tajiks, but they have a great range of variations. The Kirghiz have a still greater range of variations. The Ferghana Kirghiz are more highly pigmented than the Ferghana Tajiks and much more than the Mountain Tajiks. The Kirghiz from the highland areas of the Tien Shan are pigmented less strongly than even the Mountain Tajiks. Pamirian Kirghiz as well as Joyce's Tajiks from the southwestern Pamirs are still less pigmented. The Issyk-Kul Kirghiz are very strongly pigmented.

In general, the Mountain Tajiks are somewhat less strongly pigmented than the Plains Tajiks and the majority of other peoples of Central Asia examined in this study. The percentage of light-eyed individuals among Mountain Tajiks is almost identical with that in the other groups.

Eye color

Color	No.	Percent
Dark	59	*54.62*
Mixed	47	*43.53*
Light	2	*1.85*

D. D. Bukinich found a still larger percentage of light and mixed eyes on the Turgaiskaia steppe. S. I. Rudenko found a smaller [75] percentage of light and mixed eyes (11.0 percent). This definite admixture of depigmented eyes shows once more the presence in Asia of traces of the mysterious light-eyed type. In contradistinction to other investigators, as for example Ivanovskii, we cannot regard the Kazakhs as a pure darkly pigmented type, but as a dark type with a definite admixture of a mixed type. Among Samoyeds, Buriats, and Torguts the mixed eye color is found much more rarely than among the Kazakhs. The Telengets [76] occupy an intermediate place.

Hair color (adults)

Color	Fischer's scale	Percent
Black	27	*67.07*
Dark brown	4–5	*30.61*
Light brown	6–7	*1.32*

Hair color (males aged 18 to 23)

Color	Fischer's scale	Percent
Black	27	*52.04*
Dark brown	4–5	*46.62*
Light brown	6–7	*2.34*

Only one case of lighter hair (No. 10 on Fischer's scale) was observed among the adults. Red hair (Nos. 1-3) was not seen.

Black hair (No. 27) was relatively rare in central and eastern Darvaz, and more frequent in southwestern Darvaz. The Karategin

---

[75] IArkho comments that this. may be the result of variation in standards followed.

[76] Cf. IArkho, AZH, vol. 17, Nos. 3-4.

occupied an intermediary position. Dark brown shades were more frequently found in central-eastern than in southwestern Darvaz.

Beard color

Color	Fischer's scale	Percent
Black	27	22.61
Dark brown	4–5	60.14
Light brown	6–7	12.82
Light	8–12	3.26
Red	1–3	1.16

The geographical distribution follows that of hair color. For example, the Pendzhikent Tajiks are lighter; the Pskem Valley Tajiks are still lighter. The Issyk-Kul Kirghiz are pigmented very similarly to the Mountain Tajiks. The Uzbeks of Khwarazm, especially from Karshi and Shakhrasiab and the Karshi Jews are all more lightly pigmented than the Tajiks. In distribution of Nos. 4 and 27, the Jews are closer to the Tajiks than to the Uzbeks. Beard color is lighter according to IArkho and Oshanin. However, the beards of the Uzbeks and the Jews are darker than those of the Tajiks and do not show as much difference in hair color as among the Tajiks.

In general, the Mountain Tajiks are a light-skinned people, but have strongly pigmented hair and irides; they have a very small admixture of low-pigmented elements. The Tajiks from southwestern Darvaz are more deeply pigmented than the Tajiks from other regions.

BEARD DEVELOPMENT

The distribution of degree of beard growth as recorded on 427 males, aged 24 to 50, was recorded in percentages on the following scheme:

No.   Descriptive category
0 = complete lack of beard.
1 = very scanty growth on either chin or cheeks.
2 = weak growth on chin and cheeks.
3 = medium growth; growth on cheeks merging into growth on chin.
4 = well-developed beard, but not strongly spreading onto neck and cheeks.
5 = well-developed beard, spreading strongly onto neck and cheeks.

No.	0	1	2	3	4	5
Percentage	1.17	5.15	14.72	28.81	41.69	8.43

Although the general development of the beard was fairly strong, there were 21.0 percent with weak beards. In Darvaz a stronger beard development than in Karategin was found. Tajiks from Bukhara (Oshanin) and Ferghana (IArkho) had a weaker beard development than the Mountain Tajiks. However, a greater age range was covered by these authors.

The Uzbeks, with the exception of the Khivans, have a much weaker beard development. The Kirghiz have still weaker beards. The beards of Turkomans vary; while the Iomuds have beards as strongly developed as the Mountain Tajiks, the Chaudyrs show a weaker degree of development. The beards of Jews and the Arabs are more strongly developed than those of the Tajiks.

Regarding hair development,[77] the Darvaz have less growth on the upper lip. The eyebrows of the Darvaz are stronger than those of the Karategin. The amount of chest hair is weak, 31.99 percent being glabrous. The Darvaz had less than the Karategins. Hair on the back was very little, 78.20 percent being glabrous. Pubic hair was also scanty, the Darvaz having less than the Karategins. In general, the body hair was more abundant among the Darvaz. The form of the beard was recorded as: small waves, 49.80 percent; curly, 38.68 percent; deep waves, 9.96 percent; straight, 1.53 percent.

Curly beards were more frequent in central and eastern Darvaz than in Karategin and southwestern Darvaz, where the deep wave was more common. Straight hair was found in a few cases, only in Karategin.

Curly beards were found most frequently in the western part of the Tavil-Darya region, least frequently in the Muminabad region. The Uzbeks of Khwarazm have a much greater percentage of straight-haired beards; among the Issyk-Kul Kirghiz straight beards are in majority.

HEAD FORM

Occiput	No.	Percent
Flat	51	44.4
Round	44	37.9
Prominent	12	10.3
Indeterminate	9	7.8

Forehead	No.	Percent
Strongly sloping	22	18.33
Medium	76	63.33
Straight	22	18.33

BROWRIDGES

Category	No.	Percent
Absent or weak	13	10.83
Medium	42	35.00
Strong	53	44.16
Very marked	12	10.00

[77] The form of the head hair could not be determined because all the heads were shaved.

In comparison with the Buriats and the Tannu-Tuvans, the Kazakhs have strongly developed browridges and a slanting forehead. In addition, we find that the Kazakh group is not homogeneous with respect to this trait, and suppose that with the basic predominating "Altaic" type there had been admixed another type, frequently found among the Buriats and the Tannu-Tuvans.

FACIAL FORM

Shape	No.	Percent
Round and round-oval	14	*12.07*
Oval	60	*51.72*
Pentagonoid	34	*29.31*
Square	5	*4.31*
Others	3	*2.58*

NOSE

Root	No.	Percent
Low	24	*20.16*
Medium	90	*75.63*
High	5	*4.20*

This also distinguishes the Kazakhs from the Buriats and the Tannu-Tuvans, the majority of whom have low nasal roots.

Profile [1]	No.	Percent
Concave	4	*3.36*
Straight	56	*47.06*
Convex	59	*49.58*

Profile [2]	No.	Percent
Concave	30	*25.51*
Straight	77	*64.70*
Convex	12	*10.09*

Nasal tip	No.	Percent
Elevated	20	*16.80*
Horizontal	61	*51.26*
Depressed	38	*31.93*

Nostril	No.	Percent
Round	6	*5.04*
Triangular	46	*38.65*
Oval	63	*52.94*
Indefinite	4	*2.36*

Height of alae	No.	Percent
Low	19	*16.24*
Medium	72	*61.54*
High	26	*22.22*

[1] Of bony part of the nose.
[2] Of nasal cartilage.

This average Kazakh type of nose, possessing a medium-prominent nose root, straight or convex profile, slightly drooping tip, oval-triangular form of nostrils, medium slanting, with medium alae with below-medium flare, differs from Buriat and Tuvan Mongol type of nose, having a low root, concave-straight profile, tilted tip, rounded-triangular, almost horizontal nostrils and low alae. A strong suspicion is aroused that this group originated from the mixing of two groups, one of which had a Mongoloid, the other a Europeoid form of nose.

LIPS

The Kazakhs have thinner lips than either the Buriats or the Tannu-Tuvans.

EARS

The ears protrude markedly in 89 cases (76.07 percent), the remainder being in the medium category. The lobes do not agree with the prevailing Mongolian type. For example, 54.16 percent were tongue-shaped, 25.0 percent horizontally truncated, and 20.84 percent triangular. In general, the ears were usually egg-shaped with a certain percentage of pear-shaped forms; greatly protruding, with a well-developed helix, medium-developed anti-helix, and well-expressed lobes. All these points differ from those of the Mongoloids, and are specific for the Kazakh type.

SUMMARY

The Mongoloid peoples of North Asia fall into several distinct groups. More clearly distinguished are the "Ugrian" type described by Rudenko, having a long, narrow, low skull, and very typical structure of the soft parts of the face; and the "opposite" type, eurycephalic, with a long and broad face, typical for many Turko-Mongolian peoples. We shall compare the Kazakhs with the type of other Turko-Mongolian peoples in an attempt to find out whether these are formed on the basis of one variety of the Mongol race, or on the basis of several.

Our Kazakhs, who are very close to Kharuzin's Kazakhs of the Bukeevskaia Horde, are to be compared with the Buriats observed by Talko-Grintsevich, Porotov, the Shendrikovskii and the Tannu-Tuvans [78] measured by IArkho in Kemchik.

[78] IArkho, A. L., Kemchikskie Tannu-Tuvintsy. Severnaia Aziia, Nos. 5-6, 1929.

This peculiar combination of traits among the Kazakhs forces us to answer the query regarding the identicity of Turko-Mongolian tribes in the negative.

Thus, IArkho finds two basic types, and one mixed type. He attempts by combining forehead, lips, nose, and face form (Saian, rounded and round-oval; Altaian, oval and rectangular) to divide them by morphological characters, and finds five such combinations.

Measurements and indices of 120 Kazakhs[1] of the Altai

Measurements	Range	Mean	S. D.	C. V.
Stature	145-181	163.00	7.11	4.36
Head length	175-206	188.20	6.73	3.57
Head breadth	149-174	160.70	5.01	3.11
Head height	113-143	127.90	6.30	4.92
Bizygomatic diameter	137-167	151.40	5.67	3.80
Bigonial diameter	103-132	115.60	6.52	5.62
Nasal height	40-68	55.40	4.72	8.52
Nasal breadth	27-46	36.65	2.92	7.95
Ear length	52-76	64.30	4.41	6.85
Ear breadth	29-42	35.30	2.48	7.02
Indices				
Cephalic	75-98	85.40	3.47	4.06
Nasal	43-74	58.25	5.78	9.92
Ear	42-76	55.35	4.94	8.92

[1] Age range was 21 to 60.

The supplementary types in the Kazakhs may include, theoretically, the Ugrian and the Samoyed, as supposed by Aristov. Without any doubt there should be included the brachycephalic Europeoid type, which IArkho calls Pamiro-Ferghan, of the Tajiks and which is more frequently found among the western Kazakhs and the Kirghiz.

The Mongolian type is called provisionally the "Saianic," [79] indicating by this a complex of descriptive characters distinctive from the "Altaic."

ALTAIC TYPE

Kharuzin pointed out the Europeoidal (Caucasian) character of this type. The following facts may be adduced in support of this position:

1. Large admixture of depigmented eyes, especially if we eliminate the darker Saianic eyes.

2. Slight intensification of tertiary hair covering, i.e., beard.

[79] IArkho also describes a "Saianic" variant of the Central Asiatic racial type among the Tannu-Tuvans from Kemchik.

3. Relatively slight development of upper eye fold and low percentage of epicanthic fold.

4. Prominent nose.

Comparative table of descriptive characters

	Kazakhs	Tuvans and Buriats
Pigmentation:		
Hair	Dark.	Dark.
Eyes	Dark, with large admixture of mixed shades.	Dark with small admixture of mixed shades.
Hair texture	Coarse medium.	Coarse.
Beard quantity	Small but with admixture of higher quantity of growth.	Very small.
Occipital form	Flattened-rounded.	Flattened-rounded.
Forehead	Broad, slightly inclined.	Broad, rounded, straight.
Browridges	Strongly expressed.	Weakly expressed.
Face form	Oval or long pentagonal.	Round, round-oval, round-pentagonal.
Horizontal profile	Weak, with large percentage of medium.	Very weak.
Eye opening	Narrow, admixture of medium.	Narrow.
Upper eye fold	Medium over entire extent without reaching eyelashes.	Medium over entire extent reaching the eyelashes.
Epicanthus	Small.	Relatively frequent.
Nose root	Medium prominent.	Flat.
Nasal profile	Straight or convex.	Straight or concave.
Tip elevation	Horizontal with tendency to depression.	Horizontal with tendency to elevation.
Nostrils, form	Tendency to be elongated.	Tendency to roundness.
Nasal wings	Medium.	Tendency to low.
Nasal wings, development	Below medium.	Weak.
Lip height	Above medium.	High.
Lip thickness	Below medium, many thin.	Tends to be broad.
Teeth, anomalies	Frequent.	Rare.
Ear form	Egg-shaped or pear-shaped.	Pear-shaped.
Helix	Well developed.	Medium developed.
Lobe	Well developed.	Below medium.
Protrusion	Great.	Great.

ARGUMENTS AGAINST EUROPEOIDAL AFFINITY

1. Broad face. The admixture of narrow faces, according to IArkho, lowers the facial width proportionately to the extent of the admixture.

Author	Homogeneity	Racial affinity and composition
Kharuzin	Not homogeneous.	Formed by interbreeding of Mongolian and Caucasian type. Typical average type of Kazakh is a product of mestization.
Seland	Not homogeneous.	Agrees with Kharuzin.
Ivanovskii	More or less homogeneous.	Belongs to the Central Asian group of Ivanovskii's classification.
Deniker	?	Belong in Turkish race; together with the Ugrian race from Eurasian racial group. Turkish race (Deniker) is distinguished from Mongol race proper.
Giuffrida-Ruggieri [1]	?	Belong to *Homo sapiens asiaticus* var. *centralis* together with Buriats, Kirghiz, Torguts, etc.
Bukinich (1924)	Not homogeneous.	Original, yet closer to Mongolians.
Rudenko (1927)	Not homogeneous.	Belong in Central Asiatic group together with Altaians. Analysis of distribution curves shows non-homogeneity, in stature and nasal index.
IArkho (1927)	Not homogeneous.	Basic type is Turki (South Siberian); with this is mixed a certain percentage of Mongolian (Central Asiatic type) and a small amount of Europeoidal Pamiro-Ferghan type.

[1] He places Tannu-Tuvans in another variety, *Homo sapiens asiaticus palearcticus* var. *brachymorphus*, close to Samoyeds, but with the nasal index close to *centralis*.

2. Mandibular breadth.

3. The entire complex of characters typical for Asia.

IArkho does not believe the validity of the data on the nose and epicanthic fold. There are also insufficient data on pilosity, which may result from Pamiro-Ferghan admixture since the hairiness appears to be higher among the western Kazakhs. Depigmentation may be natural to the Altaic type or may be due to a very ancient admixture. The structure of the head and face includes the Kazakhs in the Mongoloid cycle.

The Altai variety of the Mongol race apparently coincides with Deniker's Turkish race, "supplementing and expanding its stingy but neat definitions."

The following are regarded as specialized traits: great stature; modeling of skull; prominent nose; structure of lips; ear (reduction of the helix); and probably depigmentation. This indicates that our Altaic type approaches the Turkish race as characterized by Deniker: "The Turkish race may be characterized in the following manner: stature above medium (167.0-168.0) brachycephaly (81.8-87.0); face oblong, oval; eyes non-Mongol, but frequently with an outer eyefold; hair covering moderately developed; broad cheek-bones, thick lips, straight and relatively prominent nose."

In the future we shall attempt to elucidate the role of the Mongol race in the formation of other peoples of Altai and Saian, and also shall give a craniological verification of our positions. The problem of the historical genesis of this type will be solved by paleoanthropologists. In this connection much is expected from the study of the crania collected by S. A. Teplukhov from the ancient graves in the Minusinsk region.

Since ancient crania of Turkish type have been found as far apart as Trans-Baikalia (Talko-Grintsevich) and South Russia, the distribution of this type in Eurasia must have been very wide. A mestization resulting in the origin of the Altaic type consequently is not excluded, but such a mestization may have taken place at a very early period.

Due to the localization of the described "Altaic" type in the steppe zone of South Siberia, IArkho proposes that it be named *Homo sapiens asiaticus* var. *sibirica meridionalis*.

The Saianic type (subvar. *saianica*) is a local variant of a wider complex which is best described as "Central Asiatic" (var. *centralis*).

Thus, in the foundation of the race genesis of our Kazakhs lies a basic specific type corresponding to Deniker's Turkish race. In addition, the following races took part in the formation of the Kazakh type: Central Asiatic—Mongoloid—and, to a very small degree, the Europeoid Pamiro-Ferghan complex.

WESTERN KAZAKHS

Rudenko [80] observed that the study of the Kazakhs (Kirghiz-Kazakhs) is of many-sided interest. The Kazakhs, one of the most numerous Turkish peoples, have, better than the other Turks, preserved their ancient way of life and, most probably, their physical type.

In analyzing the physical type of the Kazakhs, it may be possible to determine the basic type of the Turks as well as the foreign admixtures which entered into their composition.

All earlier measurements were based on very little material, dealing almost entirely with adult males. Zeland [81] measured 10 male and 10 female Kazakhs and 30 male Kara-Kirghiz of the Semireche (Jetty-Su) region. Ujfalvy [82] measured 11 male Kazakhs and 26 male Kara-Kirghiz of Ferghana. Matseevskii and Poiarkov [83] measured 30 male Kazakhs in Kuldzha; Tronov [84] measured 36 male and 13 female Kazakhs of the Middle Horde; Kharuzin,[85] 157 male Kazakhs of the Lesser (Bukeevskaia) Horde, Ivanovskii,[86] 126 male and 30 female Kazakhs of the Middle Horde.

Thus, we have data regarding 426 male and 53 female Kazakhs and Kirghiz taken together. Of the investigators mentioned, only Ivanovskii gives summary data for individual clans, while the clans of the groups investigated by other authors are not known.

However, we know that the Kazakhs formed an independent people, consisting of only several tribes by the middle of the fifteenth century.

[80] Rudenko, S., Osobennosti zapadnykh Kazakov, in Akademiia Nauk S.S.R. Materialy osobogo komiteta po issledovaniiu soiuznykh i avtonomnykh respublik, No. 3, pp. 83-221, 1927.

[81] Zeland, N. L., Kirgizy. Zapiski Zap.-Sibir. Otd. Russ. Geog. Ob., vol. 7, No. 2, Omsk, 1885.

[82] Ujfalvy de Mezö-Kövesd, Le Kohistan, le Ferghanah et Kuldja. Paris, 1878.

[83] Matseevskii and Poiarkov, Etnograficheskie zametki o tuzemtsakh byvshego Kuldzhinskogo raiona. Omsk, 1883.

[84] Tronov, V. D., Materialy po antropologii i etnologii Kirgiz. Zap. Imp. Russ. Geog. Ob., po Otd. Etnogr., No. 2, St. Petersburg, 1891.

[85] Kharuzin, A. N., Kirgizy Bukeevskoi ordy. Trudy Antr. Otd. Imp. Ob. Liub. Est., Antr. i Etnog. Imp. Mos. Univ., vol. 14.

[86] Ivanovskii, A. A., Kirgizy Srednei ordy..Razh., vol. 14, No. 2, 1903.

At that time, in connection with the breaking up of the Djuchi *Ulus* (that is, the domain of the elder son of Genghis Khan, Djuchi Kahn), when the independent Khanates of the Crimea and Kazan were formed in the western half of the *Ulus,* the Kazakh Federation came into being with the death of Abul Khair Khan in the third quarter of that century. The first to secede from Abul Khair Khan were the Sultans Girei and Djannibek, who were joined by some of the clans. With the death of Abul Khair Khan and the final breaking up of the eastern half of the *Ulus,* a portion of the clans forming the *Ulus* joined the Kazakhs who had rallied about Sultans Girei and Djannibek. Somewhat later, the Kazakh Federation was joined by the majority of the Dasht-i-Kipchak clans.

Thus, the Kazakh Federation was formed by various tribes and clans, whose international administration was in the hands of their elders and was based on their separate customary law.

On the basis of historical data and from the study of the present-day composition of Turkish tribes and peoples, Aristov states that the main tribes forming the Kazakh Federation were:

1. Great Horde: tribes Dulat, Kangly, Kirghiz.
2. Middle Horde: tribes Kirei, Naiman, Argyn, Kipchak.
3. Lesser Horde: tribes Alchin, Baiuly, Jettru.

In all probability, even while still in the Altai, and later, when coming into Mongolia and into the so-called Kirghiz steppe in the west, the Turkish tribes intermingled in a greater or lesser degree, forming complicated tribal and clan federations.

Nevertheless, it is most probable that the study of modern clan subdivisions of the Kazakhs will uncover their tribal origin. Without attempting to treat of the tribal and clan subdivisions of the Kazakhs in general, Rudenko enumerates such subdivisions of the Kazakhs among whom he and his colleagues have conducted anthropological investigations.

In 1921, 496 Kazakhs were measured in the Kustanai canton (*uezd*) of the Turgai region. These data have not been published. In the summer of 1924 Rudenko measured 20 male Kazakhs in the Chuiskaia steppe during the Altai Expedition of the Russian Museum. During the summer of 1926, 827 Kazakhs of both sexes were measured in the government of Aktiubinsk and, partly, in the Adaevsk canton, by the Anthropological Section of the Kazakhstan Expedition of the Academy of Sciences under the leadership of Rudenko. The following anthropometric data give an idea as to the volume of observations: 233 individuals were measured in great detail, 496 in less detail, and 594 according to a simplified schedule. The Kustanai canton and Chuiskaia steppe groups were measured by Rudenko, the Aktiubinsk and Adaevsk groups by M. N. Komarova and L. K. Kornilov. Our investigations have covered in the main the Kazakhs of the Lesser Horde; the Kazakhs of the Middle Horde were studied only in part.

The Kazakhs of the Naiman tribe, measured in the Chuiskaia steppe belong to the Middle Horde. The number of individuals measured is so small that Rudenko postpones any interpretations of these materials until more substantial investigations of the eastern Kazakhs have been made. Part of the individuals measured in Kustanai canton belong to the Kipchak tribe, which also belongs to the

Tribal subdivisions of Kazakhs measured

1. *Baiuly*
    Adai .... Akbota, Balykshi, Baipak, Begei, Esenbet, Zhary, Zhemenei, Isek, Karazhan, Krykmyltyk, Kosulak, Konanorys, Mugal, Tazike, Turkpenadai, Tobysh, Turkpen, Shegem.
    Alasha.
    Baibakty.
    Bersh.
    Zhappas .... Nauruz.
    Esentemir.
    Taz.
    Tana.
    Sherkesh.
    Ysyk.
2. *Alimuly*
    Alim .... Akbura, Maimbet, Kabak, Karash, Karakesek, Kenzhe, Mailibai, Nazar, Ryskul, Tleu, Shuren.
    Kete .... Ozhirai, Uak.
3. *Jettru*
    Zhagalbaily .... Tleu, Shagyr.
    Kerdery.
    Tabyn .... Aidyr, Kedeikul, Kozhantai, Medet.
    Tama .... Kulan.

Middle Horde. The Kipchaks are one of the ancient Turkish tribes of the group in which Rashid-ud-Din (fourteenth century) also enumerates the Uigurs, Kirghiz, Karlyks, and other tribes. Long before the Mongol invasions, the Kipchaks were a numerous tribe wandering on the steppes between the Don, Volga, and the Urals, and giving their name to the steppe (Dasht-i-Kipchak—"The Kipchak Plain"). The number of Kipchaks decreased greatly as a result of great masses of them in the west becoming a part of the Bashkirs, Nogais, Crimean and Volga Tatars, and of further groups of Kipchaks, because of their part as the mainstay of the Juchid domination, going southwest with the Sheibanid armies to form the principal part of the Uzbeks particularly in Ferghana, between Zarafshan and the Amu, and also in Khiva.

The tribal composition of the Lesser Horde is very heterogeneous, since the Horde was formed of many fragments of various Turkish tribes. According to Tevkelev's Memorandum (1740) the Lesser Horde for a long time consisted of one tribe, the Alchin, which was divided into two tribal groups, the Alimulin and the Baiulin; seven smaller tribes joined the Alchins. These seven tribes formed a union only at the end of the seventeenth or the beginning of the eighteenth century, when Khan Tiavka, who died in 1717, united them into one tribal group of Jettru "seven clans." Of the tribes forming the Jettru group, two, the Tabyn and Tama, are also found among the Bashkirs and the Uzbeks. The investigations covered the Baiuly group (north in Kustanai canton and south in the Aktiubinsk region) and the Alimuly and Jettru groups.

The above groups are exogamous within clans, but endogamous within tribes and tribal subdivisions.

PIGMENTATION

Skin color.—Using von Luschan's scale, the color of the chest on areas normally covered by clothes: light (Nos. 7-13) and dark skins (Nos. 5, 6, 14-18, 22-25) were evenly divided.

Eye color.—According to Martin's scale the eyes were predominantly brown: 85.8 percent men, 96.0 percent women; of that number, 40.1 percent of the men and 62.8 percent of the women had dark brown eyes. There was no significant difference between the tribal groups. More women than men had dark eyes.

Eye color	No.	1	2	3	4	5	6	7	8	9
Baiuly	125	1	12	39	43	12	12	3	2	1
Alimuly	143	0	18	47	37	24	2	7	8	0
Jettru	36	0	2	8	11	7	6	1	1	0
Total	304	1	32	94	91	43	20	11	11	1

Hair color.—The hair was dark in the overwhelming majority of cases; of 448 adult males only 2, and of 402 women only 3, had light brown hair with dark eyes.

Combined hair and eye color.—The dark type having eye color Nos. 1-5 and dark hair definitely predominates: 90.2 percent of the men and 96.3 percent of the women. A larger admixture of the mixed type was found among the southern Baiuly (Aktiubinsk and Adaevsk regions) and the Jettru men. Comparable results were obtained by Kharuzin for the male Kazakhs of the Bukeev ("Lesser") Horde, and Ivanovskii for the Middle Horde, 97 percent of the dark type for the former, 95 percent for the latter. This endows with a still greater interest the considerations regarding the admixture among the Kazakhs of the legendary blond race, the Dinlins, found in the Chinese chronicles.

Aristov [87] states that the history of the Tang Dynasty written in the ninth century on the basis of earlier sources, in connection with a description of the Yenisei Kirghiz, says that "the inhabitants of that land have become mingled with the Dinlins . . . are generally tall, with red hair and pink faces and blue (green) eyes. . . ."

According to Aristov, Dinlin admixture may be found among the Tele, Merkit, Kirei, and a Lesser Horde tribe, the Alchin. Judging by the name, the Alasha tribe of the Baiuly group must also be of Dinlin origin. The data on the pigmentation of the Kazakhs at our disposal do not corroborate the supposition of a blond admixture among the Kazakhs. Whatever the case, this problem can be more appropriately examined when we have data regarding the physical type of the eastern Kazakhs and the Kirghiz, among whom, on the basis of historical information, the admixture of the Dinlins was much more probable.

STATURE

In the great majority of cases the stature was medium or below medium (164.0 for men and 151.0 for women). While the individual range of variation was relatively broad, there was no significant difference between the means obtained for various tribal groups. A somewhat greater stature was found for the men of the Jettru group, which also had women of a somewhat smaller average stature than the average for the other Kazakh groups. The average stature noted by Kharuzin for the men of the Lesser Horde was 162.9, i.e., very close to our figures for the Lesser Horde. Ivanovskii found a mean stature of 165.1 for the Kazakhs of the Middle Horde, which is somewhat higher than the figure for the Lesser Horde. This may be explained by a higher percentage of the Jettru group among the former.

Group	No.	Range	Mean	Short	Medium	Tall	Very tall
Baiuly A........	132	147.0-178.2	163.68	28.8	30.3	24.2	16.7
Baiuly K........	80	146.6-179.9	163.36	28.7	27.5	30.0	13.8
Alimuly	141	146.9-179.4	164.14	25.5	26.2	29.8	18.4
Jettru	65	153.7-178.7	165.70	24.6	21.5	29.2	24.6
Kipchak	48	150.3-175.9	163.62	25.0	27.1	37.5	10.4
Total or mean..	466	146.9-179.9	164.32	26.8	27.0	28.9	17.2

[87] Aristov, N., Opyt vyiasneniia etnicheskogo sostava kirgiz-kazakov Bolshoi ordy i kara-kirgizov. Zhivaia Starina, Nos. 3-4, 1894.

From the distribution curve (bimodal maxima at 162.0 and 166.0 for the men and 148.0 and 152.0 for the women) it is possible to assume the presence of two elements, differing in stature; the low element is most sharply pronounced among the southern groups (Aktiubinsk, Baiuly) and is also found among the Kustanai Baiuly and the Jettru. The tall element is most clearly present among the Alimuly, and is also found among the Kustanai Baiuly and the Jettru.

CEPHALIC INDEX

The overwhelming majority are true brachycephals (85.86 for the men; 86.87 for the women) with a very small percentage of sub-brachycephals and only an exceptional mesocephal.

Group	No.	Range	Mean	Meso.	Sub-brachy.	Brachy.
Baiuly A..........	128	79.1-95.4	86.35	3.90	12.5	83.60
Baiuly K..........	80	75.6-91.3	84.80	6.25	20.00	73.75
Alimuly	141	78.0-96.1	86.13	4.26	15.60	80.14
Jettru	65	78.2-82.2	85.32	4.61	23.08	72.31
Kipchak	48	79.5-89.1	84.53	4.16	29.17	66.67
Total or mean...	462	75.6-96.1	85.86	4.54	17.96	77.49

Only slight variations were noticed by tribes: the Kipchak males and their neighbors, the Kustanai Baiulys, are less brachycephalic than the other tribal groups. Kharuzin gives the average index of 86.28 for the Lesser Horde (brachycephals 82.0 percent; brachycephals and subbrachycephals together 96.0 percent). Ivanovskii's Middle Horde Kazakhs (clans Kirei, Naiman, Baidzhigit, and Murun) had an average of 89.39 (91.0 percent brachycephals and 99.0 percent brachycephals and subbrachycephals together). However, Rudenko's Middle Horde Kazakhs (Kipchak clan) averaged 84.53, while 33.33 percent of individuals were mesocephalic and subbrachycephalic. No data are available for the Great Horde.

HEAD BREADTH

The mean head breadth was 160.46 for males.

Group	No.	Range	Mean
Baiuly A........................	129	147-175	160.74
Baiuly K........................	80	149-172	159.35
Alimuly	141	143-174	160.62
Jettru	65	146-177	161.06
Kipchak	48	147-174	159.92
Total or mean..................	463	143-177	160.46

The tabulation of differences by tribes does not disclose any sizable difference between groups. The Kazakh groups investigated were found to be relatively homogeneous both in head form and in absolute head dimensions.

FACIAL INDEX

The majority were euryprosopic (men, 80.80, 74.1 percent; women 80.77, 77.3 percent). Of men, 18.4 percent, and of women, 16.4 percent, were mesoprosopic. Of men, 7.5 percent, and of women, 6.2 percent were leptoprosopic.

While the number of observations is probably not quite sufficient for a positive statement, certain differences in the facial indices of various tribes have been noted. The broadest faces were found among the Kipchaks and the Kustanai Baiulys; the greatest tendency toward

Face width	No.	Range	Mean
Baiuly A	131	134-160	148.86
Baiuly K	80	134-165	149.10
Alimuly	141	128-160	148.84
Jettru	64	138-162	149.44
Kipchak	48	138-159	149.58
Total or mean	464	128-165	148.98

Facial index	No.	Range	Mean	Eury.	Meso.	Lepto.
Baiuly A	131	72.9-90.4	81.22	71.0	20.6	8.4
Baiuly K	80	69.0-92.0	79.66	81.2	10.3	7.5
Alimuly	140	69.3-90.8	81.12	75.7	19.3	5.0
Jettru	64	70.9-96.0	82.59	59.4	25.0	15.6
Kipchak	48	68.0-87.5	78.38	87.5	12.5	...
Total or mean	463	68.0-96.0	80.80	74.1	18.4	7.5

leptoprosopy and mesoprosopy was observed among the Jettru. On the basis of the distribution curve, we can assume among the prevalently broad-faced Kazakhs an admixture of some mesoprosopic element. Because of the limited character of the data, this may be definitely shown only in the case of the Aktiubinsk Baiuly (men) and Alimuly (women); the women as a rule are more broad-faced than the men. Ivanovskii's observations on facial form on the Middle Horde were made on the basis of the physiognomic index and not the anatomical, as were Rudenko's. Nevertheless, his data do not contradict those of Rudenko, the great majority of the Middle Horde Kazakhs being euryprosopic, with a very small percentage in the leptoprosopic category, and the women being more broad-faced than the men.

14

The facial index of the Kazakhs depends on their very great absolute facial breadth (mean for both women and men 148.98). No significant variation in facial breadth was discovered between the various tribal groups, with the possible exception of the somewhat less broad-faced Jettru women.

NASAL INDEX

All Kazakh groups, in spite of their broad faces, are mesorrhine with a leptorrhine tendency. The average for men is 71.64 (56.1 percent), and for women 71.62 (52.2 percent). Of men, 40.8 percent, and of women, 44.5 percent were leptorrhine. In the platyrrhine category there were 3.0 percent males and 3.3 percent females. A slight tendency toward narrower noses is discernible among the Alimuly and Jettru groups, both in the mean nasal index and in the number of leptorrhines.

The distribution curves show the undoubted presence of two elements among the Kazakhs, one leptorrhine, and the other, predominating, mesorrhine. The two elements are found in all tribal groups, but are most clearly discernible in the case of the Aktiubinsk Baiuly and Alimuly. Nasal indices for the Middle Horde recorded by Ivanovskii do not differ materially from Rudenko's groups (71.78; leptorrhine, 54.0 percent; mesorrhine and platyrrhine together, 46.0 percent). Platyrrhines account for only 8.0 percent of the women (mean 72.25).

The nasal height (nasion-subnasale) is 53.16 for males, 48.38 for females. No material difference in this respect had been observed between tribes, with the exception of the Kustanai Baiuly (men and women) who, having a nasal index similar to the other groups, had somewhat lesser absolute nasal dimensions.

Nasal length	No.	Range	Mean
Baiuly A	132	45-63	53.10
Baiuly K	79	45-60	51.73
Alimuly	140	44-67	53.52
Jettru	65	40-66	54.96
Kipchak	48	46-63	52.54
Total or mean	464	40-67	53.16

Nasal index	No.	Range	Mean	Lepto.	Meso.	Platy.
Baiuly A	132	57.4-90.0	72 30	35.6	61.3	3.0
Baiuly K	79	55.4-88.9	72.08	36.7	60.8	2.5
Alimuly	139	50.0-92.5	70.76	46.0	50.3	3.6
Jettru	65	56.3-85.5	70.32	50.7	47.7	1.5
Kipchak	48	55.9-88.6	72.96	33.3	62.5	4.2
Total or mean	463	50.0-92.5	71.64	40.8	56.1	3.0

Conclusions

Rudenko's Kazakh group is characterized by dark and light skin; dark hair and eyes; medium stature; obvious brachycephaly, euryprosopy, and mesorrhiny tending toward leptorrhiny. From the analysis of the distribution curves, it is seen that two elements are indicated among both men and women: tall and short; narrow-nosed and with a nose of medium breadth, the latter group (i.e., the mesorrhines) being also characterized by a relatively broader face.

Only preliminary considerations may be advanced regarding the racial type and tribal composition of the western Kazakhs. There are three points of view regarding these problems:

Kharuzin [88] writes that they not only lack ethnological and anthropological unity, but also do not have any numerically strong nucleus around which other elements could become grouped. According to him, the Kazakhs are in the process of being dissolved in numerous Turkish, Mongolian-Turkish, and even other (Usuns or Wusun) tribes. This conglomerate character of the Kazakhs Kharuzin explains by geographical conditions, i.e., the steppes.

In another work while denying that the Kazakhs have a strictly definite type, Kharuzin states that there is an average predominating type among them, and proceeds to describe it. In addition to this type, he also states that among the Kazakhs are encountered individuals leaning toward either the Mongolian or the Caucasian race.

Criticizing Kharuzin's position, Ivanovskii, who does not think that the anthropological data indicate a high degree of mestization, lack of pure type, etc., among the Kazakhs, favors vaguely the idea of relative homogeneity of the Kazakh type.

Aristov, after examining Kharuzin's conclusions, supposes that the predominating type described by Kharuzin among the Kazakhs must be considered to be a Turkish (Turki) type. The other two types he is inclined to consider to be the western Dinlin and the Finno-Ugrian type. At the same time he thinks that the historical, ethnographical, and philological considerations and data also indicate traces of the Samoyed type.

Comparing the anthropological traits of the Kazakhs described above by Rudenko with the corresponding, partly published data regarding the Uralian, Altaian, and western Mongolian Turks and with some of the Mongol tribes, it is not difficult to observe that they are all possessed of common morphological peculiarities, and ap-

---

[88] Kharuzin, A., K voprosu o proiskhozhdenii Kirghizskogo naroda. Etnograficheskoe Obozrenie, 1895, p. 26.

parently all belong in the same, fairly stable, race. It is very probable that there exist local and tribal variations of this race, which we shall conditionally call the "Central Asiatic race," owing to incorporation within themselves of native (sometimes of ancient origin) elements, to mestization with representatives of other races, and to the variability of their own race.

Further study is necessary, especially of the Turkish and Mongol tribes, in order to identify the race that interests us, after which it will not be difficult to discover the nature of the admixture. In order to solve the problem of the disappearance of certain racial types, such as the Dinlins or Wusuns, if the information contained in the Chinese chronicles is accurate, or even to trace the evolution of the racial type of the Kazakhs, it is necessary to study the "large families" and other similar problems.

TURKOMANS OF KHWARAZM AND THE NORTH CAUCASUS

IArkho [89] gives the following summary for the Iomuds and the Chaudyrs of Khwarazm (Khoresm) and the Caucasus:

Iomuds.—Stature: above medium. Eyes: dark, with small admixture of mixed shades. Beard: growth, more than medium; form of hair, wavy. Head form: oval. Forehead: medium slanting. Supraorbital crest: below medium. Face: oval, with strong horizontal profile. Nose: height of root above medium; strong horizontal profile; nasal profile straight or convex; cartilage straight; tip slightly elevated; nostrils slant medium, oval in cross section, medium alae, tip inclination slight. Lips thin. Ears mainly oval with more than average protrusion. Helix well-developed; lobe usually attached.

Head very narrow, long, high. Dolichocephalic. Orthocephalic narrow forehead. Medium face length. Small zygomatic and bigonial breadths. Leptoprosopic. Nose medium long, medium broad. Leptorrhine. Majority of individuals clearly Europeoid.

Chaudyrs of Khwarazm.—Stature: above average. Hair and eyes: dark. Beard: growth below medium. Head: oval but higher admixture of spheroidal and sphenoidal forms than among the Iomuds. Forehead: medium slanting. Supraorbital crest: below medium. Face: oval, but with definite admixture of pentagonoidal forms. Nose: root height below medium; horizontal profile medium; profile straight or convex; cartilage, straight or concave; tip slightly elevated; slant of nostrils, medium. Epicanthic fold: relatively frequent (20 per-

[89] IArkho, A. I., Turkmeny Khorezma i Severnogo Kavkaza. AZH, Nos. 1-2, pp. 70-119, 1933.

cent). Upper eye fold: weak. Upper lip: height above medium; thin, but thicker than that of Iomuds. Ear: more protruding than that of Iomuds; less pendulous lobe. Compared to Iomuds, Chaudyrs have less dolichocephaly, greater head breadth and less head height. They also have wider minimum frontal, zygomatic, and bigonial diameters and greater face height. The Chaudyrs have a large admixture of Mongoloid individuals.

Chaudyrs of the Caucasus.—This group is still farther removed from the Iomuds. Stature: lower. Hair: darker. Beard: growth weaker. Forehead: medium slanting, supraorbital crest. Facial profile: much weaker. Nose: root height below medium; tip elevation straight. The remaining characteristics do not show a sharp deviation from other groups. Mongoloid peculiarities of the eye are like those of Khwarazm Chaudyrs, but epicanthic fold less frequent. Great upper lip height. Ear: lower percentage of pear-shaped forms; greater ear protrusion; smaller degree of helix inversion. Still less head length, but greater head breadth than Iomuds. Mesocephalic index. Broader minimum frontal, zygomatic, and bigonial diameters. Greater nose length and breadth than the Iomuds. Very considerable percentage of individuals of Mongoloid type.

Certain group distinctions are observable among Caucasian Turkomans, the most significant being the lesser Mongolization of the Chaudyr subgroup in comparison with Suiun-Dzjadzhii and the Ygdyr.

Summary.—Our problem is to discover which of the three Mongol races of Northern and Central Asia participated in the formation of the Turkoman racial type: North Asiatic, Central Asiatic, or South Siberian.

It must be stated that our materials do not furnish a definite answer to this problem. Obviously the probability of participation of the North Asiatic [90] element is small. Since the greatest degree of Mongoloidicity among the Caucasian Turkomans is accompanied by a bizygomatic breadth of 145-146 mm., the possibility of a considerable admixture of the Ural-Altaic subtype is excluded.

The participation of the Paleo-Siberian type (subdolichocephalic, massive, broad-faced, with strongly slanting forehead and a sharply marked supraorbital crest) is impossible to deny since geographically it had been in contact with the long-headed race both in Siberia and Europe. If such were the case, its traces may more probably be found in the Caucasus than in Khwarazm, and other Mongoloid ele-

---

[90] Cf. the Ural-Altaic group including the Voguls and Shortsi.

ments must have taken part in the Turkoman admixture. The first is seen from the similar development of browridges and the inclination of the forehead of the Iomuds and of the Khwarazmian Chaudyrs. A Paleo-Siberian admixture among the Chaudyrs would have been expressed in a greater inclination of the forehead in comparison with the Iomuds. The browridges of Caucasian Chaudyrs are strongly expressed and do not contradict the possibility of the presence of a Paleo-Siberian complex.

On the other hand, this possibility is denied by the slight inclination of the forehead. The differences in type between the Caucasian and Khwarazmian Chaudyrs suggest, more or less definitely, the heterogeneous character of the Mongoloid components. Historical data indicate contacts of Turkomans and their ancestors, the Guzes, on one side, with other peoples of Turko-Mongol origin, on the other. Among these must first be mentioned the Kazakhs, Kalmyks (in the case of the Caucasian Turkomans) and the "historical Mongoloids" of Central Asia. Accordingly, it would be appropriate to discover the relative degree of participation in the formation of the physical type of the Turkomans of the Central Asian brachycephals, particularly since the great brachycephaly of the Mongol element among the Turkomans is proved through an ordinary comparison of group means.

The Khwarazm Chaudyrs, having in comparison with the Caucasian Chaudyrs a greater admixture of the Europeoidal type, are nevertheless characterized by a similar height of the nose, a greater percentage with an epicanthic fold, a similar degree of upper eye fold, and heavier browridges.

To summarize, the Central Asian type is without doubt represented among both the Caucasian and the Khwarazmian groups; to a certain degree, the possibility of participation of the South Siberian type is stronger in the Caucasus. The differences of the isolated types tend in three directions: toward the Kazakhs (South Siberian type); toward Tannu-Tuvans (Central Asiatic type); and, in the case of the Iomud group, toward the Mediterranean Europeoid complex.

To turn to another phase of the problem, let us examine the so-called Europeoidal complex. This should also show relationships to the already known type of Europeoids in Central Asia. The characteristic group, described by Oshanin and IArkho, was conditionally named the "Pamiro-Ferghanic." The distinctive traits of this group are: brachycephaly, more or less straight forehead, relatively dark pigmentation, and a moderately narrow face (138-142 mm.). However, among the Turkomans brachycephaly is connected with the Mongoloid, and not the Europeoid, complex. The Europeoid complex of the Turkomans is dolichocephalic, having the smallest cephalic index (75.0) known in the U.S.S.R.

There are some historical data showing that the dolichocephaly of the Scytho-Sarmatian tribes, and also of the Turkomans, may have been caused by a peculiar local method of artificial cranial deformation, resulting in the change in the cephalic index. During the expedition E. G. Libman and D. Iomudskaia studied the use of the felt headgear put on the heads of the nursing babies and demonstrated that the use of such a hood could not result in a dolichocephalic change of the skull, and that the children were naturally dolichocephalic.

In applying the fact of negative interracial correlation of the head length and breadth discovered by Pearson and Czepurkowski to Central Asiatic groups, we find that some groups possessing great head length have, at the same time, a smaller head breadth. The Turkomans belong in the lower left-hand corner of the correlation grid, having the greatest length and the smallest breadth. In the upper right-hand corner belong the Uigurs. According to IArkho and Debets, the lack of positive correlation between the length and breadth of a group indicates its mixed character. In this connection two facts are of interest: (a) great positive correlation of Iomuds; and (b) impairment of correlation of Khwarazmian Chaudyrs. The first verifies the racial, and not artificial, character of the Turkoman dolichocephaly. The small size of the index excludes the possibility of significant participation of any Europeoid brachycephalic type. It is possible to claim that the Europeoid base of all investigated Turkomans is homogeneous. This is explained socially by strict endogamy, national, tribal, and clannish, of the Khwarazmian Turkomans. In the Caucasus the Turkomans mix with the Turkish Nogais, Europeoid Tatars, who apparently have a Europeoid element comparable to that of Turkomans. Formerly, they used to mix with Kazakhs and Kalmyks.

A STUDY OF THE TURKISH PEOPLES, 1924-1934

In a posthumous article,[91] edited by G. Debets, A. I. IArkho [92] published a summary of a systematic anthropometrical survey continued for 10 years among the Turkish peoples of the Soviet Union.

[91] IArkho, A. I., Kratkii obzor antropologicheskogo izucheniia Turetskikh narodnostei SSSR za 10 let (1924-1934) [A brief review of the anthropological study of the Turkish peoples of the U.S.S.R. during the 10 years 1924-1934]. AZH, No. 1, pp. 47-64, 1936.

[92] IArkho's death in Turkestan during 1935 came as a great shock to his colleagues throughout the world, since he was one of the foremost Soviet physical anthropologists. His work will be quoted in many text books still

The systematic anthropological study of Turkish peoples in the U.S.S.R. was begun in 1924, little having been done previously. The Academy of Sciences of the U.S.S.R. has sponsored the study of the following peoples:

1. Chuvashes, Uzbeks, by B. Vishnevskii.

2. Tatars of the Crimea, and Nogais of Daghestan, by N. Terebinskaia.

3. Yakuts, by Schreiber.

4. Kazakhs, Bashkirs, and Teptiars, by S. I. Rudenko and S. Baronov.

5. Kirghiz, by R. Mitusova.

6. The Central Asiatic organizations of the Academy sponsored the study of the Uzbeks, Kirghiz, Kazakhs, and Turkomans by L. V. Oshanin, in collaboration with V. K. IAsevich.

7. The physical development of children was recorded by Shishlov, Goncharov, and others; that of adults by A. I. IArkho, A. Askarov, and others; while demographic studies were made by D. Iomudskaia, E. Time, and assistants.

8. The following studies were also conducted:

a. Tatar tribes of European Russia, by G. Debets, T. Trofimova, and V. Sergeev, all of MGU.

b. Turkish tribes of the Caucasus, the Karachais, and Balkarians, by V. Levin and V. Bunak, both of MGU.

c. Kumyks and Kazakhs of the Volga area (Povolzhe) by G. Debets and T. Trofimova.

d. Azerbaidzhan Turks by Debets, IArkho, and N. I. Anserov.

e. Mountain Tatars of the Crimea by IA. Roginskii.

9. The former Society for the Study of the Urals, Siberia, and the Far East collected and preserved materials on the anthropology and demography of the Shortsi, Teleuts, nationalities of the Oirot Autonomous Province, Khakass (various groups), Kazakhs, Kirghiz of Kirghizia and Uzbekistan, Uigurs, Uzbeks (various groups), Kuramins, Kara-Kalpaks, Turkomans of Turkestan S.S.R. and of the North Caucasus, Azerbaidzhan Turks, Nogais of Daghestan (IArkho), Kumyks (A. Grinevich), Karaims (B. Adler), and the Russo-Turkish mestizos of the Altai and of the Khakass Autonomous Province. The craniological research was conducted by Bunak, Debets, and Trofimova.

10. A MGU Expedition (V. Bunak and A. I. IArkho, leaders) was dispatched to Tannu-Tuva [formerly Uriankhai].

---

unwritten. I had the privilege of meeting him at MGU in September 1934, and of discussing numerous anthropological problems of the Caucasus, Turkestan, and Central Asia. (H. F.)

11. Quantitatively, the materials assembled greatly exceed the pre-Revolutionary collections. For the first time the Kumandintsis, Altai-Kirghis, Teleuts, Crimean Tatars, Astrakhan Tatars, Kara-Kalpaks, Kirghiz, Uzbeks, Kuramins, Tubalars, and Shortsis were investigated.

12. Among the few Siberian and Tatar groups still to be studied are the Karagasis, Kalmazhis, and Dolgans.

13. The study of the Turkish peoples was carried out in four fields:

a. Racial composition.

b. Physical development.

c. Mestization.

d. Demographic data.

Racial composition.—The theoretical problems of racial analysis of the Turkish nationalities have been studied mainly by Bunak (craniological data) and by Oshanin and IArkho. The majority of the data, particularly those collected by the MGU investigators (Debets, IArkho, and Trofimova), those of Central Asia (Oshanin) and of Transcaucasia (Anserov), yielded consistent results.

According to IArkho, it is already possible, through the study of the data available, to obtain a relatively accurate idea of the basic anthropological types which were combined to produce the modern Turkish peoples, although there still remain many unsolved problems.

In attempting to classify the Turks into one of the racial branches either in a Mongoloid or a Europeoid [93] race of the first order, IArkho comes to the conclusion that the racial heterogeneity of the Turks has been entirely proved. If one disregards the more recent admixture of the Russian elements, some of the Altaic peoples of Siberia and the Yakuts may be considered to be relatively pure Mongoloids. The concentration of the Mongoloid influence decreases gradually toward the west. The western Turks are characterized by feebly expressed Mongoloid traits and by practically pure European characteristics, e.g., the Kumyks (Debets); Azerbaidzhan Turks of Nakhichevan, Nukha, and Gandzha (Anserov, IArkho, and Debets); Karaims (Adler); and the Crimean Tatars from the south coast (Terebinskaia).

A large section of the Turkish language groups is of a racially hybrid character. They are mixtures of varying composition of the Mongoloid and European races of the first order, e.g., Uzbeks, Tatars,

---

[93] Term used by Soviet anthropologists to denote *Homo sapiens indo-europaeus* in contradistinction to *Homo sapiens asiaticus* (Mongoloid) and certain transitional forms such as *suburalis* and *sublappica* (sublapponoid). IArkho does not differentiate between Turks and merely Turkized stocks. (H. F.)

Bashkirs, etc. Many racial types of the second order entering into the composition of various Turkish peoples may be successfully discerned by different methods of racial analysis.

Three Mongoloid races of the second order were discovered by IArkho in the Altai-Saian highlands: Ural-Altaic, South Siberian, and Central Asian.

Rudenko states that the Kirghiz and the Kazakhs belong to the Central Asian stock. They are characterized as possessing in general South Siberian traits, with a small admixture of the European Pamiro-Alpine element, which according to Trofimova becomes increasingly strong in the west.

In Central Asia, Oshanin and IArkho distinguished brachycephalic Pamiro-Alpine, dolichocephalic Mediterranean,[94] and "Vorderasiatische Armenoid" types.

In Transcaucasia the Armenoid influence is also found simultaneously with the Pamiro-Alpine and the Mediterranean elements (Anserov, IArkho, and Debets).

The admixture of Mongoloid traits, while extremely slight, may nonetheless be traced, as for example among the Azerbaidzhan Turks in Gandzha (IArkho) and the Mughal-Turks of Kakh (Debets).

In the North Caucasus, V. Levin has described a special "Japhethic"[95] element, observed also by Debets among the Kumyks. The Mongoloid elements were found to be concentrated among the Nogais and the Turkomans (Levin, Terebinskaia, and IArkho).

In the Crimea, Pamiro-Alpine and Dinaric elements were recorded by Terebinskaia among the Crimean Tatars.

Among the Tatars of the Middle Volga region (Debets and Trofimova), in addition to a slight Mongoloid admixture (the South Siberian variant), they were found to possess the Eurasian sublapponoid component element described by Bunak and Zenkevich and also an admixture of the eastern Baltic and the northern types.

The same component elements were encountered among the Bashkirs with a far greater prominence of the Mongoloid type.

The unpublished materials on the Chuvash (Vishnevskii) disclose the presence of distinct traces of the suburalic type of Bunak.

On the basis of all available data it has been possible to discern

---

[94] The identification of a dolichocephalic Mediterranean element in Central Asia seems to me of great significance since, in addition to the Mediterranean belt which extends from Morocco to the Pacific Ocean, following a line south of the Himalayas, there must also have been connecting lines of migration into Central Asia. (H. F.)

[95] IArkho preferred the term "Caucasian proper."

not less than three Mongoloid races of the second order, six Europeoid races, and one or two transitional types. IArkho suggested immediate standardization of these definitions. Wherever craniometric studies were possible, the results conformed to a remarkable degree with those obtained on the living.

Provisionally, the zone of the original formation of Turkish languages appears to have been peopled by both Mongoloids and dolichocephalic Europeans.

On the basis of existing data, the modern Turks may be considered neither as belonging to a homogeneous race, nor as originating from a single racial base. This does not contradict the results obtained by Oshanin and IArkho, substantiated by the paleoanthropological finds of Debets, showing the contemporaneity of Mongoloid complexes with definite historical groupings and stratifications of the Turks in Central Asia and South Russia (e.g., the Polovtsy) as well as the connection found by Debets between the ancient Turkish elements in the Chuvash langauge with the sublapponoid and Mediterranean European elements.

Physical development.—A regional characterization is complicated by the lack of data [96] and the differences in recording techniques. It is possible, however, to state that the physical development of the Turkish tribes varies greatly with the geographic, economic, and social conditions, all of which have operated for long periods of time to modify the somatic peculiarities of the inhabitants.

It often happens that racially different groups in a closely similar environment retain their own peculiar traits, as, for example, the narrow chests of the Turkomans (Oshanin), while closely related groups under differing environments show different physical indices.

Among the Chuvashes, Kirghiz, Uzbeks (Libman), and the Turkomans of North Caucasus (Vertogradskaia), body temperature, rate of pulse and respiration, and blood pressure were recorded.

No specific racial peculiarities were disclosed through the study of blood samples, many of which were collected.

Mestization.—Because of the highly mixed character of the Turkish peoples with regard to the races of the first and second orders, it is possible to utilize the data regarding such tribes for the study of the problems of mestization.

A special study was undertaken by IArkho during 1924-1925 in the Oirot and Khakass Autonomous Provinces. Because of the

---

[96] Records of stature, weight, chest circumference, etc., were taken by members of the former Society for the Study of Soviet Asia and MGU. These figures are given in table 7, AZH, No. 1, pp. 47-64, 1936.

insufficiently developed program and the errors of method, the results are not valid. Nevertheless, the materials collected testify to the absence of any negative influence of mestization upon the physical development of the population. The hybrids of Altaians and Khakass with the Russians have the higher physical indices of the Russians (Belkins and IArkho).

Data regarding the physical development of definitely hybrid groups (e.g., Uzbeks, Kara-Kalpaks, etc.) demonstrate conclusively that no decrease of anthropometric indices accompanies mestization.

No materials have yet been published regarding the mechanism of variability of racial traits in the course of mestization.

Demographic data.—The demographic study of the Turkish peoples was conducted by questioning individual families and economic units.

The following areas were studied under different auspices: The UNKHU Expedition, the Society for the Study of Soviet Asia, and the Uzbek Institute of Social Hygiene in the Oirot Autonomous Province, the Kirghiz S.S.R., Uzbek S.S.R., the Kara-Kalpak A.P., the North Caucasus, the Bashkir A.S.S.R., the Karachev A.P., and in Daghestan; the Institute of Social Hygiene of the R.S.F.S.R. and the Society for the Study of Soviet Asia in Daghestan; and by the latter and the Turkoman Institute for Social Hygiene in the Kara-Kalpak A.P., and the Tatar A.S.S.R.; and the Academy of Sciences of the U.S.S.R. in the Bashkir, Kazakhstan, and the Yakut A.S.S.R. In addition, the current official statistical data of the GOSSTATISTIKA were available.

Although the theoretical interpretation of these data is under consideration by Time, Schreiber, and Baronov, the following facts may now be stated:

a. The presence of a specific demographic structure (age-sex composition) of many Turkish groups.

b. Relatively high dynamic indices of many groups.

c. Many radical demographic changes, with respect to the longevity, mortality, marrying age, etc., as a result of improvements in social-economic conditions.

d. That the peculiarities noted can in no sense be connected with the racial factors, in so far as the inheritable influences of fertility and other biodemographic indices are governed by the social-economic factors.

e. That the gradual numerical decrease of two Turkish peoples, the Nogais and the Turkomans of North Caucasus, can be explained by social-economic analysis (IArkho).

f. At the end of the First Five Year Plan the following were the unfavorable factors: Early marriages of women resulting in lowered fertility, high infant and female mortality, lower longevity (in comparison with Russians) and general higher mortality of Nogais, Kara-Kalpaks, Kirghiz, Turkomans, and others. These were doubtless due to the former low level of social-economic relations, servile status of women, etc., and are now showing signs of disappearing (IArkho).

The important tables [97] of anthropometric data have been omitted since the physical anthropologist can have ready access to them should he so desire.

PALEOANTHROPOLOGY OF THE LOWER VOLGA AREA

In 1930 G. F. Debets [98] measured ancient skeletal remains from various Volga sites preserved in the Museum of the Kuibyshev [formerly Samara] Society of Archaeology, History and Ethnography, the Regional Museum of Saratov, and in the Central Museum of the Volga-German A.S.S.R. at Engels.

The earliest well-known sites from this area, characterized by a microlithic industry, belong to a later period than the western stations yielding geometric forms. Usually associated with these microliths is pottery of the same type as the Eneolithic sites of the Drevne-IAmnaia culture.[99]

The burials contain flexed, stained skeletons, egg-shaped pottery, and isolated flint, or, rarely, copper implements. This period is characterized by the prevalence of hunting and fishing with a slight development of animal domestication toward the end of the period and a total absence of agriculture.

According to Debets the crania were not Mongoloid in spite of the great facial breadth. On the basis of the typical combination of a low, orthognathous face with low orbits and a highly prominent nose, Debets considers them to be definitely European. The great percentage of slanting foreheads with very strong browridges comparable

---

[97] Tables 1 to 4 include 20 measurements and observations on groups in Siberia, Central Asia, Caucasus, and Crimea, and the Volga area. The data, obtained during the past 15 years, are made available here in English for the first time. See AZH, No. 1, pp. 47-64, 1936.

[98] Debets, G. F., Materialy po paleoantropologii SSSR: Nizhnee Povolzhe [Materials for the paleoanthropology of the U.S.S.R.: Lower Volga area]. AZH, No. 1, pp. 65-81, 1936.

In September 1934 I met G. F. Debets at MGU, where he is the leading physical anthropologist of the younger generation. He has recorded considerable anthropometric data among widely scattered groups. His publications are already extremely valuable. (H. F.)

[99] "Culture of the Burying Grounds in Fosses."

to Australian crania or IArkho's "South Siberian" type is not represented among modern European races; the Lower Volga series in this respect may be compared only with the Upper Paleolithic series from Brünn (Brño) and Predmost in Moravia.

The "Catacomb Burial Period," succeeding the Drevne-IAmnaia culture, is characterized by a greater increase in animal domestication. These burials, almost never found on the left bank of the Volga, are probably a local form. Only four male crania of this period, from the Ust-Griaznukha excavations of T. Minaeva near Stalingrad, were studied. In general, they have both a greater cranial index and a greater height than the crania of the preceding period associated with a European facial structure.

Debets mentions that another more numerous group of brachycephalic crania from catacomb burials is known from the Slobodka-Romanovka tumulus near Odessa, described in 1915 by D. K. Tretiakov, who states that "catacomb-building brachycephals are found as an alien element wedged among the predominantly dolichcephalic populations."

The second half of the Bronze Age in the Lower Volga area is known as "Srubno-Khvalynskaia"[1] after P. S. Rykov and V. V. Holmsten, or "Stage II of gens-society" after A. P. Kruglov and G. V. Podgaetskii. This culture is characterized by the leading role of agriculture and the use of domesticated animals.

The skeletal remains differ but slightly from those of the preceding period. The crania are characterized by straighter foreheads, smaller browridges, and a somewhat smaller bizygomatic breadth. There was no apparent connection between the slight change in morphological characters and local cultural variations so that there was no reason for supposing that the people of the Srubno-Khvalynskaia culture came from outside.

Only one female skull from the subsequent period, the so-called Scythian stage, was available to Debets. This in turn was followed by the Sarmatian culture (third century B. C.—third century A. D.).

Skeletal remains from 17 sites, excavated by Zhuravlev (1), P. D. Rau (11), and P. S. Rykov (5), were studied by Debets. In 1928 B. Grekov pointed out the similarity between the Volga and the Ural burials of the Hellenistic period. The later burials, attributed to the Roman period, are connected with the preceding phase by a series of minor transitions so that burials from both periods can be considered as belonging to one "Sarmatian" culture, characterized by pastoral nomadism.

---

[1] "Log-cabin type of burial culture."

No anthropometric differences could be observed between Hellenistic and Roman crania. Regionally, however, significant differences were found between crania from the Volga-German region and the Astrakhan district. The crania from the former were mesocephalic and large; from the latter they were brachycephalic and small. While the general European character of the face is common to the two periods, the skull differs greatly in breadth and in other characteristics.

Bronze Age dolichocephalic crania were encountered at a much later period in the Finnish burial grounds of the Middle Volga. This agrees with the archeological data, which indicate a direct continuity between the two cultures. The same type of cranium is present in the "Andronovo" culture burials from the Minusinsk region of western Siberia. The Sarmatian crania stand much closer to the Andronovo crania than to those of the Volga Bronze Age. The same type of cranium was found by M. N. Komarova in burials along the left tributaries of the Ural River in Kazakhstan.

The brachycephalic Sarmatian crania from the Astrakhan district differ greatly from those of the Volga Bronze Age. The combination of brachycephaly with the slanting forehead is nearer to the Mongoloid Turkish type on one side, and to the Armenoid skull on the other. Because of the low facial height and the highly prominent nose, Debets classified these Sarmatian crania as European; not having sufficient data to compare them with the proper Armenoid type, he places them in the Eurasian brachycephalic group, the Pamiro-Alpine. The Sarmatian brachycephalic crania are also comparable to the round-headed type of the Catacomb culture, both belonging among Eurasian brachycephals.

No analysis was possible on the fourth-fifth century Sarmatian crania, because of the widespread practice of artificial cranial deformation. Only one late Sarmatian skull, attributed to the seventh-eighth centuries A. D., was available to Debets. This was of Mongoloid type with a very high face and a tendency toward dolichocephaly. It is impossible to state, on the basis of this single specimen, whether the length of the skull was typical for the given group, as it known that the dolichocephalic Mongoloids of the Paleo-Siberian type were known to penetrate into Europe, or whether it was an individual variant or a case of mestization with some European stock.

During the first half of the present millennium, the Mongoloid South Siberian type appears in great numbers near the Lower Volga region, in an almost pure form among the nomads and continuing its existence among the population of the settlements of the Golden Horde.

Debets gives the following conclusions:

1. The oldest type is represented by the skeletons of the so-called Drevne-IAmnaia culture, attributed to the third millennium B. C. This type is closely similar to the Upper Paleolithic crania of Western Europe.

2. The stage of the Catacomb culture, which apparently did not spread east of the Volga, belongs to the end of the third and to the beginning of the second millennium B. C. This culture appears to have penetrated from the west. The typical skull, belonging to the Eurasian brachycephals, stands most closely to the Dinaric group. To some degree, this type is also connected with a similar culture in the Ukraine.

3. The Srubno-Khvalynskaia culture of the late Bronze Age (second millennium B. C.) in many localities follows directly after the Drevne-IAmnaia culture; in general, the racial type is close to that of the preceding period.

4. Crania of the period between the end of the Bronze Age (ninth century B. C.) and the beginning of the Hellenistic period (third century B. C.) have not been studied.

5. The prevalent racial type of the Sarmatian culture, during the Hellenistic and the Roman periods (third century B. C.—third century A. D.) came to the Volga area from Kazakhstan; the crania and long bones appear to be most closely related to the skeletons of the Andronovo culture from western Siberia.

6. During the same period there is also found, mainly in the Astrakhan area, a type belonging to the Eurasian brachycephals, which may be connected with the type belonging to the Catacomb culture.

CRANIOLOGY OF THE TATARS OF THE GOLDEN HORDE

Trofimova [2] of the Moscow State Museum of Anthropology studied a series of 35 male crania from two sites of the Golden Horde period (fourteenth-fifteenth centuries) at Sharinnyi Bugor [hill] and Streletskaia Sloboda settlement, near Astrakhan. These crania, originating from Vorobievs' and Lesgaft's excavations about 1870 are now preserved in the Moscow State Museum of Anthropology and in the Museum of the Anatomical Institute, Kazan. The series of 11 crania from the Kazan Museum were measured by Debets, the rest by Trofimova. Rudolph Martin's measurements were used by Trofimova,

---

[2] Trofimova, T. A., Kraniologicheskii ocherk Tatar Zolotoi Ordy [Craniological outline of the Tatars of the Golden Horde]. AZH, No. 2, pp. 166-192, 1936.

and the range of variation for means as suggested by Bunak was followed.

This series was brachycephalic (greatest occipital length 176.9; greatest breadth 145.4), hypsicephalic (height 132.9), and of medium size, with a medium broad forehead. The skull was often sphenoidal, although spheroidal and euripentagonoidal forms predominated. The face was of medium height and breadth; the nose was medium broad and the orbits of medium height. The slant of the forehead was medium, the profile orthognathous, with a medium nasal prominence.

In attempting to discover the racial affinities of the series, Trofimova deduced that the facial characteristics were close to the European Armenian (Bunak's 105 crania) Abkhazian (Trofimova's 41 crania) and eight "Sarmatians" from Astrakhan (Debets). The Tatar crania, however, had a less prominent nose and a less-developed fossa canina, and a relatively large number (28.5 percent) had a fossa prenasalis type of nasal orifice. No other Mongoloid traits were present.

In general, the series was considered to belong within the Europeoidal brachycephalic groups, despite the presence of Mongoloid elements. After examining 24 crania in Moscow Trofimova divided them into two groups, one showing preponderance of Europeoidal traits, the other having Mongoloid tendencies. Of the seven crania classified as Mongoloid, only two were definitely of Mongoloid type; the others having only certain Mongoloid traits. Several crania of the European group were of the characteristic European type, the remainder manifesting a slight Mongoloid admixture.

The cephalic index of the Europeoid group is less than that of the Mongoloid, while the absolute dimensions of the Mongoloid group are greater, and the skulls higher. The crania of the Central Asiatic and the South Siberian types, which may have participated in the formation of this Tatar group, are also of large absolute dimensions and relatively low height. On the basis of further analysis, Trofimova came to the conclusion that the Golden Horde Tatars from Streletskaia Sloboda and Sharinnyi Bugor were a mestized group consisting, basically, of the brachycephalic European and the Mongoloid types.

In order to determine the component elements of the Golden Horde Tatars, Trofimova compared them with other brachycephalic crania of mixed types. For this reason she examined a series of 14 Uzbek crania from contemporaneous cemeteries of Zolotaia Mulushka near Samarkand and from Tashkent. Trofimova also examined a series of 41 Abkhazian crania (37 of which had been described in 1879 by

A. A. Tikhomirov and A. P. Bogdanov), and also Bunak's measurements on Armenians and Croats and Reicher's measurements on Danisians.

The Uzbek crania were found to be more dolichocephalic and considerably higher than these Tatars. In general, the main difference between these two closely related types were the greater cranial, orbital, and facial heights. Trofimova divided the Uzbek series into "Europeoidal" and "Mongoloid" groups. IArkho states that the Uzbeks are a typical hybrid group resulting from the mixture of the white and yellow races of the first order. They are typical representatives of the Pamiro-Ferghanian racial complex. The Uzbeks of the nontribal groups have a slight Mongoloid admixture.

According to IArkho the Pamiro-Ferghan complex is characterized by "brachycephaly, a short skull, a straight forehead and a straight or slightly convex nose, an average nasal breadth and an average hair growth. . . . It is hardly likely that this type belongs in the European racial cycle; more probably, it is connected with the short-headed population of Vorderasien and the Caucasus."

Trofimova assumes, therefore, that the Golden Horde Tatars, near in type to the Uzbeks, are also a result of the mixture between the Mongoloid and the brachycephalic European types of the Pamiro-Ferghan complex.

In order to discover the components of this mestization, Trofimova also divided the Uzbek group into European (8) and Mongoloid (9) series of crania.

Trofimova concluded that three component elements were represented among the Golden Horde crania:

1. Europeoid ....Pamiro—Ferghan group.
2. Mongoloid ....a. South Siberian.
                          b. Central Asiatic.

The presence of these elements does not explain the unusual head length of the European series and the low orbits of the entire group. These can only be explained by the presence within the group of another European type, characterized by a long head, and low orbits. Such a type can only be one of the variants of the Mediterranean race. The admission of such an element will explain fully the racial composition of the Golden Horde Tatars.

Debets also investigated five Golden Horde groups:

1. Davydovka-Augustovka tumuli (Pugachev region): South Siberian type.

2. Volga-German A.S.S.R. tumuli: South Siberian type.

3. Uvek site: South Siberian type; partly Pamiro-Ferghan, or a closely related variety of European brachycephalic type.

4. Bukeevskaia steppe: Pamiro-Ferghan of a closely related Europeoidal brachycephalic type with probable Mediterranean admixture.

5. Tiaginka village, near Kherson on the Dnieper: South Siberian.

Trofimova then gives a summary of the pre-Mongol populations of the Lower Volga:

Earliest known remains are Sarmatian described by P. S. Rykov and P. D. Rau. Previously considered to be Iranian nomads from Asia, who began their invasion during the fourth century B. C., the Sarmatians, according to Marr, Ravdonikas, etc., "were not an ethnic group, but rather a new stage in the development of society during the Scythian epoch," in the regions of the Black Sea steppes (Sauromatians) and the Volga. The Sarmatian crania described by Debets [8] are of a brachycephalic type with a medium high face, leptorrhine and wide prominent nose, definitely European, in spite of the rather great face breadth. Similar crania were described by Rudenko [4] from Prokhorovo tumuli near Orenburg, and by Komarova [5] from Bronze Age sites.

Trofimova also examined seven crania from Chilpek burial ground near Kara-kol in the Kirghiz A.S.S.R. excavated in 1929 by M. V. Voevodskii and attributed to the period between the first century B. C. and the first century A. D. They were compared by Voevodskii with the "Scythian" crania from Altai, described by Griaznov,[6] and also with the nomadic burials from Orenburg steppe excavated by Grekov. Trofimova found that six of the crania belonged to IArkho's Pamiro-Ferghan type now living in Central Asia; one was close to the Mediterranean type; one, while similar to the Pamiro-Ferghan type, possessed an Armenoid nose and a few similarities with the Mediterranean type.

The second series attributed to the Sarmatian period, described by Debets from the Volga-German A.S.S.R., was of the so-called Andronovo type.

---

[8] Debets, G., AZH, No. 1, 1936.

[4] Rudenko, S. I., Opisanie skeletov iz Prokhorovskikh Kurganov [Description of skeletons from Prokhorovo tumuli]. Materialy Arkheologii Rossii, No. 37, 1938.

[5] Komarova, M. N., Cherepa bronzovoi epokhi iz mogil po levym pritokam reki Ural [Bronze Age crania from the graves on the left tributaries of the Ural River], Leningrad, 1927.

[6] Griaznov, M. P., Raskopka kniazheskoi mogily na Altae [The excavation of a prince's tomb in the Altai]; Pazyrykskoe kniazheskoe pogrebenie na Altae [A prince's burial from Pazyryk, Altai]. Priroda, No. 11, p. 971, 1929.

When these Sarmatian crania were compared with the European group of the Golden Horde Tatars, one thousand years later, Trofimova discovered an exceptional degree of similarity between them. This agrees with the archeological evidence collected by Rykov, who concludes that the culture of the Sarmatian epoch "grew over into" the Golden Horde culture in the Lower Volga.

This brachycephalic type is still preserved in Central Asia among modern inhabitants of Uzbekistan and Tadzhikistan.

According to Debets, the dolichocephalic European type, widespread in the steppes of the Ukraine during the Scytho-Sarmatian[7] period, is also represented in the Saltovo burials of the eighth and ninth centuries, variously classified as "Alanic" or "Khozarian";[8] another type, present in Saltovo, were brachycephalic European crania of Dinaric affinities. It was curious that no Mongoloid crania were found in this series of "Tatar" burials.

The only Mongoloid South Siberian crania attributed to the Torks (?) were found in Gorodtsov's excavations in the Izium and Bakhmut regions of the Ukraine. These crania were attributed to the eleventh century A. D. Debets, who studied this series of 15 crania, stated that there were 3 European dolichocephalic crania and 4 of the mixed type.

The only other Mongoloid crania from eastern Europe from any period are the fourth century A. D. Hun crania from Hungary described by Bartucz.[9]

CONCLUSIONS

The Golden Horde Tatars were a strongly mestized group composed of Europeoid and Mongoloid elements. The city-dwellers' crania from Sharinnyi Hill and Streletskaia Sloboda, as well as those from Uvek belong mainly to the Pamiro-Ferghan European type. The Mongoloid element present in the series belongs overwhelmingly to the South Siberian (Deniker's "Turkish") type. The latter is typical for the Golden Horde nomad crania from sites in the Pugachev region and from the Volga-German A.S.S.R., where there appears a European admixture.

---

[7] Bogdanov, A. P., O mogilakh skifo sarmatskoi epokhi i o kraniologii skifov [The tombs of the Scythio-Sarmatian epoch and Scythian craniology]. Antropologicheskaia vystavka, vol. 3, pt. 1, p. 263.

[8] Debets, G., Cherepa iz Verkhne—Saltovskogo mogilnika [Crania from the Upper Saltovo burial ground]. Antropologiia, VUAN [now ANU], vol. 4, Kiev, 1931.

[9] Bartucz, Lajos, Über die anthropologischen Ergebnisse der Ausgrabungen von Moson Szent Janos. SKYTHIKA, vol. 2, Prague, 1929.

The European brachycephalic type of the Lower Volga, of the foothills of the Urals ("PriUral'e"), western Kazakhstan, and Central Asia represents the ancient population of these regions during the Sarmatian epoch. This type was preserved during the Golden Horde epoch mainly among the city-dwelling Tatars but still exists among the Karagash Tatars [10] of the Lower Volga region and among various groups of Central Asia.[11] It is also probable that IArkho's Pamiro-Ferghan type represented among the contemporary Kazakhs [12] of the Altais is also a vestige of this ancient population.

In the light of these materials [13] it is possible once more to deduce that the Mongolian conquest may by no means be regarded as a significant mass migration, but as merely a military and political expansion of the Mongolian Empire. According to Barthold [14]: "The overwhelming majority of the Mongols returned to Mongolia; the Mongolians who remained in the conquered land, rapidly lost their nationality."

At the time of the partition of the Empire of Genghis Khan among his heirs, the majority of the Mongolian warriors remained in the Ugedei *Ulus* (Mongolia proper) and only 4,000 warriors remained in the entire territory of Djuchi *Ulus* including eastern Europe and the modern territory of Kazakhstan and Khwarazm. Thus, the numerous Mongol troops, mentioned by Plano-Carpini, most probably consisted of subjugated Kipchaks and other eastern European nomadic tribes. According to Barthold,[15] "The formation of the Mongolian Empire was not accompanied, as in the instance of the German invasion of the Roman provinces, by the migration of the people."

In the light of the anthropological data it is interesting to note the

[10] Based on T. Trofimova's unpublished data obtained during an MGU Expedition in 1932.

[11] Oshanin, L. V., K sravnitelnoi antropologii etnicheskikh grup prishlykh iz Perednei Azii [Contribution to the comparative anthropology of ethnic groups originating in Western Asia]. Materialy antropologii naseleniia Uzbekistana, No. 1, Tashkent, 1929.

[12] IArkho, A. I., Kazaki Russkogo Altaia [The Kazakhs of the Russian Altai]. Severnaia Aziia, Nos. 1/2, p. 76, 1930.

[13] IAkubovskii, A., Stolitsa Zolotoi Ordy Sarai Berke [The capital of the Golden Horde Saiai Berke]. GAIMK, Leningrad, 1932.

[14] Barthold, V. V., Istoriia turetsko-monogolskikh narodov [History of the Turko-Mongolian peoples], p. 17, Tashkent, 1928.

[15] Barthold, V. V., Isotoriia kulturnoi zhizni Turkestana [The cultural history of Turkestan]. Acad. Sci. U.S.S.R., Leningrad, 1927, p. 86.

contemporaneous evidence of the Arabic author Al Umari,[16] who wrote in the beginning of the fourteenth century:

> In antiquity this state [the Golden Horde] was the land of the Kipchaks [Polovtsy] but when it was conquered by Tatars, the Kipchaks became their subjects. Afterward they [the Tatars] mingled and intermarried with them [the Kipchaks] and the land prevailed upon their [the Tatars'] natural and racial qualities, and they all became even as like the Kipchaks as if they were of the same clan; for the Mongols [Tatars] had settled in the land of the Kipchaks, intermarried with them, and remained to dwell in their land.

The Mongoloid population of the Golden Horde also had its origin during the pre-Mongolian period. Thus the presence of South Siberian and European types, among the Tork subjects of Kiev, and the same types in Sarkel [17] permitted Trofimova to connect the infiltration of these tribes onto the Caspian-Black Sea steppes with the epoch of formation of the Pechenegs, and later the Polovetsian (Kipchakian) feudal-clan unions in Kazakhstan and the eastern European steppes.

The complete absence of the typical Central Asian racial types among the populations of the Golden Horde, with the possible exception of Mongoloid admixture in the case of the Sharinnyi Hill crania, adds probability to this supposition.

Trofimova concludes that the Mongolian conquest, in the course of which there was formed the new political federation of the Golden Horde, and which exercised an enormous political and social-economic influence upon the conquered areas, apparently did not greatly change their racial and ethnical composition. The isolated dolichocephalic European elements discovered in the series of the city-dwellers' crania from Sharinnyi Hill may belong to either the pre-Mongolian period, or to the Khazar state with its mixed population.

CRANIOLOGY OF THE KALMYKS

Levin and Trofimova [18] state that the earliest descriptions of single Kalmyk crania were published in the middle of the eighteenth century by Fischer, Kamper, and Blumenbakh. A complete bibliography of

---

[16] This is quoted from V. Tizengauzen (W. Tiesenhausen), Sbornik materialov otnosiashchikhsia k istorii Zolotoi Ordy [Collection of materials for the history of the Golden Horde], vol. 1, p. 325. St. Petersburg, 1884.

[17] Debets, G. F., Chelovecheskie kostiaki iz pogrebenii v Sarkele [Human skeletons from the Sarkel burials]. [In ms.]

[18] Levin, M. G., and Trofimova, T. A., Kalmyki: kraniologicheskii ocherk [A craniological description of the Kalmyks]. AZH, No. 1, pp. 73-81, 1937. [English summary.]

Kalmyk craniology was published by A. A. Ivanovskii,[19] who also described a large series of crania.

Studies on Kalmyk craniology have been published recently by M. Reicher [20] and N. K. Lyzenkov,[21] but these investigations were either published as comparative materials (Reicher) or were based on an insufficient amount of material (Lyzenkov: 5 male crania.)

The present investigation by Levin and Trofimova is based on a series of 61 crania in the Museum of Anthropology of Moscow First University.

A large portion of the series is described for the first time; there are 21 male and 9 female crania from the Kalmyk cemetery near Bodek settlement in the Manych area, which were brought to the Museum in 1925 by members of the Kalmyk Expedition from the State Institute for Social Hygiene. The remainder, already described by Ivanovskii and Reicher, come from the older collections of the Museum (11 crania collected by Lesgaft from cemeteries of Astrakhan, *Ulus* [nomad community] Khoshutovskii, and Zamianskaia Cossack settlement; and 20 crania collected by Walter and others).

The series of 61 contains 43 male and 18 female crania. The measurements and descriptions used are those of Rudolph Martin; the sex was determined cranioscopically. The three series were studied separately and collectively.

The Kalmyk type is described (pp. 76-77) in the following terms: Of medium length and relatively great breadth; brachycephalic, bordering on mesocephalic; the head not high; the face long and broad with a medium facial index; orthognathous; the nose long and not very prominent with a medium nasal index; the orbits high; and the forehead medium slanting. The browridges, fossa canina, and spina spinalis are weakly developed.

In general, the series might be regarded as Mongoloid, only seven skulls having some Europeoid traits (two from Manych, two collected by Walter, two Astrakhan). In attempting to analyze this Europeoid element, the author dismisses the possibility of a Russian admixture and agrees with the conclusions of Cheboksarov,[22] who

[19] Mongoly-Turguty Trudy Antropologich. Otd. IOLEAE, vol. 13, 1893.

[20] Untersuchungen über Schädelform der alpenländischen und mongolischen Brachycephalen. Zeitschr. Morphol. und Anthrop., vol. 15, No. 3, pp. 421-562; vol. 16, No. 1, pp. 1-64, 1913.

[21] Materialy k kraniologii Kalmykov [Craniology of the Kalmyks]. AZH, Nos. 1-2, 1933.

[22] Cheboksarov, N. N., Kalmyki Zapadnogo ulusa [The Kalmyks of the western *Ulus* (subdivision of a horde)]. AZH, No. 1, 1935.

classified the Europeoid element among his group of western Kalmyks as being of the western Caucasian mesocephalic type ["Pontic race" after Bunak [23]].

A series of Torgut skulls from Jugar investigated earlier by Reicher were reexamined by Levin and Trofimova. Although the Torguts were the principal component of the Kalmyks in the seventeenth and eighteenth centuries, no traces of Europeoid admixture were discovered. From this the authors conclude that Europeoid elements were absent in the composition of the Central Asian immigrants into the Volga region, who formed the chief component element of the Kalmyk people.

Thus, the authors conclude that the Kalmyks acquired these Europeoid elements after their emigration and during the subsequent periods of formation of the Kalmyk feudal union on the territory of the Lower Volga and the North Caucasus. The "Pontic" elements in this area are found since the Scytho-Sarmatian period,[24] later being present among the Tatars of the Golden Horde [25] and among the modern Nogais,[26] who were close neighbors of the Kalmyks.

The same Europeoid admixture is also found among the western Circassians.[27] There is also some trustworthy historical testimony regarding intermarriage between the Kalmyks and the Adighe. Thus, historical and anthropological data agree.

According to Palmov,[28] Shcheglov,[29] IArkho,[30] and Cheboksarov, the Kalmyk racial type was strongly affected by intermixture with the Turkomans [of North Caucasus].

Levin and Trofimova examined IArkho's conclusions identifying the Europeoid element among the Turkomans of the Mangyshlak Peninsula with a dolichocephalic element present in its purest form among the Iomud Turkomans of Central Asia. They came to the con-

---

[23] Bunak, V. V., Crania Armenica. Moscow, 1927.

[24] Debets, G., Materials for the paleoanthropology of the Lower Volga. AZH, No. 1, 1936.

[25] Trofimova, T. A., Craniological description of the Golden Horde Tatars. AZH, No. 2, 1936.

[26] Molkov, A. V., Kalmyki [Kalmyks]. Moscow, 1928.

[27] Levin, V. I., Ethnogeographical distribution of certain racial traits amongst the populations of North Caucasus. AZH, No. 2, 1932.

[28] Palmov, N. N., Studies in the history of Volga Kalmyks. 4 vols. Astrakhan, 1926-1929.

[29] Shcheglov, I. A., Turkomans and Nogais in the Government of Stavropol. Stavropol, ISID.

[30] IArkho, A. I., Turkomans of Khoresm [Khwarazm] and North Caucasus. AZH, Nos. 1-2, 1933.

clusion that this Europeoid element was closer to Bunak's "Pontic" type than to the more dolichocephalic, narrower-faced Central Asian Europeoid type.

The interrelation between the mesocephalic ("Pontic") and the dolichocephalic variants of the eastern branch of the Mediterranean race have not yet been determined. IArkho suggested a connection between the dolichocephalic Turkoman groups and such dolicho-cephalic Caucasian groups as the Kurds and Azerbaidzhan Turks, without, however, making an analysis of the relationships. Although Cheboksarov differentiated between the mesocephalic component of the western Circassians and the extremely dolichocephalic type com-mon among the Iomud Turkomans, yet he followed IArkho in seeking only the latter element among the Turkomans of North Caucasus. This does not explain the absence of the dolichocephalic type among the Kalmyks, who were fixed with the Turkomans.

After comparing the Mongoloid elements with other Mongoloid groups, Levin and Trofimova arrived at the following conclusions:

The average for the series agreed with the measurements of Tannu-Tuvans from Kemchik, measured by Debets;[81] the Kalmyks pos-sessed more slanting foreheads, higher orbits, and slightly more promi-nent, but narrower, noses. These characters are similar to those of Buriats from Kudinsk, measured by Debets (loc. cit.), and are gen-erally common for the South Siberian types (e.g., the Kazakhs) who, however, are extremely brachycephalic and have very large absolute cranial dimensions. A similarly strong frontal slant was also found by Roginskii[82] among the Lake Baikal Tungus, who are, however, extremely dolichocephalic and have flat noses.

On individual evaluation of the crania in the Mongoloid portion of the series, a group of four aberrant crania was isolated (three from Manych, one from Lesgaft's collection from Zamianskaia). These four crania are dolichocephalic, with very high and wide faces, strongly slanting foreheads, and medium-prominent (for a Mongoloid group) noses. Without any doubt these four crania belong to the Paleo-siberian race represented among the Tungus of Lake Baikal, the Ostiaks, the Voguls, and the Shortsi.

In the absolute dimensions of the skull and the facial and frontal characters, the Kalmyks are close to the Tungus. In the majority

[81] Debets, G., Craniological description of Tannu-Tuvans. Severnaia Aziia, Nos. 5-6, 1929.

[82] Roginskii, IA., Materials for the anthropology of Tungus of the northern Lake Baikal area. AZH, No. 3, 1934.

of the relative dimensions of the skull and in the orbital and nasal measurements the Kalmyks are close to the Voguls.

Thus the Mongoloid components of the series are limited to the Central Asiatic and the Paleosiberian, in the larger sense of the word. These differ from Cheboksarov's series in the presence of the latter [Paleosiberian] and in the absence of the South Siberian type. This difference may be explained by geographic reasons, since the author's data are limited to the central portion of the area inhabited by the Kalmyks, while Cheboksarov studied the populations of the western regions, where the Kalmyks were strongly mixed with the Nogais among whom the South Siberian type is strongly represented (cf. Trofimova, 1936).

The presence of the dolichocephalic Mongoloid element, discovered by the authors, may be explained historically. The territory of the formation of the Oirot feudal union in ancient times formed part of the Great Hun State.[33] One of the craniological types of the Huns described by Bartucz [34] was found by Roginskii to be very close to the Paleosiberian type. The relations of the Oirot Union in the later period with the more northerly regions could also account for the introduction of the Paleosiberian type among the Kalmyks.

THE ULCHI (NANI) CRANIAL TYPE

Levin [35] of the Institute of Anthropology, Moscow University, examined 16 male and 11 female crania from Ulchi burials near Ukta, Mongoli, Dudi, and Kolchom settlements in the Amur region. These crania, presented to the Museum in 1936 by A. M. Zolotarev, form the only collection from this area. Golds, Udekhe, Oraks, Negidals, and Amur Giliaks are nowhere represented in Soviet Museums. The crania were mesocephalic, being short, narrow, and of medium height. They had medium slanting foreheads, with weakly developed frontal bosses. The frontoparietal index was low. The occiput of the majority of the crania was angular.

The face was high and medium broad, with an index of 55.7. The nose was high and medium broad, with a mesorrhine index. The glabella was low. The orbits were high and medium broad, the intra-

---

[33] Iakinf, Historical survey of the Oirots or Kalmyks from the fifteenth century until the present time. Journal of the Ministry of the Interior (Russia), vol. 8, pt. 1, p. 33.

[34] Bartucz, Lajos, Über die anthropologischen Ergebnisse der Ausgrabungen von Moson Szent Janos. SKYTHIKA, vol. 2, Prague, 1929.

[35] Levin, M. G., Kraniologicheskii tip ulchei (Nani) [Cranial type of the Ulchi (Nani)]. AZH, No. 1, pp. 82-90, 1937.

orbital distance being relatively great. The face was orthognathous, with a slight tendency to alveolar prognathism. The development of the fossa canina was slight.

The series was not homogeneous, there being a wide range of variations.

Measurements on the living agreed with the craniological data.

The Ulchi (they call themselves "Nani") number only 723 individuals, according to the 1926 census. They live in the region of the lower Amur River between the regions occupied by the Giliaks and the Golds. They are described as a complex of clans of different origin, consisting of the Gold, the Orochi, the Ainu, the Manchu, and the Giliak.

Both in language and in culture the Ulchi are related to the Gold, but they have also been influenced by the Orochi and the Giliak, whom they most resemble craniologically. However, the Ulchi skulls possessed a lower cephalic index and a more retreating forehead than skulls of the Orochi and the Gold. Levin states that even Ainu admixture, if present, would not be sufficient to explain these differences, and suggests that the long-headed component of the Gold, who appear to be related to the North Chinese, may also be present in the Ulchi.

He also advances the hypothesis that this lower cephalic index among the Ulchi represents a Paleoasiatic admixture, present among many groups of the Evenks (Tungus). Recapitulating his characterization of the Pacific Ocean type of the Mongoloid race, which the Ulchi resemble, Levin states: "This type, scattered widely among the peoples of the Amur region, seems to be the basis on which the further formation of both Paleoasiatics and the Tungus-Manchus proceeded."

TWO TYPES OF YAKUT CRANIA

A. N. IUzefovich [86] states that the presence of two anthropological types among the Yakuts has been recorded by all investigators since Middendorff.[87]

According to A. N. Nikiforov the Yakuts begin a description of a person by stating whether he has a long or a round face. Mainov [88] wrote that a "small percentage of the Yakuts have somewhat different

---

[86] IUzefovich, A. N., Dva tipa IAkutskikh cherepov [Two types of Yakut crania]. AZH, No. 2, pp. 65-78, 1937.

[87] Middendorff, A., Puteshestvie na sever i vostok Sibiri [A voyage to the north and east of Siberia], pt. 2. St. Petersburg, 1869.

[88] Mainov, I. I., Naselenie IAkutii [The population of Yakutia]. Leningrad, 1927.

facial traits from those of their compatriots. The aquiline nose of such Yakuts makes them somewhat resemble the American Indians."

Previous to IUzefovich's report, however, only four Yakut crania had been described (one uncertain Yakut, by Virchow in Crania Ethnica, 1882; and three by A. I. Kazantsev in Trudy of the East Siberian Medical Institute, 1935).

IUzefovich (1937, pp. 65-78) studied 34 crania that the Institute of Anthropology and Ethnography (IAE) of the Academy of Sciences of the U.S.S.R. had acquired between 1858 and 1928. Six of the series belonged to Dolgan Yakuts, who are considered to be Mongol-speaking Tungus and are treated separately.

From his study of the 28 remaining crania IUzefovich concluded that two distinct types actually exist among the Yakuts. He tabulated their characteristics as follows:

Type 1	Type 2
Brachycephalic.	Mesocephalic.
Small cranial height.	Great cranial height.
Chamaecephalic.	Hypsicephalic.
Tapeinocephalic.	Metriacephalic.
Broad-faced.	Very broad-faced.
Long-faced.	Very long-faced.
Mesoprosopic.	Leptoprosopic.
Mesenic.	Leptenic.
Hypsiconch.	Mesoconch.
Mesorrhine.	Leptorrhine.
Chamaestaphyline.	Orthostaphyline.
Mesognathous.	Orthognathous.

The first group reveals a strong likeness to the Tungus of the North Baikal region described by Roginskii.

The second group is characterized by feebly expressed Mongoloid characters. IUzefovich states, however, that this weakness of Mongoloid traits cannot be attributed to any Europeoid admixture.

He suggests that two types took part in the formation of the Yakuts, one of which had also played an important role in the development of the Tungus physical type.

CRANIOLOGY OF THE OROCHIS OF THE MARITIME AREA

M. G. Levin,[39] of the Anthropological Institute of the State University in Moscow, remeasured a series of 19 Orochi crania at the

---

[39] Levin, M. G., Materialy po kraniologii Primorskikh Orochei [Materials for the craniology of the Orochis from the Maritime Area]. AZH, No. 3, pp. 323-326, 1936.

State Anthropological Museum which Ranchevskii [40] described in 1888. The collection was presented by the eastern Siberian branch of the Russian Geographical society.

The series consisted of nine male and eight female crania. Two children's crania were included.

Levin found the series to be relatively homogeneous. The crania were short, very wide, and of medium height. The cephalic index was 84.0. The forehead was straight, not broad, and the supraorbital region was of medium development. The prevailing skull forms were sphenoidal and broad-pentagonal. Muscular relief was slight. The occiput was flattened. The face was high, broad, and orthognathous (F.I. 52.8) ; the nose, medium (N.I. 46.8) and slightly prominent; the orbits, medium high. Horizontal and vertical facial profiles, as judged from the development of fossae caninae, were weak. Nine out of seventeen crania possessed a prenasalis.

Six crania had asymetrical occipita. Levin was unable to conclude whether or not the deformation was artificial, that is, a result of the use of native cradles.

Three crania had "Inca bones."

After comparing these crania with those of other peoples of northeastern Asia such as Giliaks (Trofimova), Tannu-Tuvans and Kemchik (Debets), Buriats and Kudiaks (Debets), Ainu (Trofimova), Tungus and North Baikal (Roginskii), and Aleuts (Tokareva), Levin concluded that the Orochis belong to the Central Asiatic variant of the Mongolian race but that they differed from other representatives of that type, such as the Tannu-Tuvans, in smaller head length, greater brachycephaly, and smaller cranial capacity. He therefore classifies them as belonging to the Pacific Ocean variant of the Central Asiatic type, to which Debets,[41] following Montandon,[42] attributed the Giliaks, the Aleuts, and the Tlinkits. Levin argues that the Aleuts differ greatly from the Orochis and the Giliaks in such essential characters as frontal, facial, and nasal angles, cranial height, and bizygomatic breadth. The Orochis and the Giliaks differ in growth of beard, the Sakhalin Giliaks including a heavy bearded type, which Debets found also among the so-called Amur Orochi.[48] Debets was not of the opinion that this characteristic was due to Ainu admixture.

---

[40] Morskoi sbornik, meditsinskoe pribavlenie, 1888.

[41] Debets, G. F., Anthropological composition of the population of Baikal area in the late Neolithic period. AZH, vol. 19, Nos. 1-2, 1930.

[42] Montandon, G., Anthropologie paléosibérienne. L'Anthropologie, Nos. 3-6, 1926.

[48] Debets, G. F., Ulchi. AZH, No. 1, 1936.

16

CRANIOLOGY OF THE ALEUTS

Tokareva [44] studied the osteological materials from the excavations of W. I. Jochelson [45] in connection with the Kamchatka Expedition of the Russian Geographic Society, 1908-1910. Jochelson, who excavated in the Aleutian Islands during 1909 and 1910, found 78 crania, 19 skeletons, and 617 bones in burial caves on the islands of Attu, Atka, Umnak, Amaknakh, and Uknadakh, and in burial huts on Unimak Island. Tokareva is now preparing for publication an extensive monograph on this material.

Tokareva summarizes the theories regarding the origin of the Aleuts. The early explorers believed them to be immigrants from Asia: Steller on the basis of some cultural elements, such as headdress; Veniaminov (1840), on Aleut traditions. Schrenk classified the Aleuts as belonging to his Paleoasiatic group of peoples.

Dall was the first of the modern investigators to express the belief that the Aleuts came from America. He thought them to be of Eskimo ("Innuit") origin, but did not base his conclusions on any anthropological evidence beyond recording the extreme variability of the Aleut crania, ranging from dolichocephalic to brachycephalic. Jochelson, while criticizing Dall's theories regarding Aleut prehistory, shared his ideas concerning the American origin of the Aleuts. According to his conception of the history of the peoples of North America and Asia, the Paleoasiatic tribes of northeastern Asia (Chukchi, Koriaks, Kamchadals) are an Americanoid branch, closely connected culturally with the tribes of northwestern America.

According to Jochelson all these tribes represent the remains of an ancient cultural layer, the unity of which was disrupted at a definite period by the intrusion of a new ethnic group, the Eskimo. Constituting the apex of the Eskimo wedge, which divided the autochthonous population into an American and an Asiatic group, were the Aleuts.

According to Tokareva, Jochelson did not give adequate attention to the racial peculiarities of the Aleuts. Jochelson [46] pointed out the existence of a series of sharp differences between the Aleut and the Eskimo type (brachycephaly), and suggested that these differences

[44] Tokareva, T. IA. (State Museum of Anthropology, Moscow), Materialy po kraniologii aleutov [Materials for Aleut craniology]. AZH, No. 1, pp. 57-71, 1937.

[45] Archaeological investigations in the Aleutian Islands. Carnegie Institution of Washington, 1925; History, ethnology and anthropology of the Aleut. Carnegie Institution of Washington, 1933.

[46] Jochelson, W. I., History, ethnology and anthropology of the Aleut. Carnegie Institution of Washington, 1933.

could be explained either as a result of mestization with a highly brachycephalic group (Athabaskan Indian), or in the course of local development under conditions of isolation.

L. S. Berg also shares Jochelson's views regarding the American origin of the Aleuts, without, however, touching upon the anthropological affinities.

Hrdlička has stated that the Aleuts belong to the Eskimo stock and has explained their physical differences from the Eskimos, particularly their brachycephaly, as the result of mestization with the Athabaskans. He bases this explanation on the postulate of a southerly migration of Eskimos from Alaska to the Aleutian Islands.

Montandon,[47] working with extremely limited material, connects the Aleuts with the Giliaks, and unites them into the "Aleut-Giliak type," a branch of the greater Mongoloid race. Biasutti shares this view, terming this branch "Aleutian."

Tokareva selected for investigation 32 male and 22 female crania, and 5 crania segregated into a special group as not typically Aleutian. This number of crania may be deemed sufficient for study, since the total number of Aleuts in 1937 was only about 2,000.

Jochelson attributed these crania to the period prior to the Russian invasion, i.e., during the middle of the eighteenth century. This eliminates the possibility of Russian admixture.

The age groups represented were as follows: 28 adult, 1 mature, and 3 subadult males; and 12 adult, 7 mature, and 3 subadult females. Measurements were taken according to Rudolf Martin's technique.

Neither artificial cranial deformation nor pronounced cranial asymmetry was observed. Three crania were affected by syphilis.

Preliminary examination revealed a group of five crania (three male, one female, one child) that differ sharply from the rest. As compared with the rest of the series, these crania have a straight forehead, a greater head height, a greater facial angle, and a lower face.

The extremely homogeneous male series of the main group, consisting of the 32 typical crania, has been described. These crania are medium in size, length (181.0), and breadth (146.57). The head height is exceptionally small, 127.05 (range 116-139).

A characteristic feature is the slanting forehead (66.2°) with a medium-developed browridge (1.52) and a well-developed glabella. The form of the head is subbrachycranial, while the pentagonal outline predominates. The bizygomatic breadth is 143.44 (range 137-

---

[47] Montandon, Georges, Craniologie paléosibérienne. L'Anthropologie, 1926.

153). The upper facial height is medium to high, 72.14 (range 65-81). The facial index of 51.57 (range 46.5-56.5) is mesoprosopic. The facial angle of 83.04 (range 76-90) is mesognathous. The facial form is elliptical, with medium-developed (1.84) fossa canina. The nasal index of 45.4 (range 35.5-53.4) is mesorrhine with a medium-developed nasal bone. The orbital height is above medium but tends toward being mesoconch.

The female crania are of smaller dimensions, both as to size and facial measurements. They are more brachycephalic, the frontal angle being smaller. The face is more protruding. The glabella, brow-ridges, and fossa canina are less developed.

After comparing Aleut measurements with the scheme proposed by Debets for Mongoloid, Europeoid, and Australoid (after Morant) races, Tokareva concludes that the Aleuts belong to the Mongoloid group, having neither Europeoid nor Australoid traits. Tokareva then compares the Aleuts with the racial groups of the second order, beginning with the Eskimo.

According to Jochelson,[48] the Aleutian langauge originates from a source common to all Eskimo dialects, and in all probability represents by itself one of the most ancient Eskimo dialects. The culture of the Aleuts is very close to that of the Eskimo. According to Tokareva there is, however, very little in common between their physical traits.

According to Jenness[49] the Eskimos are characterized by a relatively high skull, considerable dolichocephaly accompanied by a broad face, an exceptionally narrow nose and large cranial capacity. In all these traits the Eskimo skulls sharply differ from the average Aleut cranium.

There exists a much greater degree of similarity when Aleut crania are compared with those of the Tlinkits of northwestern America. The two series are very close together in size, bizygomatic breadth, facial height and index, and frontal angle. The main difference consists in Tlinkit crania having a greater head height and in being more brachycephalic. In head length and breadth as well as in facial and orbital indices both Aleut and Tlinkit crania resemble Hrdlička's[50] "mixed" group of Alaska.

Tokareva then compares the Aleut measurements with the cranial

---

[48] Jochelson, W. I., Unanganic (Aleutian) language, the language and writing of the northern peoples, pt. 2, 1934.

[49] Jenness, Diamond, The American aborigines, Toronto, 1933.

[50] Hrdlička, Aleš, Catalogue of human crania in the United States National Museum collections. Proc. U. S. Nat. Mus., vol. 63, art. 12, 1924.

measurements of other groups: Lake Baikal Neolithic Type A,[51] Tungus,[52] Tlinkits,[53] Chukchi (Hrdlička), Eskimo of Alaska (Hrdlička), Giliaks (Trofimova), Ainu,[54] Tuvinians,[55] and the Telengets (Bunak).

The Telengets have only the frontal angle and the facial height in common with the Aleuts. The Tannu-Tuvans, representing the Central Asian variety, have a much straighter forehead, a higher skull, a greater degree of brachycephaly, a higher face, a smaller bizygomatic breadth, and a narrower nose. The Aleuts, therefore, cannot be included in either of the two basic Mongoloid races of Siberia.

When the Aleuts are compared with the Giliaks (whom Montandon considered to belong to one race), it is found that the two types differ greatly; that the Giliak skulls are higher, more brachycephalic, possess straighter noses, greater facial angles, and broader faces than the Aleuts.

The Chukchis also differ from the Aleuts, having a smaller cephalic index, greater skull capacity, higher face, higher orbits, and a smaller bizygomatic breadth.

The Ainu has a straighter forehead, smaller facial height and breadth, and is more dolichocephalic.

The most amazing fact in connection with the determination of the racial affinities of the Aleuts was the discovery of their indubitable similarity in a number of traits with the populations of Lake Baikal area, particularly with the Tungus described by Roginskii. Both the Tungus and the Aleuts have exceedingly low skulls. According to Roginskii "The trans-Baikal Tungus are apparently one of the lowest-headed groups in the world." However, the Aleut skull is still lower than the Tungus (Tungus, 129.6; Aleuts, 127.75). Both these groups have great similarity in the frontal angle, in the orbital and nasal indices, and in the bizygomatic breadth. The facial index of the Aleuts is but slightly less than that of the Tungus, the latter possessing a slightly greater facial height.

The only differences between these two groups are the greater head

[51] Debets, G., Anthropological composition of the population of Baikal area in the late Neolithic period. AZH, Nos. 1-2, 1930.

[52] Roginskii, IA., Materialy po antropologii tungusov severnogo Pribaikalia [Materials for the anthropology of the Tungus of the northern Baikal area]. AZH, No. 3, 1934.

[53] Fridolin, Amerikanische Schädel, Arch. Anthrop., 1898.

[54] Trofimova, K Ainskoi probleme [A contribution to the Ainu problem]. AZH, No. 2, 1932.

[55] Debets, G., Kraniologicheskii tip Tannu-Tuvintsev [The craniological type of the Tannu-Tuvans]. Sovetskaia Aziia, Nos. 5-6, 1930.

length of the Tungus, resulting in their dolichocephaly, and the greater facial angle.

A closely comparable type was found by G. F. Debets in the Neolithic sites of the Baikal area.[56] This is the so-called Neolithic "Type A" which almost coincides with the contemporary Tungus type of this region. The similarity to the Aleuts of the "Type A" skulls includes also the pentagonal form of the skull, of the lower border of the apertura pyriformis, and of the fossa prenasalis.

The main differences between these Neolithic and Aleut crania are the same as between the latter and the Tungus, the greater head length resulting in the accentuated degree of dolichocephaly of the Neolithic crania.

Trofimova compared the female Aleut skulls with six Asiatic groups.

Conclusions

The Aleut series of crania is of an unusually homogeneous character, disrupted only by the series of five skulls with straight foreheads.

Tokareva omits them on the basis of archeological evidence, concluding that they were very late arrivals (white color of crania present only in the higher strata at Atka Island).

A homogeneity of the main series then testifies to the absence of alien admixtures in the population of the Aleutian Islands during pre-Russian periods.

Tokareva quotes IArkho [57] and also Dubinin and Romashek [58] in support of the role of isolation as a factor "conditioning the development of the racial type of the Aleuts along a specific path, and stimulating the emergence of their distinguishing somatic characteristics."

Tokareva, while disagreeing both with the theory of the origin of Aleuts through mestization as proposed by Hrdlička and with that of Montandon about their kinship to the Giliaks, believes that the Neolithic type is still preserved among the Aleuts, having been modified as a direct result of island isolation.

The origin of the brachycephaly is due to genetic-automatic processes.

---

[56] See also Hrdlička's "Crania of Siberia."

[57] IArkho, A. I., Ocherednye zadachi sovetskogo rasovedeniia [The problems before Soviet race science]. AZH, No. 3, 1934.

[58] Dubinin and Romashek, Geneticheskoe stroenie vida i ego evoliutsiia [The genetic structure of the species and its evolution]. Biologicheskii Zhurnal, Nos. 5-6, 1932.

ORIGIN OF THE MONGOL

Roginskii [59] begins his study of the origin of the Mongol by giving a brief review of the literature.

In 1927 Hrdlička [60] expressed the supposition that modern man originated in the Neanderthal type. Later, Bartucz [61] pointed out the remarkable similarity between the skeletal type from the Hun burials of the fourth and fifth centuries and the dolichocephalic variety of the Tungus, on the one hand, and Neanderthal man, on the other. More recently, Weidenreich [62] stated the opinion that Sinanthropus possessed certain Mongoloid traits.

In an attempt to solve these problems, Roginskii [63] studied anthropometric data on the dolichocephalic peoples of Siberia, particularly the Tungus. In the Anthropological Institute of the University of Moscow he examined the mandibles and teeth of the Ulchi crania (cf. M. G. Levin) collected by A. M. Zolotarev in the Amur region in 1936, and of the Ostiak crania collected by D. T. IAnovich near Obdorsk in 1911. He also made a study of the geographic localization of some of the Mongol characters in eastern Asia and of the intragroup correlations between them. As a result he came to the following conclusions concerning the origin of the Mongol type.

A comparison of physical characters of modern Mongoloid peoples in Siberia with those of *Homo neanderthalensis* revealed such differences as absence of the torus superciliaris, general weakness of the supraorbital crest, small dimensions of the molar pulp, and development of the chin. On the other hand, modern Mongols were found to resemble the Neanderthal type in their retreating forehead, very high mean height index, a slight development of the fossa canina, and large dimensions of the mandible.

Archeological evidence from the Neolithic and later periods indicates that the geographic area inhabited by the Mongol race was considerably smaller than it is today.

---

[59] Roginskii, IA., Problema proiskhozhdeniia mongolskogo rasovogo tipa [The problem of the origin of the Mongol racial type]. AZH, No. 2, pp. 43-64, 1937.

[60] Hrdlička, Aleš, in Ann. Rep. Smithsonian Inst. for 1928.

[61] Bartucz, Lajos, Moson Szent Janos, Seminar. Kondakovianum, Prague, 1929.

[62] Weidenreich, Franz, Peking Natural History Bulletin, vol. 10, pt. 4, 1936.

[63] Roginskii, IA., Materialy po antropologii tungusov severnogo Pribaikalia [Materials for the anthropology of the Tungus of the northern Baikal area]. AZH, No. 3, 1934.

ORIGIN OF THE ESKIMO

Basing his opinion on the new evidence from Point Barrow, northwestern Alaska, the Bering Sea region, St. Lawrence Island, and other sites excavated by Collins, Zolotarev [64] accepts Mathiassen's views, in preference to those of Birket-Smith, regarding the origin of the Eskimo. From his study of the archeological materials he arrives at the following conclusions:

The most ancient proto-Eskimo culture is that of the Bering Sea. The archeological characteristics of this culture are distinct, although it is impossible at present to draw any conclusions regarding its social and economic status.

This culture came to the area of Bering Strait from the west, most probably progressing along the Arctic coast of Siberia. The art preserves a strong Paleolithic tradition, but the degree of its material production does not attain the level of fully developed Neolithic. It is very tempting to connect this culture with the ancient culture of the IAmal Peninsula. An assumption to this effect would find support in the close relation of the Samoyed and the Eskimo languages.

The theory of the Asiatic origin of the Eskimo receives a firm foundation in this new archeological evidence.

Having reached America during the stage of the "Bering Sea Culture," the ancestors of the Eskimo migrated eastward along the Arctic shore of America. There they formed the Thule culture, out of which developed the modern cultures of the Central, Polar, and Greenland Eskimos.

The culture of the contemporary Eskimos of Alaska was formed from the Bering Sea Culture. Having passed the Punuk stage, it was possibly affected by influences connected with the reverse movement of some of the Thule groups.

Examining the anthropological evidence,[65] Zolotarev draws further conclusions. The most ancient Eskimo type, homogeneous in the main, is dolichocephalic, with a high carinate skull. This type obviously came from Asia.

This type was displaced in Alaska in relatively recent times by tall brachycephals approaching the Paleoasiatic type.

Recognition of the dolichocephal as the most ancient Eskimo type

---

[64] Zolotarev, A. M., K voprosu o proiskhozhdenii Eskimosov [On the origin of the Eskimo]. AZH, No. 1, pp. 47-56, 1937.

[65] Cf. Hrdlička, Aleš, Anthropological survey in Alaska, 46th Ann. Rep. Bur. Amer. Ethnol., 1930; and Melanesians and Australians and the peopling of America, Smithsonian Misc. Coll., vol. 94, No. 11, 1935. Also Diamond Jenness, The American Aborigines. Toronto, 1933.

once more poses the problem of the connection of the Eskimo with the dolichocephalic populations of the Upper Paleolithic period. Preservation of the Paleolithic tradition in Eskimo art permits the formulation of a hypothesis according to which the ancestors of the Eskimo were in the van of the northward movement of South Siberian populations, beginning at the end of the Paleolithic and the beginning of the Neolithic period.

OBSERVATIONS ON THE TIBIA

Zenkevich,[66] of the Section on Human Morphology and Genetics at the Anthropological Institute of the State University of Moscow, studied 56 tibiae belonging to middle-aged males who died from accidents. Zenkevich established the absence of any correlation between the form of the bone and its chemical composition. At the same time the correlation between massiveness, i.e., the ratio of the circumference measured in the middle of the shaft to the length of the bone, and chemical composition was significant. The more massive bones contained a lesser quantity of inorganic components (especially calcium) and more water and organic components (especially fat) than the smaller bones. The more massive bones were somewhat flatter in cross section.

HEAD FORM AND GROWTH IN UTERO

Madame Shilova,[67] of the Second Medical Institute in Leningrad, studied 725 human embryos and fetuses. She recorded a constant rise in cephalic index during the whole uterine life, there being a slight fall only after parturition. In 339 of 725 cases (56.2 percent) the child was brachycephalic (C.I. 80.0-84.9) at birth.

Shilova concludes that during uterine life the cranium passes from dolichocephalic to brachycephalic, that is, it undergoes the same changes as have the heads of the human race in general during the last millennium.

She points out the following details of this change: During the

---

[66] Zenkevich, R. I., K voprosu o faktorakh formoobrazovaniia dlinykh kostei chelovecheskogo skeleta, I. Variatsii formy secheniia bolshoi bertsovoi kosti v sviazi s udelnym vesom i khimicheskim sostavom kosti [On the factors of formation of long bones in the human skeleton, I. The variations of the form of cross section of the tibia and its specific gravity and chemical composition]. AZH, No. 1, pp. 26-46, 1937.

[67] Shilova, A. V., Materialy o formie golovy i roste v utrobnoi zhizni [Materials on the form of the head and growth during uterine life]. AZH, No. 1, pp. 3-25, 1937.

first 3 months the cephalic index constantly increases, the prevalent skull form during this period being mesocephalic. From the fourth to the tenth month the index varies slightly, brachycephaly prevailing. The index decreases during the tenth month, as a result of parturition.

The fluctuation of cephalic index in different embryos may vary greatly in point of time. This is true with twins in the majority of cases.

In no instance does head breadth exceed head length. The curves of the absolute length and breadth are very similar to the curves of their absolute growth, by month. Head length increases more than head breadth up to and including the fifth month, which shows the greatest difference in increase of any month.

A definite periodicity governs the absolute increase of length and breadth of head, as well as length of body and leg. Up to the fifth month there is successively greater increase; from the sixth to the ninth month the increase fluctuates; the pre-parturient period is characterized by a sharp rise.

Sex dimorphism is clearly expressed. The cephalic index of girls in utero is lower than that of boys except during the last 2 months, when that of girls becomes greater. In general, newborn girls are more brachycephalic than boys. During the first half of uterine development girls surpass boys in their growth. The growth of all their dimensions is more evenly distributed between the two halves of uterine life than is that of boys, whose growth is shifted more to the second half.

A STUDY OF BLOOD GROUPS IN THE CAUCASUS [68]

Anthropological study of blood groups in Georgia was begun in 1925 by the Hematological Department of the Georgian Bacteriological Institute. The blood groups of all patients in the Hematological and Wassermann Departments were recorded, together with data regarding sex, age, and nationality.

One thousand measurements disclosed tentatively the prevalence of Group I (O) among the Georgians and of Group II (A) among the Armenians. The extreme western and eastern groups represented the maximum range of brachycephaly and dark pigmentation. The highest degree of both was found in the east, the lowest in the west.

[68] Semenovskaia, E. M., Izuchenie grup krovi narodov Kavkaza [Study of blood groups in the Caucasus]. Sovetskaia Etnografiia, Nos. 4-5, pp. 213-215, 1936.

Group II (A) became proportionately more rare toward the west, while Group I (O) increased in frequency.[69]

In 1929 the editorial office of the "Problems of Biology and Pathology of Jews" sponsored a study of the blood groups of Georgian and Persian Jews. The material was collected in Tbilisi and Kutaisi. Altogether 3,409 examinations were made on various Georgian tribes and 1,422 on Jews. The four blood groups were normally represented, while the distribution of percentages was similar for Georgian and Persian Jews and for Romanian, Balkan, Russian, and Polish Jews. Blood groups of the Jews did not correspond to blood groups of the Georgian tribes. This was explained by the absence of interbreeding between the two peoples, owing to religious handicaps. On the other hand, Dzhavachishvili [70] states that the Georgian Jews are anthropologically a metamorphic Georgian group, who have for many centuries lived alongside the Georgians and adopted their language.

In 1930 an article [71] on the blood groups of Georgians appeared.

On the basis of more than 6,000 examinations, it was discovered that Group I (O) predominated in the west, while Groups II (A) and IV (AB) were rarely present. Percentages for Group II (A) increased strongly to the east, together with those for Group III (B), owing to the influence of Armenians, 50 percent of whom belong to Group II (A), and the influence, especially in the east, of Mongoloid elements. Not all the peoples of the Caucasus have been examined, owing to the inaccessibility of many of the mountain tribes. A number of expeditions now in progress are expected to complete the survey.

In 1930 Dr. Ukleba conducted an expedition to Svanetia for the First Clinical Institute of Georgia, Tbilisi. Five hundred and seven measurements were taken, and it was discovered, strangely enough, that percentages for Group I (O) increased in the more mountainous regions.

In 1932 Dr. Kvirkelia, a member of an expedition led by Professor Machavariani, collected materials among the Adzhars, Gurians who have been Islamized. The distribution of blood groups was found to be typical for western Georgia, with an increase of Groups II (A) and III (B) in the regions nearest the Turkish frontier.

---

[69] Cf. AZH, vol. 15, Nos. 3-4.

[70] Ost-Rundschau, No. 9, 1930, and Problems of Biology and Pathology of Jews, No. 3, pt. 1, Leningrad, 1930.

[71] Ukrainisches Zentralblatt für Blutgruppenforschung, vol. 4, pt. 4, 1930.

Blood groups (from Semenovskaia) ⃰

Peoples	Individuals	I (O)	II (A)	III (B)	IV (AB)
Adzhars	700	51.57	36.57	5.71	0.15
Svanetians	507	56.21	34.91	6.90	1.97
Mingrelians	519	54.72	32.75	8.48	4.04
Imeretians	663	50.52	35.14	10.86	3.47
Lechkhums	20	11	6	3	
Gurians	265	51.31	36.98	9.81	1.88
Rachins	183	40.43	37.70	17.48	4.37
Kartalinians	611	41.72	40.59	51.29	6.38
Kakhetians	489	36.19	42.74	16.15	4.9
Khevsurs	2	4	4		
Mokhe . ⸰...............	7	3	2	2	
Tushins	6	1	3	2	
Lezghians	1	1			
Daghestan mountaineers...	1			1	
Chechens	4	2	2		
Osetes	142	38.02	41.14	15.49	6.33
Georgian Jews............	1239	26.95	43.09	19.12	10.73
Persian Jews.............	127	20.49	47.57	23.62	8.65
European Jews...........	95	25.26	48.42	20.01	6.31
Assyrians	6	1	3	2	
Armenians	906	28.80	51.76	10.81	8.6
Russians	315	31.42	38.41	17.79	12.38
Poles	14	6	3	3	2
Mordvinians	1		1		
Komi	2		1		
Esthonians	1		1		
English	1		1		
French	2		1	1	
Germans	15	5	8	1	1
Latvians	2	1	2		
Lithuanians	3	1	1	1	
Greeks	19	13	5	1	
Gypsies	2			2	
Chinese	1	1			

⃰ Figures in italics are percentages. Note errata in Khevsur, Komi, and Latvian groups.

On the basis of 3,775 examinations on Georgians, the following percentages were obtained:

Group	Percent
I (O)	50.32
II (A)	36.31
III (B)	10.33
IV (AB)	3.02

The formula for the groups was O>A>B. Among the Kakhetians A>O>B was particularly characteristic. This ratio was also noted as present among the Armenians, Osetes, and Georgian Jews. Among the more easterly groups the percentage of Group III (B) also increased, and it was particularly high among the western Georgians and Imeretians. It reached 15 percent in the Shorap region, through which the high mountain road passed, and among the Rachins, east Georgian people who were pushed westward.

In spite of the position of the Caucasus between Asia and Europe, neither the Georgians nor the Armenians were found to belong to the intermediate serological type, both being generally classed among the European peoples. A tendency toward the Pacific type was noted in western Georgia. The Armenians and the Georgian Jews showed a greater percentage of A than O groups. The Turks alone could be considered as an intermediary type, owing to the admixture of Mongoloid elements.

Blood grouping [72] was continued during 1936 by the Tiflis [now Tbilisi] Branch of the Russian Institute for Blood Transfusion and by various medical expeditions in Georgia.

ISOAGGLUTINATION OF THE TURKOMANS

Ginzburg [78] studied blood samples from 562 Turkomans of various regions, which he collected during an expedition in 1936 under the sponsorship of the Anthropological Institute of Moscow State University.

This expedition investigated two of the three large, historically known groups of Turkomans: the eastern Turkomans, seventeenth-century settlers along the middle course of the Amu River, in the Chardzhui and Kerkin regions of the former Khanate of Bukhara, now forming the eastern portion of the Turkoman S.S.R.; and the Transcaspian Turkomans of the region between the Caspian Sea and the Amu. The Transcaspian Turkomans were divided into a central group, dwelling along the Murgab and Tedzhen Rivers, and a western group, living near Ashkhabad and farther to the west.

A third large group, located in the former Tashauz region of the Khanate of Khiva (now the northerly section of the Turkoman

---

[72] During 1936-1938 the Anthropological Section of IAE obtained copies of individual measurements described in this article. Other materials have been forwarded from the Central Blood Transfusion Institute, Tbilisi, and from Dr. V. N. Chuprinin, of that city. At the present time the Anthropological Section has 16,000 catalog cards of individual blood measurements from the Caucasus. This collection is increasing rapidly.

[78] Ginzburg, V. V., Izogemoaggliutinatsiia u Turkmen [Isoagglutination of Turkomans]. AZH, No. 2, pp. 79-82, 1937.

S.S.R.), had been studied by an expedition under the leadership of IArkho,[74] who also collected blood samples.

From his own data and those of the other investigators, Ginzburg draws the following conclusions:

Group A is predominant over group B in all districts, the general formula being A>O>B. The ratios of blood groups among Turkomans of different tribes and different geographic areas are relatively similar. Group B increases slightly toward the east, Group A toward the west. In spite of great tribal and clan isolation and unceasing intertribal feuds supported by the chiefs, contact exists between various groups. The wide expanse of territory does not, apparently, present any obstacle to intercourse among separate tribes; wives are purchased from other districts, strangers are received into the clans, and slaves are captured during raids.

It is not possible to determine race from a study of blood groups, as the direction of variability does not always coincide with that of physical type. This study is of value, however, for ascertaining the degree of isolation of given tribes or populations of given territories.

THE TARDENOISIAN SKELETON FROM FATMA-KOBA, CRIMEA [75]

In 1927 S. N. Bibikov and S. A. Trusov conducted a preliminary sounding in the Fatma-Koba rock shelter in Baidar Valley, 3 kilometers northwest of Urkusta, between Sevastopol and Yalta.

There, in a specially dug pit, they discovered the Tardenoisian skeleton, which G. A. Bonch-Osmolovskii [76] excavated during the same year and reported in a preliminary account of the excavations. The burial was removed in a block to Leningrad, where it is on exhibit [77] in the Geological Museum of the Academy of Sciences. The skull, which had been shattered, was reassembled, and the other-

---

[74] IArkho, A. I., Turkmeny Khorezma i Severnogo Kavkaza [The Turkomans of Khoresm [Khwarazm] and of North Caucasus]. AZH, Nos. 1-2, 1933.

[75] This section is translated and summarized from the article by G. F. Debets, Tardenuazskii kostiak iz navesa Fatma-Koba v Krymu [Tardenoisian skeleton from Fatma-Koba rock shelter, Crimea]. AZH, No. 2, pp. 144-165, 1936.

[76] Bonch-Osmolovskii, G. A., Itogi izucheniia krymskogo paleolita [Results of the excavations of the Crimean Paleolithic period]. Trudy, First INQUA Conference, Fasc. 5, 1934.

[77] I saw this skeleton on October 17, 1934. My scanty notes do not differ from Debet's observations. The artifacts appeared to belong unquestionably to the transitional period. A monograph has been written on the Fatma-Koba skeleton, which I examined in Leningrad on July 2, 1946. Mrs. David Huxley has translated the French summary of the detailed study of the hands of this skeleton by Bonch-Osmolovskii. (H. F.)

wise well-preserved skeleton has been left in the position in which it was found, the right side partly embedded in the earth. Only the left arm and leg bones and the skull could be examined.

The skeleton was flexed; the head pointed south-southeast. It was covered with large stones. Debets expresses the opinion that the highly flexed position may indicate that the corpse had been hamstrung.

The pit, lying under two unbroken strata containing implements of Upper Tardenoisian type, was dug in another stratum containing the same type of implements. No artifacts were found, however, in direct association with the skeleton. In the underlying stratum a hearth was associated with implements of the Shan-Koba type (Azilian stage). Debets concludes that the stratum containing the skeleton and the uppermost cultural deposit belong to about the same period, a late facies of the Tardenoisian stage.

He suggests that the skeleton was that of a man approximately 40 years of age. The sutures of the skull were open except for a slight obliteration of the sagittal suture. A few teeth were well worn, but caries was absent. The enamel remained only on the crown of the molars and the incisors were approximately half eroded.

Debets records almost 200 measurements on the skull and skeleton. He states that the Fatma-Koba skeleton has all the characteristics of *Homo sapiens*. The full development of a large number of traits distinguish it from *Homo neanderthalensis*.

Debets enumerates the following points in which this skeleton differs from the Neanderthal type: cranial height, slant and convexity of forehead, development of browridges, occipital projection, slant of the main portion of the occipital bone, facial height, breadth of the ascending ramus, size of teeth, condylo-diaphysial angle of the humerus, bowing of the radius, platycnemic index, bowing of the femur, popliteal index, retroversion of the tibia, and tibio-femoral index. The chin and fossa canina were moderately developed. Prognathism was present but within the range of *Homo sapiens*. The situation of the radial tuberosity in relation to the volar plane, although not highly characteristic of man, was also within this range.

In a few points concerning massiveness of bones, that is, in the index of robusticity and the size of the epiphyses of the long bones, and in the development of muscular attachments, the Fatma-Koba skeleton resembled *Homo neanderthalensis*.

The only cranial trait approaching that of *Homo neanderthalensis* was the angle of the plane of the foramen magnum.

On account of its low face, pronounced horizontal profile, high glabella, nasal prominence, and broad nasal bones, slightly narrowed in the middle, Debets classified the Fatma-Koba skeleton as belonging to the Europeoid racial group. The proportions of the extremities also approached those of the contemporary Europeoid, with the exception of the somewhat greater length of the tibia.

Only a moderate degree of general, but not alveolar, mesognathism differentiates the Fatma-Koba skull from the Europeoid type. According to Debets, the possession of this Negroid characteristic places this skull in the category of secondary Europeoids with slight Negroid affinities.

Debets adds that such tendencies are present in the Grimaldi crania, Combe-Capelle, skull No. 4 from Predmost, skulls from the Portuguese kitchen middens of Mugem and Cabeco da Arruda, the child's skull from Genière grotto in the Rhone Valley, the Moniat skull from Belgium, Ostorf Island (Jutland) crania described by Schlitz;[78] Chamblande's skulls from Switzerland, Silesian crania described by Reche, crania from Conguel described by Hervé, Verneau's[79] two crania from Caverno del Sanguinetto in northern Italy, and some modern Italian crania.

These traits, according to Debets, are the vestiges of an ancient stage of development common to all Eurafrican races.

---

[78] Schlitz, A., Die Steinzeitlichen Schädel des grossherzoglichen Museums Schwerin. Arch. Anthrop., vol. 7, pts. 2-3, 1908.

[79] Verneau, R., Les grottes de Grimaldi, vol. 2, pt. 1. Monaco, 1906.

AKHSHTYR CAVE, 120 METERS ABOVE MZYMTA RIVER, ABKHAZIA

SMITHSONIAN MISCELLANEOUS COLLECTIONS　　　　　　　Vol. 110, No. 13, Pl. 2

GENERAL VIEW OF MZYMTA GORGE FROM AKHSHTYR CAVE, ABKHAZIA

Mrs. S. N. Zamiatnin in foreground.

DR. AND MRS. S. N. ZAMIATNIN AND DR. A. E. JESSEN OUTSIDE AKHSHTYR CAVE, ABKHAZIA

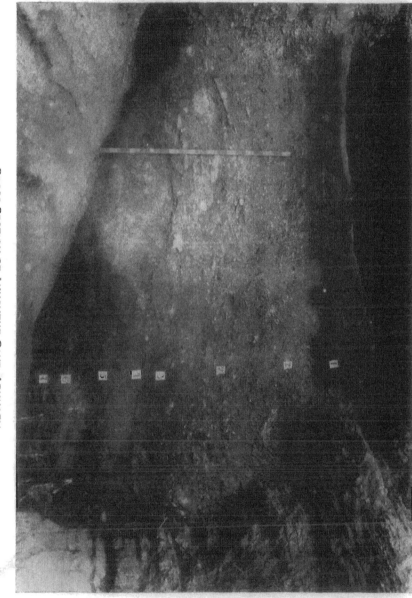

CROSS SECTION OF AKHSHTYR CAVE, ABKHAZIA

1, Ashy stratum containing pottery (Circassian, early medieval, and first centuries A.D.); 2, brown rubble containing, in the upper part, Neolithic, in the lower, Upper Paleolithic, objects; 3, yellow rubble and talus of stalagmite, with Mousterian culture; 4, purplish-brown clay, sterile; 5, gray calciferous clay, Mousterian finds; 6, gray-green silty clay, single Mousterian flints in the upper part; 7, ocher-yellow clay containing crystalline and shale gravel, sterile.

DR. M. E. MASSON (RIGHT) AND DR. L. V. OSHANIN EXAMINING SKULLS, APPROXIMATELY 1,500 YEARS OLD, FROM KHWARAZM, UZBEKISTAN

CPSIA information can be obtained
at www.ICGtesting.com
Printed in the USA
BVHW041442060619
550361BV00016B/811/P